Angry Parents, Failing Schools

Other books by Elaine K. McEwan from Harold Shaw Publishers:

The ABCs of School Success

Attention Deficit Disorder

"The Dog Ate It": Conquering Homework Hassles

"I Didn't Do It": Dealing with Dishonesty

Managing Attention and Learning Disorders: A Guide for Adults

"Mom, He Hit Me": What to Do about Sibling Rivalry

"Nobody Likes Me": Helping Your Child Make Friends

Solving School Problems

When Kids Say NO to School: Helping Children at Risk of Failure, Refusal, or Dropping Out

Books from Corwin Press:

The ADHD Intervention Checklist

How to Deal with Parents Who Are Angry, Troubled, Afraid, or Just Plain Crazy

Leading Your Team to Excellence: How to Make Quality Decisions

The Principal as Counselor (with Jeffrey Kottler)

The Principal's Guide to Attention Deficit Hyperactivity Disorder

The Principal's Guide to Raising Reading Achievement

Seven Steps to Effective Instructional Leadership

Angry Parents

Failing Schools

What's Wrong with the Public Schools & What You Can Do About It

Reading
Writing
Arithmetic

Elaine K. McEwan, Ed.D.

Harold Shaw Publishers
Wheaton, Illinois

(C) 1998 by Elaine K. McEwan-Adkins

Scripture quotations marked NLT are taken from the Holy Bible, New Living Translation, copyright (c) 1996. Used by permission of Tyndale House Publishers, Inc., Wheaton, Illinois 60189. All rights reserved.

Scripture quotation marked RSV is from the Revised Standard Version of the Bible, copyright © 1946, 1952, 1971 by the Division of Education of the National Council of the Churches of Christ in the U.S.A., and used by permission.

ISBN 0-87788-019-0

Cover design by David LaPlaca

Library of Congress Cataloging-in-Publication Data

McEwan, Elaine K., 1941–
    Angry parents, failing schools : what's wrong with the public schools and what you can do about it / by Elaine K. McEwan.
        p.   cm.
    Includes bibliographical references and index.
    ISBN 0-87788-019-0
    1. Public schools—United States—Evaluation.   2.Education-
-Parent participation—United States.   3. Education changes—
United States.   I. Title.
    LA217.2.M397   1998
    371.01′ 0973—dc21   98-23773
                                                                                            CIP

03 02 01 00 99 98
10 9 8 7 6 5 4 3 2 1

To Mary Damer and Barbara Shafer,
For your courage and commitment
to public education.

To my husband, Raymond,
For your unfailing encouragement and support.

To my editor, Joan Lloyd Guest,
For your inspiration, dedication, and insight.

Table of Contents

Introduction:
Are Public Schools Really Failing Our Kids?

Public schools are in my blood, and I have always been a cheerleader for them. The news that I am writing a book detailing the failures of those schools will probably come as a shock to those who know me. Over a career that has spanned three decades, I've been a teacher, librarian, elementary school principal, and assistant superintendent for instruction. I've written nearly a dozen books about the public schools for both parents and educators as well as authored a weekly newspaper column on educational issues. I've answered hundreds of questions for parents on radio call-in shows and spoken to a variety of parent groups. All the while I remained certain from my own personal experiences that when parents and educators worked together, problems could be solved and positive things would happen for students. I believed that unresponsive school boards, stonewalling administrators, fuzzy curricula, abysmal test scores, ineffective instruction, and sagging standards were the exception, not the rule.

I'm afraid I was rather naive and very sheltered. My retirement from public education has afforded me both the time and perspective from which to view what is happening in classrooms across America, and the big picture is both disheartening and frightening. Here's a brief snapshot of what I've found:

- parents who are angry, troubled, and even afraid of what they see happening in public schools (both urban and suburban)
- children who can't read, write, or do math
- test scores that are in decline
- parents, including current and former public school educators, who are abandoning the public schools and choosing other options for their own children
- educators who are deliberately ignoring, frustrating, and circumventing concerned parents
- national literacy rates that are a disgrace
- costly innovations that are not validated by research
- activist groups, parental websites, and charter schools that are growing in number and impact.

My journey to this point began when I was writing a book for school administrators to assist them in better understanding, empathizing, and communicating with parents (*How to Deal with Parents Who Are Angry, Troubled, Afraid, or Just Plain Crazy,* Corwin Press, 1998). During my research I discovered more than a few angry parents. And they had good reasons to be angry. Their children weren't learning and no one seemed to care. They posed intelligent questions and received the runaround. They joined task forces to become involved, and their input was ignored. They asked for accountability and were handed educational "gobbledygook" instead. They ran for seats on the school-board and encountered dirty politics and smear campaigns. They came with honesty and were often met with deception.

There are those in the education establishment who desperately want to agree with professors David Berliner and Bruce Biddle who, in their 1995 book, *The Manufactured Crisis: Myths, Fraud and the Attack on America's Public Schools,* argue that the problems these parents are encountering in their schools are really a figment of someone's imagination, be it the "Far Right, the Religious Right, or the neoconservatives."[1]

But the parents who have been talking to me are just ordinary folk who want their children to learn to read and write and are becoming increasingly incensed at what is "not happening" in their public schools. After listening to dozens of their stories, I decided to chime in with my educator's perspective for these reasons: 1) to encourage those parents who are still fighting the good fight to keep it up; 2) to sound an alarm for those parents who have never questioned whether their children's education is in good hands; 3) to give all parents some solid information and tools to help them bring about change in the public schools; and 4) to help parents turn honest anger into positive action.

Chapter 1 sets the stage for our journey into the brave new world of education on the brink of the twenty-first century and asks the question: Do you know what your children are doing in school today? Chapter 2 explores the countless reasons why so many parents are angry, frightened, and troubled, and tells the stories of some parents who aren't willing to look the other way. Chapter 3 describes how the schools have gone wrong from a historical perspective, tracing the contentious relationship between the *progressivists* and *traditionalists*. Chapter 4 discusses what I believe to be one of the most pervasive problems in our public schools today: the way we are teaching our children to read. Chapter 5 analyzes the second major curriculum debate that is looming on the horizon—so-called fuzzy math. Chapter 6 will help you analyze your neighborhood school to determine how many of the "virulent viruses" of innovation have invaded your community and what you can do about them. Finally, chapter 7 contains fifty-plus things you can do to make a real difference in public education. Forget baking cookies, working the fun-fair dunking booth, or cutting out stars for the first-grade bulletin board. We're talking involvement and activism here. You'll meet parents and teachers who are winning small but important battles in the education wars. Once you finish reading chapter 7 you'll be ready to dust off your apathy and get to work.

Throughout this book you will find Tales from the Trenches—brief commentaries, vignettes, and observations from those most concerned about what's happening in today's schools—parents, students, and community activists. You'll also find several helpful resources: websites, reading lists, and materials to help you tutor your own children. Before you begin reading, I must offer one word of warning. Although the book is written in a conversational style, I've included dozens of footnotes because I don't want you to take just my word. This book is based on the collective research of many authors, and you can locate all of the sources for yourself if you choose. Where I've changed the name of an individual who requested anonymity, I have followed that name with an asterisk the first time it is used. Otherwise all names and locations are actual.

I am deeply appreciative of the many dedicated people around the country who shared information and anecdotes by e-mail, sent materials to me by "snail mail," and "introduced" me to experts around the world. People have been unfailingly generous with their time and their resources. (Wherever individuals' personal communications are quoted, I have not given a reference in the notes.) I would not have been able to write this book without the assistance of the Education Consumers ClearingHouse and its founder Dr. J. E. (John) Stone. The ClearingHouse provides a unique and valuable resource for anyone trying to find honest answers about the current state of public education.

Notes

1. David C. Berliner and Bruce J. Biddle, *The Manufactured Crisis: Myths, Fraud, and the Attack on America's Public Schools* (Reading, MA: Addison-Wesley, 1995) 133-38.

Reading
Writing
Arithmetic

TALES FROM THE TRENCHES

Fruit Salad

Michele Zuckerman
Parent
Education Activist

American Education Week is a very big deal here in Loudoun County. All the schools have special programs going on, and parents are invited to come to their children's classroom at specific times to observe. This is all very carefully planned, of course, so that schools put their best foot forward.

I've been treated to cookies and bedtime stories with my younger son's first-grade class, but my most memorable experience was with my older son's second-grade class. The teacher had asked each child to bring in a piece of fruit. As the parents arrived, we were asked to join our children, who had pushed their desks together into tables with about five or six students each. There was a large bowl in the middle of the table and some plastic utensils. I tried to anticipate what the lesson would be. Perhaps a geography lesson about where different kinds of fruit grow. Maybe a math lesson on fractions.

Finally, the teacher gave the directions. We were making fruit salad! Each of us was to cut our piece of fruit and put it in the bowl with the others. Then we could dish it out and eat it. That was it. For this, 90 percent of the parents took off from work—to come and eat fruit salad with their children. Was this just poor planning? Or was it another example of American public school education at its finest?

Do You Know What Your Children Are Doing in School Today?

1 Reality Check

> By the year 2000, all children in America will start school ready to learn. . . . The high school graduation rate will increase to at least ninety percent. . . . Students will leave [school] having demonstrated competence in challenging subject matter, including English, mathematics, science, history, and geography. . . . They will be prepared for responsible citizenship, further learning, and productive employment. . . . U.S. students will be the first in the world in science and mathematics.
>
> —*Charlottesville Summit on Education, 1990*

Do you know what your children are doing in school today? You probably assume they're learning to read and write, doing some math, picking up a little American history, and developing study skills. You no doubt want them to understand and remember what they learn and then be able to apply this learning. These are modest goals to be sure. Calculus, physics, world history, and a foreign language would be nice, but let's get the basics mastered first, you think. Right? Well, think again. It is precisely those basics that are becoming more difficult to find in today's public-school graduates. Do you know if *your* children have mastered them?

Don't believe that your kids are doing fine because they're getting good grades. The annual Public Agenda poll for 1998, aptly titled "Reality Check," reports that employers and college professors who teach freshmen are disenchanted with the graduates coming out of today's high schools. Almost two-thirds of the employers and 76 percent of the professors surveyed indicated that a high school diploma is no guarantee that a student has learned the basics. Nearly seven in ten employers feel that graduates aren't ready for work, and more than half of the university professors think that those graduates aren't ready for college. High school graduates, according to employers and college professors, rank fair to poor in the following areas: grammar and spelling, essay writing, basic math skills, and work habits like being organized and on time.[1]

Don Crawford, professor of special education at a major university in the Pacific Northwest, laments the lack of student preparation. "I see large numbers of college students who cannot spell accurately or write effectively. And the quality of the insights that come from their reading are on the level I would have expected from high school students when I started teaching in the '70s."[2] Sadly enough, Dr. Crawford's students are teachers in training for careers in special education in which they will be teaching students with learning disabilities. Some of these teachers will eventually get jobs in public schools, including public schools in affluent areas. Maybe even in your public schools.

> "I see large numbers of college students who cannot spell accurately or write effectively."

Dr. Jerry Rosen, mathematics professor at California State University at Northridge, has encountered the same scenario while teaching the basic "math for teachers" course. "A number of these students do not know basic arithmetic," he reports. "I have seen students who didn't know that ½ and 50 percent were the same. [S]ome of these students have told me they learned arithmetic on the calculator. Although a number of them do excel and will be good math teachers, there are many who, I believe, are not qualified to teach math to elementary school students."[3]

Findings such as these are causing parents who formerly equated a high property tax bill with good schools to ask questions about what's really going on in classrooms today. Jud Martinson,* the father of two early-elementary students in a wealthy and highly respected suburban school district in the Pacific Northwest, did just that.

"I started from scratch and read everything in sight. I found that for at least seventy years we have seen a progressive takeover of our education system by those who essentially reject the idea of a 'liberal arts' [subject-matter oriented] education." Jud is upset about what he has discovered in his self-directed tutorial on education as well as by what he has observed firsthand in his children's classrooms.

When Is an A Not an A?

There are lots of parents who think that the schools, especially the ones their children attend, are doing just fine. The Public Agenda survey reports that most parents believe the schools are doing well at enforcing academic standards. And the Gallup poll taken annually reported in the fall of 1997 that four in ten Americans grade their local schools with an *A* or a *B*.[4] These parents cannot be blamed for operating under the assumption that their children's good grades mean they are learning something in school.

Their children know better, however. In the Public Agenda survey "students confirm that in practice it doesn't take much to avoid a failing grade. Almost three in four

(73 percent) say most students do the bare minimum needed to get by, and 39 percent say their teachers 'hardly ever give F's even when that's the grade kids deserve.'"[5] Even though they think their children are doing well, nearly half of the parents polled by Public Agenda had no way of comparing how their own children's achievement measured against other students in their state. Slightly more than half had no idea how their children's performance compared nationally, and seven in ten did not know that in recent international math and science rankings the United States scored 28th and 17th, respectively.[6] So, ask yourself, do you really know where your children rank?

> "Parents are being fooled by 'fraudulently high grades.'"

J. E. Stone, professor of educational psychology at East Tennessee State University and coordinator of the Education Consumers ClearingHouse,[7] believes that although parents are as concerned as they ever were about their children's achievement, they are being fooled by "fraudulently high grades." His explanation for the inflation: "The grades are a result of low academic expectations and misguided attempts to avoid making the child (and the parents) unhappy."

Dr. Stone goes on to explain:

> Grade reports are the most fundamental form of educational accountability and parents are the members of the public most interested in school quality. Their impression of teaching and learning in the local schools is inevitably influenced by the grades they see. Standardized test results and statistical reports may accurately portray student achievement, but weaknesses and mediocrity reflected by these measures can be discounted in the face of reassuring grade reports. Recognition of "real" achievement levels may not arise until students undergo external "reality checks" [e.g., entrance tests for college, pri-

vate school, or a tutoring center]. When over half of the high school graduates entering college need remedial work, it seems evident that there is a substantial discrepancy between grades received and grades deserved.

Randy Moore, editor of *The American Biology Teacher,* would agree with Stone's conclusions. Moore reported that in 1966 high school teachers gave twice as many *C*s as *A*s. By 1978, the ratio had changed in an astounding way, with the number of *A*s given exceeding the number of *C*s. By 1990, 20 percent of entering college students reported an *A* average for their entire high school career.[8]

Chester Finn, in writing about what has come to be known as "the Lake Wobegon effect" (all our children are performing above the national average on standardized achievement tests), reports that even though we keep hearing gloom and doom about schools as a whole "we have continued to receive upbeat reports about the education of our own children and almost constant claims that our local and state school systems are doing a good (and even an improving) job." He suggests that "unfortunately, much of this retail information is untrustworthy, the product of the system's preference for favorable public relations and the profession's fervent belief in positive reinforcement and encouraging feedback, reality to the contrary notwithstanding."[9]

Since 1987, the percentage of students taking the Scholastic Aptitude Test (SAT) who report their grade point averages as *A*- or better has grown from 28 percent to 37 percent, while SAT scores for this same group have fallen, a sure sign of grade inflation. An editorial in *Investors Business Daily* pointed out that "all too often, educators react to students' failures by lowering the bar, though they usually pretend to be doing something else, like making the test more useful or culturally relevant."[10]

What it amounts to is this: If you don't like the results you're getting, then just change the average score so that more students can be above average. In 1994 the Scholastic Aptitude Test did just that. With a sweep of the pen SAT officials declared that the then current average scores (424 for the verbal section and 478 for the math) would instead be "recentered" to 500.[11] Officials "blamed" the change on students, parents, and teachers who, SAT officials stated, incorrectly believed that students who scored less than 500 were below-average achievers and not college material.

Gregory Cizek in a commentary on this shift observes: "Intuitively, something doesn't seem right about changing 400s into 500s with just a wave of the wand. Sure, we could all stand on a box when a physician measures our height so that we'd all look six inches taller. Or we could scratch new lines in the thermometer so that everyone with a fever would appear to be healthy. Of course, the problem with these remedies is that they're only cosmetic—despite the 'enhanced' procedures, we'd still be short and sick."[12]

Dr. Patrick Groff, professor emeritus of education at San Diego State University, takes the fun a bit farther and offers a tongue-in-cheek recommendation for reforming all of our school problems. "By far the least expensive way to 'reform' our schools would be simply to proclaim that what are customarily seen as disabling problems needing immediate attention and resolution are in fact nothing more than normal expectations. The movement represented by the S.A.T.'s intention to eliminate certain academic problems by ruling them as normal thus may presage the way the nation can afford to rectify what ordinarily has been said to be its educational woes."[13] With all of the rescaling, renorming, recentering, redoing, retesting, and reforming, do you really know where *your* kids stand and if they have the skills to succeed? Or will *your* children need remediation and retraining just to get into college or obtain a job?

According to the Public Agenda poll, 66 percent of high school teachers are confident that most or all of their students have the skills necessary to succeed at work.

Unfortunately, about the same percentage of employers polled and slightly more college professors believe just the opposite.[14] Some of today's educators could use a good dose of psychologist Jerome Bruner's advice from the early '60s: "Let us not confuse ourselves by failing to recognize that there are two kinds of self confidence . . . one a trait of personality, and another that comes from knowledge of a subject. It is of no particular credit to the educator to help build the first without building the second. The objective of education is not the production of self-confident fools."[15]

> **"The objective of education is not the production of self-confident fools."**

Apparently, huge numbers of American students can be described as just that. University of Michigan professor Harold Stevenson has studied the differences between American and Asian students in both skills and self-esteem. He reports: "Our University of Michigan research group spent the last decade studying the academic performance of American students, and one of our most consistent findings is that the academic achievement of our students is inferior to that of students in many other societies. . . . The low scores of the American students are distressing, but of equal concern is the discrepancy between their low levels of performance and the positive evaluations they gave of their ability in math."[16]

In addition to inflated grades, parents are also being fooled by confusing report cards filled with meaningless narratives and checklists that report little having to do with real learning. In response to a Reading Strategy Inventory (the modern version of the old-fashioned "report card") sent home with his first-grade son, Jud Martinson wrote this reply to the teacher: "It would be entirely possible from the inventory list to look carefully at each item, then take all the items together, and still not be able to answer the basic questions: 'Can Lucas* read?' and 'How well?'"

As one might expect, students in urban public schools are even more shortchanged in terms of what they are learning. They are failing to acquire the most rudimentary skills in reading, math, and science, with fewer than half scoring at the basic level.[17] But just because you have the resources to live in a more affluent area, don't make the mistake of thinking that your children are safe from mediocre and failing school systems. The sharp decline of scores on the Stanford Achievement Test and the Scholastic Aptitude Test (now called the Scholastic Assessment Test) over the past two decades should sound a wake-up call to suburban parents who have been thinking that hefty property tax bills would protect their children from educational malpractice.

> Our best and brightest students "suffered the most dramatic setbacks over the past two decades."

Herbert Rudman, professor of educational psychology at Michigan State University and co-author of the Stanford Achievement Test, explains that while students scoring in the bottom quartile have shown slow but steady improvement since the 1960s, the overall average scores have dropped because of the performance of those in the top quartile. In other words, our best and brightest students, those who attend the finest elementary and high schools and whose plans include attending selective colleges, have, according to Rudman, "suffered the most dramatic setbacks over the past two decades."[18]

So Where ARE the Good Schools?

Jud and his wife, Sally, are experiencing this phenomenon firsthand. When they relocated to the Pacific Northwest, they purchased a home in the "best" district they could find, paying for the privilege of living in an affluent community next to neighbors who believed their schools were topnotch. Jud has been dismayed at what he's found in the classrooms of his first-grade son and third-grade daughter.

"It seems the schools spend a lot of time trying not to teach. The teachers are all 'good.' That is, they are concerned, not evil. They care about my children. They are just wrong. They went to schools that were intellectual wastelands, that touted one line of drivel without any rigor or real investigation as to whether it works or not. So, they accept on faith that these methods work, not having ever been presented with anything else." The Martinsons' children are still in the public schools but Jud tells people, when they ask, that he home-schools his children and uses the public schools for daycare. "My kids' education is too important to trust to these people."

Martinson is not the only one who is angry and frustrated about having to take over the academic training of his children because the school "would rather focus on problem solving and higher order thinking skills." He is not alone in his feelings of resentment that he has to "unteach" so much of what "the teachers try to stuff in my kids' minds that is either ideologically tainted or factually incorrect." The *Wall Street Journal* reported in March 1996 that growing numbers of suburban parents, people who bought their houses precisely for the educational advantages their high property tax dollars would buy, are abandoning the public schools. The article goes on to report that "fueling their anxiety is more than concern over class size or test scores. They worry that their children are being shortchanged by inadequate teaching and by the focus on classmates with special needs, as well as by the drug use and violence they associated with urban schools."[19]

Suburban parents are also worried about a growing trend to "dumb down" even the finest schools. Many parents of students at prestigious New Trier Township High School in Winnetka, Illinois, where the per-pupil expenditure is $16,500, were aghast when a new school superintendent abolished class rankings and tried to get rid of "ability grouping."[20]

Do you know exactly what your kids are learning in their "good" schools? Even the "best" ones leave a lot to be desired these days. There's only one way to find out how your schools measure up: investigate. Here are some questions to guide you.

1. Are your children spending increasing amounts of time with assignments that contribute little to learning?

To those of us who remember reading books, taking notes,

> **Fifth grade assignment: "Find a rock. Decorate your rock and make it special."**

making outlines, and writing research reports, some of the assignments children are bringing home nowadays seem downright silly. Michele Zuckerman's fifth-grade son brought home this science assignment from his northern Virginia school: "Choose a chemical element and write two paragraphs telling why it is your favorite. Be creative." Only weeks earlier he brought home another winner: "Find a rock. Decorate your rock and make it special. Write a story about your rock." Michele hit the ceiling, and I can't say that I blame her. Do you know what *your* children are doing for homework tonight?

Sandy Carmine's* children attend one of the best schools in Sullivan County, about two and half hours from New York City, but she bemoans the "less than the best" assignments her sixth-grade daughter brings home.

"My daughter got her choice of either creating a scene from the book she read as an edible diorama or making an object from the book using clay, nontoxic dough, papier mache, toothpicks, or popsicle sticks accompanied by one paragraph explaining why she chose one art medium over another."

Are your children spending valuable time on silly assignments? It's time to find out why.

2. Are you being asked to assume teaching responsibilities that were once the teacher's job?

In the Binghamton, New York, public-school fifth graders were assigned reports on famous Americans who have made our country great in the fields of literature, exploration, inventions, and the arts. This sounds like a real "back-to-basics" assignment designed to polish reading and writing skills. The only catch is that the entire assignment was to be done at home with parents. Parents were given a written set of instructions and a miniature model of the report booklet the children were to make. Children were given a specific famous person and a list of required research tools such as the computer, an encyclopedia, and biographical books. In the old days, the school librarian and teacher worked with students at school to teach the skills, provide the resource materials, and supervise the independent completion of the project.[21]

Are you teaching school most nights of the week? It's time to find out why.

3. Are increasing numbers of students in your community enrolled in tutoring programs?

Parents formerly hired tutors to remediate students who were having difficulty in school or to coach them for the SAT or ACT. But as many schools assume fewer responsibilities for teaching children the basics of reading, writing, and math, parents are turning to commercial learning centers like Sylvan, Huntington, and Kumon Math, home tutorial programs, as well as private tutors to teach the basics of reading and math to students who aren't getting phonics and math operations at school. The burgeoning growth of tutoring centers in shopping centers has only begun. In a cover feature on tutoring and its widespread use around the country, *Newsweek* magazine speculated that parents are flocking to tutoring centers with their children because of the "mush-brained educational innovations of the last 30 years."[22]

Did you just write a whopping check to a tutor or a learning center? It's time to find out why.

4. Are your schools using dumbed-down textbooks and assigning less independent reading?

Textbooks today are far easier to read than they were when our grandparents and great-grandparents went to school, according to a study done by two Cornell University researchers, Donald P. Hayes and Loreen T. Wolfer.[23] They concluded that the "long-term use of simplified texts produces a cumulating deficit in the breadth and depth of children's general knowledge and vocabulary." Translation: Reading today's textbooks could be dangerous for your child's academic achievement.

Science and math textbooks contain more illustrations and anecdotes than scientific and mathematical concepts. Reading textbooks are even less demanding. If you don't believe me, do your own research. Mary Damer did. "Two years ago I started seeing my school district assign easy books like *Charlie and the Chocolate Factory* and *Mary Poppins* to seventh graders," she relates. "I began to look at what students read back in the early part of the century to make some comparisons.[24] I concluded that the decline in the difficulty level of what students are assigned by teachers was somewhat gradual until just recently when the floor has dropped out." Mary reports that one fourth-grade boy in the 1930s read seventy books during the school year and recorded the titles and authors in a diary required by his teacher. His reading list would make the average high-school student squirm: *Men of Iron* by Pyle, *Treasure Island* by Stevenson, *The Last of the Mohicans* by Cooper, *Through Europe and*

> When was the last time your child read a "real" book?

Egypt with Napoleon by Marshall, and *Lochinvar Luck* by Terhune were just a few of the titles.

When Nancy Stevenson* of Oregon discovered what a dismal high school English experience awaited her children (fewer and easier books with almost none of the classics), she developed her own reading list. Although the school required that her children read only three books per year, she required one book per month, chosen from her reading list. The family even reads the classics aloud together because the school curriculum has dropped them; the books are too difficult, they report, and the kids don't like to read them.

When was the last time your child read a "real" book? It's time to find out why.

5. Are your schools using curricula and teaching methods that don't work?

If your schools are using whole-language as their primary reading instructional philosophy or have adopted mathematics programs that discourage computational expertise and focus instead on discussing and writing about math rather than "doing it," your children are being shortchanged. It's time to find out why.

6. Do you have the uneasy feeling that your own children aren't learning as much as you did in school?

I recently received a phone call from the parent of a second grader, worried about why her daughter wasn't reading very well. "The teacher tells me that everything's fine and not to worry," the anxious parent explained. "But I know something is wrong." This parent has every right to be alarmed. Her daughter is reading well below grade level. You would think this instructional deficiency would be of concern to the child's teacher, but unfortunately, she, like so many others, has been taken in by instructional methods like whole-language (see chapter 4 for a complete discussion of whole-language) and educational innovations like multi-age classrooms with developmentally appropriate practice (see chapter 6 for more on DAP and multi-age classrooms). This worried mom has not only decided to teach her child to read at home but has also enrolled her in a Kumon math program.

Are your children lacking the basic skills they should have mastered in first and second grades? It's time to find out why.

7. Are the teachers in your schools spending instructional time on projects unrelated to academics?

A Tucson, Arizona, teacher decided to bring current events into her sixth-grade social studies class. On the front page of the *Arizona Daily Star,* with accompanying color photos, was the headline "Clinton Trial Has Drama—-All G Rated."[25] The teacher used class time that could have been devoted to actual learning to orchestrate a mock trial of President Clinton. The pupils at Booth-Fickett Magnet School studied the ins and outs of the sex scandals and auditioned for roles in a trial that would decide the fate of the president. Schools advertise academics, but in the case of this magnet school for gifted children, they are delivering something else.

8. Are academic excellence and recognition of individual achievement discouraged in your school district?

Many parents are dismayed about what they perceive to be outrageous teaching methodologies that discourage competition, academic rewards, individual accomplishments, and accelerated instruction while focusing instead on phony self-esteem. Even parents who proudly advertise their child's honor roll accomplishments are under attack. Mark Mlawer proclaimed the honor roll an unfair institution in an *Education Week* commentary in which he wrote: "Both the educational practice of maintaining an honor roll and the parental practice of public proclamations of this status create and reinforce certain species of unfairness, one which necessarily causes resentment."[26]

Mlawer's sentiments are echoed in this chilling statement from prominent Harvard educator Charles Willie, who believes that the goal of education should not be excellence, because that is a matter of personal choice. Rather, he says, schools should be concerned with "adequacy."[27] Peggy McIntosh, a Wellesley College educator, preaches that "excellence" is a dangerous concept for schools and argues they need to stop giving out "gold stars" and other honors because they reflect an outmoded white male culture of "vertical thinking."[28] Today's classrooms emphasize cooperation and group grades over individual accountability and personal responsibility.

Is your school anti-competition and anti-recognition? It's time to find out why.

9. Does your district make excuses for poor or declining student achievement?

Elaine Arest,* a Tennessee parent, has tried in vain to "wake up" the administrators at her son's middle school with regard to test scores and accountability. She tried to convince them that a highly respected statistical model called the Tennessee Value-Added Assessment System (TVAAS), which uses the scores from the Tennessee Comprehensive Assessment Program (TCAP) to track the impact that school systems, schools, and individual teachers have on the yearly academic growth of all students,[29] would help them be more effective in evaluating student performance. But they were not interested. Elaine observes that "when it comes to accountability, school systems have learned to be slippery. You have about as good a chance of pinning them down about problem areas as you would have standing on your head and gargling greasy BBs."

Does your district explain away test scores with educational jargon and empty excuses? It's time to find out why.

10. Is your district continually implementing unproven innovations and untested curricula?

In many districts around the country, the energies of talented teachers who signed contracts to teach reading, math, and history are consumed with implementing innovations like "block scheduling," "Outcome-Based Education," "School-to-Work," and "multi-age classrooms." Usually unproven, often more related to a "social engineering" agenda than to academic goals, and frequently working at cross purposes with one another, these innovations leave the school treasury drained and administrators, teachers, and students exhausted from trying to do what makes sense along with what has been mandated by the state and district. Chapter 6 contains descriptions of many innovations that are distracting teachers from teaching the subject matter they were hired to teach.

> **If you don't like the test score, change what "average" means!**

Is your school inundated with innovations? It's time to find out why.

11. Is your district phasing out standardized testing for new, more creative tests?

Perhaps the term *performance-based assessment* is a new one to you. In the jargon of today's educators it means that instead of knowing something (e.g., factual knowledge), a student has to do something to demonstrate proficiency (e.g., solving a "real world" problem). Performance-based assessments don't typically have right or wrong answers, unlike multiple choice tests. Rather, they are scored with rubrics that give students credit for a range of answers. The scorers attempt to figure out what students were thinking, and creativity or divergent thinking may often get even more credit than a straightforward, correct response.

Parents in Arizona (and in many other states) recently said good-bye to the good old-fashioned standardized test and are welcoming a new, more "user-friendly" test. Marianne Moody Jennings, parent of four and professor at Arizona State University's College of Business, wrote in her column in the *Arizona Republic* that "the standardized test, the final vestige of classical education and the one no-holds-barred method for determining whether our children are actually learning, is disappearing. These tests are the victims of market forces generated by educrats using their theories on integration, open-ended questions with flexible grading rubrics, and tests as the destroying angel of self-esteem. The education market wants bunk and the test companies, with their fully commissioned sales staffs, are delivering. Arizona was a loyal customer of ITBS (Iowa Test of Basic Skills), the test that has been with us since little houses on the prairie and which remains the most traditional in format and content. That word 'basic' in the name of ITBS must have frightened our education leaders, so come this spring, Arizona's children will experience the SAT 9." Jennings goes on to describe the SAT 9 as a test that "conveys a disdain for basics and oozes creativity."

Have standardized tests become dinosaurs in your district? It's time to find out why.

Do you really know what your children are doing in school today? It's time to find out. Perhaps your own research will sound a wake-up call for you to join the growing cadre of parents and community activists who have discovered that their children's school days are no longer filled with learning, that their schools no longer care about academic achievement, and that their tax dollars are not buying challenging texts and proven programs. These parents are doing their homework, asking questions, and demanding answers. Chapter 2 details the somewhat disturbing ways that the educational establishment is responding to their activism.

Notes

1. Editorial Projects in Education, "Public Agenda: Reality Check," *The Urban Challenge: Public Education in the 50 States,* Quality Counts '98 (Washington, DC: Editorial Projects in Education, 1998) 72-75.

2. All direct quotations from individuals in this book were obtained through personal communication via e-mail, phone, and letter. All are reprinted by permission. No further footnotes will be provided for these quotations.

3. Mathematically Correct, quoted in "The Northridge Chronicles: A Virtual Play," online. Available: http://www.mathematicallycorrect.com

4. Lowell C. Rose, Alec M. Gallup, and Stanley M. Elam, "The 29th Annual Phi Delta Kappa/Gallup Poll of the Public's Attitudes Toward the Public Schools," *Phi Delta Kappan* Sept. 1997: 41-58.

5. Editorial Projects in Education, "Public Agenda" 74.

6. Ibid.

7. To subscribe to Education Consumers ClearingHouse, e-mail Dr. John Stone at education-consumers@tricon.net

8. Randy Moore, "Grades and Self-Esteem," *American Biology Teacher* Oct. 1993: 388.

9. Chester E. Finn, Jr., *We Must Take Charge: Our Schools and Our Future* (New York: Free Press, 1991) 99.

10. "National Testing Is No Magic Bullet," *Investors Business Daily* 3 Sept. 1997: A32.

11. Karen Diegmueller, "S.A.T. to Realign Scores for the First Time in Half a Century," *Education Week* 22 June 1994, online. Available: http://www.edweek.org

12. Gregory J. Cizek, "S.A.T. 'Recentering': Baby Boomers Get a Break," *Education Week* 21 Sept. 1994, online. Available: http://www.edweek.org

13. Patrick Groff, "Letter to the Editor," *Education Week* 3 Aug. 1994, online. Available: http://www.edweek.org

14. *Editorial Projects in Education* 74.

15. Jerome Bruner, *The Process of Education* (Cambridge, MA: Harvard Univ. Press, 1963) 65.

16. Harold W. Stevenson, "Children Deserve Better Than Phony Self-Esteem," *Education Digest* Dec. 1992: 12-13. Harold W. Stevenson and James W. Stigler, *The Learning Gap: Why Our Schools Are Failing and What We Can Learn from Japanese and Chinese Education* (New York: Summit Books, 1992).

17. Office of Educational Research and Improvement, U.S. Dept. of Education, NAEP 1994, *Reading Report Card for the Nation and States*. NAEP 1996, *Math and Science Report Card for the Nation and States* (Washington, DC: U.S. Dept. of Education).

18. Daniel J. Singal, "The Other Crisis in American Education," *The Atlantic Monthly* Nov. 1991: 60.

19. Jonathan Kaufman, "Suburban Parents Shun Many Public Schools, Even the Good Ones," *Wall Street Journal* 1 March 1996: A1, A6.

20. Carol Innerst, "Students Fall Behind All Along the Way," *Washington Times* 20 Oct. 1997: A1.

21. Dorothy Zandt, "Reports on Famous People Bring Learning into Homes," *Binghamton Press & Sun Bulletin* [NY] 6 Mar. 1998: 1B.

22. Jerry Adler, "The Tutor Age," *Newsweek* 30 March 1998: 48.

23. Donald P. Hayes and Loreen T. Wolfer, "Was the Decline in SAT Verbal Scores Caused by Simplified Texbooks?" Unpublished manuscript prepared for the *Journal of Educational Research,* 31 Aug. 1993.

24. Evangeline Colburn, *A Library for the Intermediate Grades* (Chicago, IL: Laboratory Schools of the Univ. of Chicago, 1930).

25. Jill Jorden Spitz, "Sixth-grade Jury Deadlocked on President's Guilt," *The Arizona Daily Star* 29 Jan. 1998: 1A, 5A.

26. Mark A. Mlawer, "My Kid Beat Up Your Honor Student," *Education Week* 13 July 1994, online. Available: http://www.edweek.org

27. Glynn Custred, "Onward to Adequacy," *Academic Questions* Summer 1990.

28. Dennis Farney, "For Peggy McIntosh, Excellence Can Be a Dangerous Concept," *Wall Street Journal* 14 June 1994: A1, A5.

29. William L. Sanders and Sandra Horn, *An Overview of the Tennessee Value-Added Assessment System* (Knoxville, TN: The Univ. of Tennessee, n.d.).

TALES FROM THE TRENCHES

The Educrats' Alphabet

Joan Batey
Parent
Education Activist

Perhaps the term *educrat* is a new one to you. It's a combination of two words, *educator* and *bureaucrat*. Educrats are people who have been around education so long they've forgotten who the schools really belong to. They've lost sight of what made them want to be educators and board members in the first place, and have been seduced by the power and perks that accrue to insiders.

A is for Always Assess (everything but our own mistakes);

B is for Build empires that are indestructible;

C is for Control by Consensus;

D is for Demolish all opposition by any means;

E is for Endlessly reinvent the wheel in reinventing conferences and seminars;

F is for Fooling the public;

G is for Grants, the primary purpose of education;

H is for Human Capital [students], which we will move according to our whim, using capital that humans will provide;

I is for Innovations that roll out of far-flung planning committees;

J is for Just schedule meetings at times convenient for school personnel without worrying about parents or taxpayers who have work or family time conflicts. . . .

(For letters K–Z see Appendix E.)

2 The Customer Is Never Right?

How Teachers, Administrators, and School Boards Infuriate Parents

> Everybody chooses weapons when dealing with the difficulties of life, and the choice of weapons determines the distinction with which you meet your trials. You can arm yourself with ignorance, indolence, and pessimism—or with wisdom, discipline, and hope.
>
> —*Eric V. Copage*, A Kwanzaa Fable

If you're concerned about what is happening in your school or district and decide to go looking for answers and explanations, there are no guarantees that you'll receive either a straight answer or a warm reception from the principal, central office administrator, or school board member. In fact, most of the parent activists I've interviewed have been met with suspicion and downright hostility when they've had the temerity to question the status quo. This sad state of affairs is truly depressing to me as a professional educator. When I was a principal, I had a slightly different mindset about parents than many of my fellow administrators. My attitude was developed during my growing-up years when I worked for my father, who owned a department store. He ran his business with the credo: *The customer is always right.*

When I was hired for my first principalship, I decided that parents were my "customers"; I would follow in my father's footsteps and run my school with the same philosophy that had worked for him in building a successful business. In the beginning my staff had a difficult time adjusting to my consumer-oriented philosophy. I held teachers accountable for their behavior and would not make excuses for poor instruction. We communicated our expectations for learning to our parents and contracted with them to deliver. I was an advocate for parents and students, as all administrators should be, particularly those families who were disenfranchised by an English-speaking bureaucracy or were angry and frustrated at how they had been treated by educators in the past. I constantly encouraged parents and teachers to listen and learn from each other in order to ensure that children achieved.

I now serve as a consultant helping administrators learn to listen, empathize, and understand how alienating certain behaviors can be, such as a fierce defense of the status quo, an unwillingness to perform the role of public servant, an aversion to accountability, and an inability to see situations from the consumers' point of view. Parents must not be shocked if they are greeted with skepticism, arrogance, or resentment when they ask, "What are my children doing in school today?" Here are some administrative responses you might encounter.

Circling the Wagons

Automatically defending the system or backing the teachers without really hearing or trying to understand the parents' perspective makes parents furious. I call this practice "circling the wagons." Many administrators believe that their first responsibility is to defend the status quo, no matter how compelling the evidence to the contrary may be. But when teachers are ineffective, the curriculum is undemanding, and kids aren't learning, parents are hard-pressed to understand why an administrator would defend and/or cover up. Imagine a manager at McDonald's defending the counter clerk rather than the customer who got somebody else's order. This kind of behavior would be ridiculous in the business world, yet it occurs all too often in the public schools.

Stonewalling

When educators say they'll deal with a problem and do nothing or promise to return a phone call and then conveniently misplace the message, parents climb the walls. Knowing that an issue is approaching emergency status (e.g., a teacher is harassing a student; instruction is ineffective; the classroom is out of control; a child is failing) and then choosing to ignore it out of fear, indifference, or just plain indecision is guaranteed to send parents either straight up the wall or to their attorneys' offices.

Can you imagine a grocery store manager knowing about a "wet-cleanup" problem in aisle 4 and not getting someone to mop it up immediately? Yet in the public schools, administrators often ignore an "emergency" hoping both the emergency and the parent will miraculously vanish.

Labeling and Stereotyping

Putting labels on parents because they question what's happening in the schools makes parents angry, and justifiably so: "Just because I go to church and want my children to learn phonics, don't call me a right-wing Bible thumper." A majority of the parent activists with whom I spoke found that educators felt perfectly justified to engage in labeling and name calling even though parents asked reasonable questions about curriculum, teaching methodologies, and accountability. J. E. Stone of the Education

> **Tarring critics with labels such as "right winger," "extremist," "religious nut" is the easiest defense.**

Consumers ClearingHouse thinks that tarring critics with labels such as "right winger," "extremist," "religious nut" is the easiest defense available. When you're dealing with a "nut," you're not obligated to take a question seriously or consider that a concern might be valid.

In the business world, treating people differently because of their "demographics" is strictly illegal. Denny's, the headquarters for all-night breakfasts, is still smarting from the embarrassment of a suit charging discrimination against customers based on ethnicity. Yet in schools we label students and their parents routinely with scarcely a thought for the humiliation these labels may create for parents and children.

Making Them Feel Guilty

If labeling the parents who question the educational establishment as ultraconservative right-wingers doesn't work, educators have found a new way to vilify concerned parents. Accuse them of being selfish, demanding, and spoiled—parents who are more concerned for their own children than for all of the children in the community. Make them feel guilty. In a lengthy article in *Phi Delta Kappan,* Alfie Kohn explains this new way to intimidate complaining parents into shutting up—make them feel guilty for not caring about all children learning.

> It is common knowledge that the Christian Right has opposed all manner of progressive reforms. They may act stealthily to get themselves installed on school boards, and they may read from identical scripts in auditoriums across America about how outcome-based education and whole-language will destroy our way of life. But they are ultimately identifi-

able, and, once their core beliefs are exposed and their claims refuted, their impact (at least in many places) can be limited. Far less attention has been paid to the damage done by people whose positions on other social issues are more varied and more mainstream—specifically, the affluent parents of successful students, those whose political power is substantial to begin with and whose agenda [can be summarized thusly]: "they are not concerned that all children learn: they are concerned that *their* children learn."[1]

Kohn refers to such parents humorously as "Rich Parents Against School Reform," but you can be assured that educators everywhere are filing this article away to pull out and read aloud to the next parent who complains about outrageous innovations.

Why can't the school assume the attitude that successful businesses have? "We can meet the needs of a variety of customers. One size doesn't fit all, and we're willing to tailor our products and services to meet your needs."

Obfuscating with "Educationese"

When administrators speak in incomprehensible jargon rather than use straight English, it makes parents mad. When a phrase like "facilitative, inclusive, outcome-driven, cognitive, systems-thinking, interdisciplinary, performance-based, action research" is thrown at today's parents, they are intimidated and likely to wonder about the wisdom of leaving their child in a school where English is a second language.

Educator Donna Smith calls it "edubabble." Smith, who recently retired after twenty-three years in the classroom, asks this pointed question in a commentary for the Oklahoma Council of Public Affairs:

Ever wonder how those in the higher echelons of the educational system plan to dupe John Q. into supporting their outlandish proposals? As someone who has taught for 23 years, served on local and state education committees, edited an association newsletter, and now serves on a local school board, I have discovered their plan. These espousers of global citizenry, national testing, school-business partnerships, and reduction of traditional American values are conning JQ with polibaloney edubabble.[2]

Businesses go to great lengths to make "consumer-friendly" products. Companies that sell highly technical products promise twenty-four-hour customer service hotlines to decipher directions. On the other hand, educators seem to go out of their way to make education confusing, causing parents to wonder what really is happening behind those closed classroom doors.

Intimidating, Isolating, and Controlling

When nothing else works, educators often try intimidation, isolation, and control. A typical response: "You're the only parent who has a concern." Marilyn Weller,* a Pennsylvania parent, experienced what can happen when you challenge the power structure at the wrong time. Invited to participate in a school district task force to evaluate the effectiveness of an early childhood program that featured developmentally appropriate practice (DAP), Marilyn took seriously her assignment to submit concerns and questions to the curriculum and instruction administrator before the next meeting. And she had plenty of questions, especially concerning the progress of students. Her first suspicions regarding the program were aroused when a hired consultant told the group that "if it's high test scores you're looking for, then this is not the program for you." Because Marilyn didn't want to rely totally on her own judgment, she polled the parents in her school and visited DAP classrooms around the district. Then she submitted twenty-four questions. At the next meeting she asked the meeting facilitator if she could give each of the parents on the committee a copy of her questions. He turned to her and yelled, "Absolutely not. Take those papers and sit down. You're not giving those questions to anyone." Although he later apologized for his behavior, the message was clear. "This is my turf and your interference is not welcome."

> **"Take those papers and sit down!"**

Undaunted, Marilyn questioned why the program had been launched in the first place without adequate study and evaluation and why the curriculum varied so much from school to school. She questioned the teaching methodologies she had observed during her classroom visits. While Marilyn spoke, the elementary curriculum supervisor rolled her eyes and sighed out loud, sending a clear message to the rest of the task force that Marilyn was obviously uninformed, unbalanced, and out of place.

Although the professional educators acted most unprofessionally in their attempts to intimidate and control Marilyn, she kept her cool and made her point: "I'm on this task force because other parents have concerns like mine. The program is wrong. Children are not learning. This is a public school and parents have a right to decide how their children will be educated. I am not asking the district to do away with the program, but to give me a choice."

Marilyn confesses that although she held her ground, she was close to tears and exhausted after the ordeal. Should this be the experience of taxpaying parents who volunteer to help in the public schools?

Marketing managers often use focus groups to help discover how their products and services can be improved. Can you imagine business professionals insulting and intimidating the very customers they've invited to assist them? Yet it happened to Marilyn, and it happens to parents around the nation when they seek to be involved in their kids' education.

Acting Arrogant

Educators often have the most amazing capacity for arrogance. When parents question methodologies or refuse to support one more unproven innovation, educators seem surprised and even affronted. They profess fear for the very foundations of public education if they have to endure these unwarranted attacks from fanatical parents. They scurry to mount public relations campaigns rather than consider the possibility that the "public" to whom the schools are accountable just might have something worthwhile to say.

Mary Damer is a reasonable, education-savvy, and very articulate parent who wonders daily where the arrogance of administrators and board members will end. The organization she cofounded, Taxpayers for Academic Priorities in St. Charles (Illinois), recently released an eleven-page analysis of the district's test scores that laid the blame for steadily declining performance squarely on the deleterious impact of a constant cycle of unproven innovations implemented over a seven-year period. The school board ignored the report but came calling immediately to ask the group to support a multimillion-dollar referendum. Mary is astounded. "How dare the school district ask the taxpayers for more money! Many of us are paying private tuition or home-schooling because the district is not responsive to parental concerns regarding its untested curriculum. How can they have the chutzpah to think I would vote to give them even more funds for more reforms?" It is very difficult for parents, even reasonable ones like Mary, to keep their anger under control when confronted with such arrogance.

When businesses exhibit arrogance or condescension, customers let their money do the talking by walking with their dollars to a competitor. Market forces keep businesses from taking their customers for granted. Unfortunately, public schools do not view the world according to market forces. There is no penalty in public education for treating parents disrespectfully.

Demeaning and Detracting

Parents would like to be given some credit for knowing what constitutes a good education and understanding the needs of their own children. They get upset when educators assume that they, the experts, know best. Bonnie Smythe,* an Oregon parent, has been helping to educate parents about reform in the state since before her third-grade daughter entered school. She has experienced such condescension firsthand. "Before my daughter even started school I volunteered in kindergarten to get the 'lay of the land.' I went to all of the school board and site council meetings and talked with teachers." Bonnie wanted to get involved and rolled up her proverbial sleeves.

"My suggestions regarding phonics programs, volunteer cadres to assist in classrooms, and adult mentoring programs for students were met not only with resistance but even hostility. Rather than a climate of partnership there was the attitude that 'we are the professionals and you don't know anything about education.'"

Sheryl Mueller*, who lives in suburban Pittsburgh, experienced "control" when she served on a Parent Advisory Council. "A group of eight parents met twice to decide on the 'issues' that had to be presented to the faculty ahead of time. Then they were given a single one-hour meeting with teacher representatives from each grade. They had a timer and assigned each issue a certain number of minutes. It was dreadful. No room for open, honest communication. Just more of the 'we're the teachers, we're perfect, we know all, leave us alone' type of thing." Sheryl has a thriving after-school tutoring business, a master's degree in education, and substitutes regularly in her community's schools. Can you blame her for being irritated at this kind of treatment?

Many hotels and restaurants I visit in my travels solicit my input and ideas. They provide questionnaires for me to complete. My car dealer calls me every time I bring my car in for servicing to find out if I was satisfied with the work. Business owners appreciate and listen to my ideas. Customers with product loyalty are treasured and their opinions are valued. In contrast, schools too often consider parent involvement and input as interference. Loyalty is synonymous with silence and is often interpreted as a willingness to accept whatever the school district chooses to implement.

Perhaps you're already frustrated at what you've seen occurring in your public schools. You may have suspected that something is amiss but haven't been able to put a finger on just what. If what you've been reading in chapters 1 and 2 comes as a surprise to you, however, and you're feeling confused by the barrage of bad news, you're not alone. Maybe you're wondering: "Where have I been? When did this happen? How could I have been so blind?" I can relate to your feelings. I'm an educator and this sad state of affairs has my mind boggled. It was all around me, and I didn't comprehend the depth of the problem.

A brief history lesson will help put things in perspective for both of us. Chapter 3 provides just that.

Notes

1. Alfie Kohn, "Only for My Kid: How Privileged Parents Undermine School Reform," *Phi Delta Kappan* Apr. 1998: 570.
2. Donna Smith, "Schoolteacher Wants 'Just the Facts,'" Oklahoma Council of Public Affairs, 1997, online. Available: http://www.ocpathink.org

TALES FROM THE TRENCHES

The First Day of First Grade

Barbara Tennison
Parent
Education Activist

I was excited about my child's first day in first grade, and I was looking forward to hearing the goals for the school year. The teacher greeted the assembled parents warmly.

"Education has changed radically since you were a student," she told us. "There's nothing wrong with the education you had. It was okay for your times, but it won't be good enough for the kids who are moving into the global economy of the 21st century." This sounded ominous. My husband and I just wanted our child to learn to read.

The teacher explained that so much more is known today about how children learn and that instruction in her classroom would be "developmentally appropriate" to each student's learning style. I felt mystified, but I concentrated hard on the discussion of left- and right-brain learning. I wondered when we were going to start talking about reading, writing, and arithmetic.

"Your children will have an especially interesting year as we invite members of the business community in to spend time with us," she explained. "They have volunteered to be mentors and are opening up their businesses for off-campus instruction and field trips." I was still wondering when we would get to reading, writing, and arithmetic.

Then, as if she had read my mind, the teacher moved on to classroom instruction. *Aha,* I thought to myself, *now I'll find out what this teacher intends to teach.* But she began to talk about forging a partnership with parents. I had been listening for almost twenty minutes to flowery descriptions of school-business and parent-school partnerships, but I had not yet heard anything about how my child would learn to read.

How Politics, Profits, and Professors Are Taking Control of Education

3 Where Did the Schools Go Wrong?

> When you leave here, don't forget why you came.
> —*Adlai Stevenson, to a Princeton University class*

When it comes to explaining what has gone wrong in many of our public schools, Adlai Stevenson may have the answer. In some cases professors, administrators, and board members have forgotten why they got into the education business to begin with.

I still remember in vivid detail a very disturbing experience as a principal. One of my most effective teachers resigned from her sixth-grade teaching position in the late spring to have her first child. I hired a brand-new graduate from a local college who came highly recommended. Since there were only four weeks remaining in the school year, I told this bright-eyed novice in no uncertain terms to maintain the status quo. The students would feel most comfortable, I explained, if she followed the routine their teacher had established. This sweet young woman decided that she knew better. The classroom was too structured (our "factory-model" deeply offended her), and the students needed more freedom to express themselves. She threw the carefully maintained grade book in the wastebasket and planned to "make up" grades for the final report card. She ignored the meticulously prepared lesson plans left by the former teacher and tried some exploratory learning. By the end of her first week, the students were in revolt, the parents were ringing my phone off the hook, and I was ready to send this new teacher straight back to her college of education for retraining. Unfortunately, her training was a big part of the problem. For the last week of the school year, I hired an experienced, "old-fashioned" substitute and gave the young woman a filing job in the office.

Sadly enough, she never "got it." She thought we were wrong and she was right. She thought that I was an old fuddy-duddy and that the parents were clearly out of bounds to tell her how to do her job. She thought the children had been repressed and ruined by a teacher-directed classroom. She remained blithely unaware of how she had been indoctrinated by her professors. I don't know what happened to her after she left my school. I made sure she wasn't hired in my district. Perhaps she's teaching one of your children even as we speak. My disagreement with this eager educator represented the same conflict that has been a part of the American educational landscape for a century and a half—the same conflict that is still going on in school districts across the country. The protagonists today are very similar to those who held opposing viewpoints on the issues more than a century and a half ago: the *progressivists* and the *traditionalists*.

Proponents of progressive education, both today's variety as well as the early founders of our system of free public education, view the schools as the means by which to alter the structure, values, and ethics of society. Proponents of traditional education, on the other hand, want the schools to reflect the values and goals of the community; therefore, parental desires and local control should hold sway. These are the major philosophical differences in a nutshell. There are also curricular and instructional differences that have characterized these two viewpoints through the years and continue to create debate. The progressivists believe that children should construct their own learning and truth through real-world projects that build self-esteem. Teachers merely serve as nondirective facilitators, and the educational process is far more important than the educational product. The classroom is learner centered.

> **Proponents of progressive education view the schools as the means by which to alter the structure, values, and ethics of society.**

On the other hand, traditionalists believe that adults have a body of knowledge worth transmitting to the next generation and that children are capable of scholastic achievement when taught directly and explicitly in a system that holds both teacher and child accountable. Although volumes have been written about both of these educational philosophies, these simple definitions will help you begin to understand why many of our current schools and classrooms are in disarray. The districts most at risk for a total takeover by progressivism in the new millennium are those districts with multiple resources—substantial property tax bases, upwardly mobile parents, smart kids, and a desire to be on the "cutting edge."

As might be expected, the battle for control of our nation's classrooms produces both winners and losers. More often than not the winners of the "school wars" have been the critics, reformers, philosophers, professors, politicians, publishers, and consultants—the specialists in innovation and ivory tower solutions. These folk have published books, made speeches, earned tenure at universities, and lined their pockets with our tax dollars. The unions and educrats, the once dedicated educators who in

> **Proponents of traditional education want the schools to reflect the values and goals of the community.**

the course of losing their vision turned into apathetic bureaucrats, likewise have pocketed their share of the spoils with contracts and tenure of their own. The losers, of course, are those with the most at stake—parents, their children, and the many dedicated educators who have not abandoned their principles.

The Big Guns Join the Fight: Government and Corporations

Recently, two well-financed goliaths have joined the battle on the progressivist side in more surreptitious ways: the federal government and corporate America. Although Uncle Sam and the CEOs are certainly not newcomers to educational policy decision making, their newest plans for the little red schoolhouse may dwarf anything we've seen to date and if not held in check will dramatically change the way our schools are structured. Big Brother and Big Business appear poised to move forward without significant opposition.

The well-meaning and very dedicated teachers and principals currently working in our public schools are like citizens of the mythical kingdom in one of my favorite fairy tales, "The Emperor's New Clothes." You'll recall that story in which some clever and unscrupulous weavers convince a vain and stupid emperor that the completely imaginary suit of clothes they've produced for him out-shines anything he's worn to date. He wanders through the kingdom while his intimidated subjects praise the elegance of his near nakedness. Only an innocent child dares to tell him the truth.

There are hundreds of thousands of educators out there who know down deep that the emperor isn't wearing any clothes, that many of the faddish instructional methods and educational innovations we have embraced don't work. But, like the emperor's subjects, they're fearful of not being "politically correct." Instead of being permitted to make instructional decisions, they are bullied by the "theoreticians and their supporters in professional associations."[1]

William Durden, executive director of the Institute for the Academic Advancement of Youth at Johns Hopkins University in Baltimore calls it "intellectual acquiescence in the face of political and emotional deck-stacking."[2] Teachers are worried about their evaluations and are afraid of being transferred out of schools where they've spent their careers. They have seen what can happen when people don't "climb aboard." They're simply hanging on until retirement. But there are many others who are loudly and courageously proclaiming the truth: "The emperor has no clothes." They are causing people around the country to sit up and take notice.

Parents might be willing to speak out if they had more time or understood the issues more clearly. Often, however, they are intimidated by the educational establishment—shut down and shut out by phony consensus-building committees or stonewalling administrators. Worse, they are afraid of what might happen to their children if they make too much of a fuss. Or at least that used to be the case. When you meet parents like the Tennisons in Oregon, Julie Anders, Carolyn Steinke, and Gayle Cloud in California, Richard Innes in Kentucky, Barbara Shafer, Marilyn Keller Rittmeyer, Mary Damer, Sarah Phillips, and Dawn Earl in Illinois, Donna Garner and Jeanne Donovan in Texas, Chuck Arthur in Oregon, and Steve Goss in Arizona, you will see how perfectly ordinary parents and teachers have become extraordinary activists. These folks, some with advanced degrees but many with only high school diplomas and a healthy dose of common sense, each began by observing, researching, and questioning what they found in their child's school-room. Today they are writing newsletters, lobbying legislators, forming charter schools, appearing in national newspapers, and making their presence felt far beyond their local districts.

Before you can become an activist or at the very least understand what is happening in your child's classroom, you'll need to do your homework. The parents and teachers I mentioned earlier have all taken the time to become informed. This process includes understanding a bit about the history of the "education wars" we just described.

There are several key tensions that exist between the progressivists and the traditionalists, yet many parents still feel they don't have to choose. They fall into the trap of believing that their children will get it all at school—everything the progressivists have promised to deliver (e.g., cooperation, team building, creative problem solving, discovery learning, plus marketable job skills) as well as the ideals of the traditionalists (e.g., self-discipline, a competitive edge, basic skills, plus all of the academic knowledge that the past has to offer).

> **Education has resembled an imbalanced seesaw, fluctuating wildly between the ups and downs of innovation.**

You are no doubt saying to yourself: "This is exactly what I want for my children. I want it all—both ends of the continuum and everything in between." The problem with wanting "both ends and everything in between" is that rarely does one encounter the balance that is required to have it all. Education has more often resembled an imbalanced seesaw or a pendulum, fluctuating wildly between the ups and downs or back and forths of innovation.

The battle in education today is about determining just where on the philosophical continuum the line will be drawn that defines the student we want to graduate from our schools. That defining point is the subject of intense debate, and in some cases the schools have moved the line so far away from where it used to be that in most cases you won't even be able to find it. The discipline, academic knowledge, basic skills, ability to compete, and subject-matter competence that you think your children will acquire in school are vanishing faster than the pygmy owl and bighorn sheep are in my Arizona neighborhood. Critical thinking, marketable job skills, global citizenship, and cooperation are the new buzzwords. Readin', writin', and 'rithmetic "ain't" in. Neither are grammar and spelling.

Some parents and educators still believe, as I did until recently, that we didn't have to draw a line at all; we *could* have it all. A vanishing group of educators is still naively holding on to this dream and is trying under tremendous pressure and odds to do the right thing. But the politicians, businessmen, and educational policymakers are playing high-stakes poker with our children's futures and finding the impulse to gamble with the public trust irresistible. The dollars flowing from state houses and Washington are enticing local districts to the table where they (and their parents) will find the stakes have been raised and the rules have been changed.

The Beginnings of Public Education

Let's take a brief look at how the progressivist-traditionalist conflict has evolved since a free, public education first became available to the students of Massachusetts in the early 1800s. Horace Mann, recognized by most as the father of the common school, revolutionized public school organization and teaching. His unbounded faith in the power of education gave him a religious zeal that was contagious.

> The Common School is the greatest discovery ever made by man. . . . Other social organizations are curative and remedial; this is a preventive and an antidote. . . . Let the Common School be expanded to its capabilities, let it be worked with the efficiency of which it is susceptible, and nine-tenths of the

crimes in the penal code would become obsolete; the long catalogue of human ills would be abridged . . . all rational hopes respecting the future brightened.[3]

You can plainly see that from its infancy American public education had as its goal righting the wrongs of the world and curing the ills of society. Learning was definitely important, but it shared the billing with improving the lot of the "common man."

Professional educators were in charge, and they knew best how to select teachers and choose curriculum. These were weighty matters that only trained educational scientists could oversee. John Swett, California state superintendent of instruction, held the same opinion of parents in the 1860s that many educators today have:

> The vulgar impression that parents have a legal right to dictate to teachers is entirely erroneous. . . . The only persons who have a legal right to give orders to the teacher are his employers, namely the committee in some states and in others the directors or trustees. . . . If his conduct is approved of by his employers, the parents have no remedy against him or them.[4]

> **After two hundred years of public education in Massachusetts there were more criminals and suicides per capita.**

But there were always courageous souls who recognized the importance of parental authority and wisdom. During the Senate confirmation of Zachary Montgomery for U.S. Attorney General in 1886, his views on public education were unpopular. His nomination was denied. Montgomery used the 1860 census figures to demonstrate that after two hundred years of public education in Massachusetts there were *more* criminals and suicides per capita (using only native white inhabitants) than in the state of Virginia where education was still left totally in the hands of parents. The cause? Montgomery explained:

> We maintain that there are chiefly two causes, both of which are intimately connected, the one, in fact springing from the other. The first cause which we proposed to consider is the loss of parental authority and home influence over children, through and by means of a State-controlled system of education. The second cause, and one which, as just stated, is closely allied to the first, is a neglect of moral and religious education and training.[5]

The distinct differences between progressivists and traditionalists emerged early in our country's history. Although the arguments are more sophisticated today and the methodologies more legislated, the key issue remains unchanged: Should the public schools reflect parental and community values, or should they be a political tool to impose a national agenda and create a thriving economy?

Progressivism Makes Headway

At least one thing was clear near the turn of the century—academics weren't totally ignored. Educators generally agreed that knowledge was critical, college was a worthwhile goal, and every student should complete a rigorous course of study. The Committee of Ten, created by the National Education Association and chaired by Charles W. Eliot, president of Harvard University, recommended that what pupils learned in high school should permit them to go to college if they should later make that decision. "Colleges and scientific schools should be able to admit any graduate of a good secondary course, regardless of his program." The course of study suggests four years of English, four years of a foreign language, three years of history, three years of mathematics, and three years of science as a minimum.[6]

The progressivist movement was gathering steam, however. Near the turn of the century, Francis W. Parker, the founder of the University of Chicago School of Education, demonstrated the zeal of an evangelist in his enthusiasm for the benefits of progressivism: "The child is not in school for knowledge. He is there to live, and to put his life, nurtured in the school, into the community."[7] John Dewey, an even more influential progressive philosopher and educator, asserted that "no disciplines were intrinsically endowed with liberating or cultural powers. If properly taught, a wide range of subjects were capable of producing "intellectual results." He urged educators to devote more attention to vocational subjects, on the grounds that they were valuable for exploring the characteristics and meaning of an emerging industrial society.[8]

Charles Eliot's nine committee members were no doubt shaking their heads in wonder at these outrageous statements. The educational pendulum swung wildly once again in 1918 as a second panel formed by the National Education Association rejected the recommendations made by its former panel, the Committee of Ten. In *The Cardinal Principles of Secondary Education* the panel watered down academic requirements. Its reason: "The character of the secondary school population has been modified by the entrance of large numbers of pupils of widely varying capacities, aptitudes, social heredity, and destinies in life. The needs of these pupils cannot be neglected." The academic goals of education were temporarily laid aside to deal with our country's social woes.

Meanwhile, another influential progressivist, William Heard Kilpatrick, was hard at work in the education department at Columbia University. During his extensive career he would train a generation of education leaders by attacking subject matter "fixed in advance" in favor of teaching methods that used projects drawn from students' immediate environments and interests.[9] Inane assignments, time-wasting projects, fuzzy curriculum, and student-centered classrooms were born in the classes of John

Dewey at the University of Chicago and of William Heard Kilpatrick at Columbia University. Those they trained would pour forth into the schools to preach progressivism. One of the most popular texts used for teachers in training of the day, *Elementary Principles of Education* by Edward Thorndike and Arthur Gates, enlightened teachers with this statement:

> Traditionally the elementary school has been primarily devoted to teaching the fundamental subjects, the three R's and closely related disciplines. . . . Artificial exercises, like drills on phonetics, multiplication tables, and formal writing movements, are used to a wasteful degree. Subjects such as arithmetic, language, and history include content that is intrinsically of little value.[10]

Progressive educators had still not forgotten the power of the school as an instrument of social change, and in 1932 George S. Counts, professor at Columbia University and an expert on Russian education, suggested that the schools could build a new social order: "Teachers should deliberately reach for power and then make the most of their conquest," so as to

> "Teachers should deliberately reach for power and then make the most of their conquest."

> influence the social attitudes, ideals, and behavior of the coming generation. . . . Our major concern consequently should be. . . to make certain that every Progressive school will use whatever power it may possess in opposing and checking the process of social conservatism and reaction. . . . The growth of science and technology has carried us into a new age where ignorance must be replaced by knowledge, competition by cooperation, trust in Providence by careful

planning, and private capitalism by some form of socialized economy.[11]

Traditionalist spokespersons were like prophets crying in the wilderness. Charles Beard lamented in 1939 that "education would cease to be education if it ruled out of consideration Plato's Republic, the Bible, or the writings of all such thinkers as Thomas Aquinas, John Ruskin, or Ralph Waldo Emerson."[12] Beard's dire prediction would prove to be prescient when one considers what today's classrooms are like. These classrooms more closely represent Boyd Bode's description of progressive education:

> The strongest and most evangelistic movement in American education at the present time is . . . progressive education. A visitor to our schools ordinarily has no difficulty in recognizing a so-called progressive school. . . . In academic language, the progressive school is a place where children go, not primarily to learn, but to carry on a way of life.[13]

Need Your Life Adjusted?

In 1945, the "life-adjustment" movement was born with the adoption of the "Prosser Resolution" by the U.S. Department of Education. The report stated that 60 percent of the nation's secondary school students were not suited to training for college or for skilled occupations and that they should be provided instead with "life-adjustment training," such as "functional experiences in the areas of practical arts, home and family life, health and physical fitness, and civic competence."[14] The academic rigor suggested by Charles Eliot's Committee of Ten in 1893 had all but disappeared in half a century. Beard's prediction was becoming a reality. Education seemed to have ceased being education.

The traditionalists, however, had not died, and there were definitely pockets of resistance and educational activists who yearned for a return to the "cultural literacy" of the past century. Mortimer Smith, a former school board member in Connecticut, critiqued the progressive movement:

> Here was a doctrine that released the teacher from his responsibility for handing on the traditional knowledge of the [human] race, a doctrine that firmly implied that one need not adhere to any standards of knowledge but simply cater to individual interests. . . . With the acceptance of this doctrine American public school education took the easy way to meet its problems.[15]

Progressive educators were less concerned with teaching and learning than with their role in remaking society. A 1949 issue of the journal *Progressive Education* published the following statement by American Education Fellowship president Kenneth Benne: "Teachers and school administrators [should] come to see themselves as social engineers. They must equip themselves as 'change agents.'"[16]

Do not think for a moment that the "dumbing down" of American schools is a recent phenomenon. This process has been occurring on and off for nearly fifty years. Consider this defense of the "dumbed down" curriculum by a progressive junior high school principal in the early '50s.

> Through the years we've built a sort of halo around reading, writing, and arithmetic. We've said they were for everybody . . . rich and poor, brilliant and not-so-mentally endowed, ones who liked them and those who failed to go for them. The Three R's for All Children, and All Children for the Three R's! That was it. We've made some progress in getting rid of that slogan. But every now and then some mother with a Phi Beta Kappa award or some employer who has hired a girl who can't spell stirs up a fuss about the schools . . . and ground is lost. . . . When we come

to the realization that not every child has to read, figure, write and spell . . . that many of them either cannot or will not master these chores . . . then we shall be on the road to improving the junior high curriculum.[17]

> "Not every child has to read, figure, write and spell."

The progressives felt pretty smug and secure in the early '50s. They believed that American schools were far superior to those of the 1900s.[18] But the decade would bring a barrage of attacks on progressive education by traditionalists, among them a scathing attack on the current state of education by Albert Lynd, *Quackery in the Public Schools.*

> Whether you like it or not, the Education bureaucracy has relieved you of all basic decisions about the aims and methods of the schooling in your town. The professors at the center of the system, who have been elected by nobody, control the qualifications of your teachers by fixing them in terms of their own course offerings. . . . An ambitious young administrator in a small town would be a fool to spend much time trying to find out what the parents and citizens would really like. . . . He will move along much faster in the profession if he performs so as to draw the favorable attention of the pundits in some influential School of Education.[19]

Lynd raised the issue that is still confounding educational activists attempting to gain an audience with professional educators—how to get educators to pay attention to parents and citizens.

In 1953, Arthur Bestor mounted an attack on progressive education in his book *Educational Wastelands:*

> I stand for an American public school system that

shall be educational. There is an antique play on words that still seems to tickle the fancy of professional educationists. "We do not teach history," they say, "we teach children." The implication that those who teach history teach it to no one is a manifest impossibility. . . . But it *is* a distinct possibility, alas, that educationists, following their own maxim, may succeed in teaching children—nothing. . . . Can we afford to entrust to men [and women] who think and act like this, the power to direct the first 12 years of American schooling . . . the years in which young men and women must learn to think clearly and accurately if they are to learn to think at all?[20]

Where Would the Rocket Scientists Come From?

Although books like Bestor's created a stir in some circles, their dire warnings fell on largely deaf ears in the educational community until the attention of the American public and its leaders were riveted on education by the launching of the Sputnik satellite by the Russians. Our educational system was one-upped in 1959. It was measured and found lacking. Suddenly the federal government began pouring millions of dollars into schools. We had to catch up to the Russians, and academics were the answer. Money for library books, science programs for gifted students, and grants for mathematics education were there for the taking, and schools suddenly tightened their requirements, notched up the teaching, and raised the standards.

Progressive educators were unfazed, however. Their firm belief that children know what is best kept them calm when all about them, politicians were worried about academic achievement. A. S. Neill, founder of the English progressive school Summerhill, continued to beat the drum for child-centered schools in 1960. "Parents are slow in realizing how unimportant the learning side of school is. Children, like adults, learn what they want to learn. All prize-giving and marks and exams sidetrack proper personality development." Neill goes on to explain that "a child is innately wise and realistic. If left to himself without adult suggestions of any kind, he will develop as far as he is capable of developing."[21]

The state of California, often the stage upon which our national educational battles are played out in microcosm, brought forth Max Rafferty in 1963. The colorful and outspoken California state superintendent of education made this case for content over process:

> Only through mastery of the great tools of English, history, languages, science, and mathematics can the citizens of the future possess the key to tomorrow. This means study and hard work. There is no royal or easy road to mastery of content. . . . For those who really wish to break away from the dead hand of progressive education, then, the rules are simple. Stress subject matter, all subject matter, provided it has been placed in the curriculum of the schools by the representatives of the people.[22]

Nevertheless, another strong voice for progressive education, author John Holt, joined A. S. Neill in casting his vote for student-centered classrooms. "True learning—learning that is permanent and useful, that leads to intelligent action and further learning—can arise only out of the experience, interests, and concerns of the learner."[23]

During this period of renewed emphasis on academics, progressive educators never relinquished their hold on the leadership of the educational community. Consider this statement by NEA president Catherine Barrett in 1972: "We are the biggest potential political fighting force in this country and we are determined to control the direction of American education."[24] The National Education Association, the largest of the teachers' unions, has never been shy about their agenda. Teachers, not parents, control education.

Meanwhile, the progressive movement continued to flood the market with books that educators read and loved. John Holt was a favorite author, and he continued to be a strong apologist for the progressive movement throughout the '70s:

> Young people should have the right to control and direct their own learning, that is, to decide what they want to learn, and when, where, how, how much, how fast, and with what help they want to learn it. To be still more specific, I want them to have the right to decide if, when, how much, and by whom they want to be *taught* and the right to decide whether they want to learn in a school and if so which one and for how much of the time."[25]

In the '70s, the Association for Supervision and Curriculum Development began to flex its muscles and picked up the progressivist baton in powerful ways through its journals, books, staff development programs, and national agenda. In its yearbook for 1977, titled *Feeling, Valuing and the Art of Growing,* William Hedges and Marian Martinello stated:

> [School time] cannot be spent well if individuals are constantly striving to live up to others' expectations and views of what they should do or be. [Time] cannot be spent well if external norms become more important than personally satisfying values. . . . The school . . . must help learners . . . to do more than memorize others' meanings and unthinkingly adopt others' values. . . . When questions of valuing arise, they can be invited to think about what is just and good for themselves and their peers. . . . Curriculum must . . . seek more than proficiency in the 3 R's or adoption of all that is traditionally held sacred.[26]

The seeds for the child-centered, learner-directed, "value-less" classroom of the '80s and '90s were sown anew.

Whose Outcomes Do We Want?

Shortly thereafter, Benjamin Bloom of the University of Chicago had the germ of an idea that would launch the educational movement to be known as Outcome-Based Education (see chapter 6) when he wrote that "the purpose of education and the schools is to change the thoughts, feelings and actions of students."[27] This would become the '80s version of the progressive movement's "social engineering" of the '30s.

> "[U.S.] preeminence in commerce, industry, science and technological innovation is being overtaken by competitors throughout the world."

The progressives were once again thwarted, however. In 1983, the National Commission on Excellence of the U.S. Department of Education released a report that was the biggest bombshell to be dropped on education since the Russians launched Sputnik, *A Nation at Risk:* "Our Nation is at risk. Our once unchallenged preeminence in commerce, industry, science and technological innovation is being overtaken by competitors throughout the world." Analyst Paul Copperman concluded that "for the first time in the history of our country, the educational skills of one generation will not surpass, will not equal, will not even approach those of their parents"[28]

Thomas Shannon, executive director of the National School Boards Association, condemned the "stridently negative view of public education and the near-hysterical narrative" of *A Nation at Risk.*[29]

But there were those who took note of the increasing cultural illiteracy in our country. Pat Oliphant, the political cartoonist who lampoons just about everything and everybody in his offbeat drawings, lamented the demise of the educated reader. "The problem is that as education becomes more and more of a mess in this country, and people learn less and less about the arts and history, the possibility of using those sorts of metaphors [familiar artistic and literary icons] is disappearing. It will get to a stage where eventually you won't be able to use the classics at all, or allusions to historical events.[30]

Alan Bloom, a scholar and a University of Chicago professor, recognized that something was terribly wrong with American education. He saw the results in the university students whom he taught. In *The Closing of the American Mind,* he wrote:

> There is now an entirely new language of good and evil, originating in an attempt to get "beyond good and evil" and preventing us from talking with any conviction about good and evil anymore. . . . The new language is that of value relativism, and it constitutes a change in our view of things moral and political as great as the one that took place when Christianity replaced Greek and Roman paganism.[31]

Even popular columnist William Raspberry felt compelled to comment on public education. Speaking for parents in his syndicated column in the *Washington Post* in 1990, he wrote:

> What parents seem to want are public schools, traditionally organized, that work as well for the children who attend them as the private and parochial schools work for their enrollees. . . . But mostly the educationists don't ask parents what they want. They merely ask us to support—and press our legislators to finance—whatever vague schemes they come up with, no matter how little evidence there may be to suggest that it will make any appreciable difference.[32]

The professional educators would not go down without a fight. In the book *The Manufactured Crisis,* education professors David Berliner and Bruce Biddle assured us that nothing was really wrong. They asserted that statements like "college-student performance has recently declined in America" or "American schools fail in comparative studies of students achievement" were myths and that "organized malevolence" was underway.[33]

If so, E. D. Hirsch, Jr., is part of that organized malevolence. In what has become a must-read book for every parent and educator concerned about the future of American education, Hirsch explained in *The Schools We Need and Why We Don't Have Them* how parents and educators have once again been misled by the false claims of progressivism:

> *To stress critical thinking while de-emphasizing knowledge reduces a student's capacity to think critically.
>
> *Giving a child constant praise to bolster self-esteem regardless of academic achievement breeds complacency, skepticism, or both, and ultimately, a decline in self-esteem.
>
> *Schoolwork that has been called "developmentally inappropriate" has been proved to be highly appropriate to millions of students the world over, while the infantile pabulum now fed to American children *is* developmentally inappropriate (in a downward direction) and often bores them.
>
> There is scarcely a district or school across the nation in which progressive education has not left its calling cards, particularly during the past twenty years. Lowered expectations, watered down curriculum, and an emphasis on "feeling good" over "working hard" are the rule, not the exception.[34]

Who's to Blame for This Shocking State of Affairs?

Who's responsible for a nation that is more at risk today than when *A Nation at Risk* was issued in 1983? There are four principal culprits who have each contributed their share to the educational mess we're in: politicians, professors, profits, and professional organizations. Although some might hypothesize dark conspiracies, evil cabals, or sinister takeovers of our children's minds, it is not difficult for even the most reasonable people among us to recognize the real source of the problem. There is an almost blind acceptance by the public of the complicity between the educational establishment, government at many levels, and a variety of groups that profess to have our children's best interests at heart.

> If this educational monopoly were a company, the Justice Department would be filing suit.

A vast interlocking network of teacher training institutions, teacher organizations and their publications, state and federal departments of education, school officials, and publishers of school textbooks exists on which it is exceedingly difficult for outsiders to have an impact. If this educational monopoly were a company, the Justice Department would be filing suit against it for violation of the antitrust laws. Instead, the monopoly seems to be moving forward at the speed of light to control education from early childhood throughout our work lives.

Politicians

There are three categories of politicians who have contributed to the educational system: 1) the elected officials like national and state legislators, governors, and state school superintendents; 2) the career government types (policy analysts, legislative aides, Washington groupies, advisers, and speechwriters) who work behind closed doors, are unaccountable to the voters, and have seemingly unlimited resources (our tax dollars) to use as carrots and sticks in the battle to accomplish their agendas; and 3) board of education members, many of whom are dedicated community servants with the best interests of the kids at heart, but a growing number of whom have become pawns in the hands of the professional educators.

Professors

Academic types are a second major contributor to the problems we face. They are protecting their own self-interests: tenure, opportunities to publish, and the golden carrots of government-funded research. E. D. Hirsch calls this an "intellectual monopoly" and suggests that university professors, especially those in departments of teacher education, exert an enormous influence that does not always serve the best interests of students. "Despite the myth of local control, the intellectual monopoly ruling American K-12 education is more pervasive and harmful than the merely bureaucratic control exercised in other liberal democracies. Its prevailing ideas are more extreme and process-dominated than those found in systems that are more successful than our own."[35]

A recent Public Agenda poll, "Different Drummers: How Teachers of Teachers View Public Education,"[36] offers a peek into the yawning chasm that exists between what parents want their schools to do and what the "teachers of teachers" believe the educational aims should be. J. E. Stone, professor of educational psychology at East Tennessee State University and founder of the Education Consumers ClearingHouse, explains:

> The public wants schools with orderly classrooms that produce mastery of conventional knowledge and skills. Teacher-educators, by contrast, consider the public's expectations outmoded and mistaken. They want classrooms in which the top priorities are positive attitudes toward learning and the presence of activities intended to encourage "learning how to learn." In their view, learning how to read, write, and do math is secondary to whether students find their

classroom experience a satisfying one. Their ideal is schooling without schoolwork.

Today's professors of education value the "process" of learning over the content and are more concerned with self-esteem than with systematic instruction. Only one in five professors surveyed in the Public Agenda poll think teachers should stress correct grammar, spelling, and punctuation. Over 90 percent say that "teachers should see themselves as facilitators of learning who enable their students to learn on their own," while a mere 7 percent think teachers should be "conveyors of knowledge who enlighten their students with what they know." Even more revealing is the finding that only 37 percent of the professors of teacher education surveyed consider "maintaining order and discipline" as important and only 12 percent expect their students to be polite and on time. Nearly eight in ten education professors think the traditional approach toward learning is "outmoded and mistaken."[37]

The young people who go through teacher training institutions today are led to believe that what the public desires in an educational experience for their children is old-fashioned and ineffective, even detrimental to the intellectual development of children. Phonics and math facts are known as "drill and kill." Direct instruction by the teacher is referred to as "the factory model of learning." J. E. Stone explains:

> Favored methods are designed to produce what John Dewey called "intellectual growth." Instead of building proficiency in basic knowledge and literacy skills, their first priority is to promote "critical thinking" and "creativity." Theoretically, fundamentals are integrated later, on an as-needed basis. Unfortunately, they often achieve neither the fundamentals nor the creativity. Implemented fully, learner-centered methods discourage teacher direction and minimize orderly, results-oriented activity. Resources are wasted

and precious learning opportunities are squandered. Despite inherent ineffectiveness and inefficiency, almost every graduate of an "approved" teacher training program is given to understand that such methods are grounded in the latest research, known to be practical and effective, and indeed, are the only responsible approach to teaching.

I believe that most teachers are well-meaning, dedicated, and hard working. But they have not received rigorous training in their schools of education, and when hired they did not find effective instructional leadership starting with the principals in their schools and going right on up to the state departments of education.

Profits and Money

> **Education is a multimillion dollar business, and no one is willing to bite the hand that feeds it.**

The third contributing factor to failing schools is money, not so much the lack of it, but rather the vast business empire that education has become. Textbook companies, hardware and software providers, and thousands of consultants are constantly trying to figure out which way the money is flowing. Then they develop programs, staff development seminars, and conferences to bring the latest innovations to the teachers in the trenches. This is a multimillion dollar business and no one is willing to bite the hand that feeds it.

Professional Organizations

The final group that is to blame for our educational ills is the sorriest. These are professional educators who have sold out to unions, politics, and progressive education. The policies, standards, and practices they have been espousing over the past hundred years qualify as educational malpractice. The National Education Association (NEA), the National Council of Teachers of Mathematics (NCTM), the Association for Supervision and Curriculum Development (ASCD), the International Reading Association (IRA), and the National Council of Teachers of English (NCTE) are just a few of the more powerful and pervasive ones. I've belonged to some of these organizations in the past, and many dedicated educators still pay their dues today.

These professionals remind me of the proverbial frog in the folk tale. The story goes that when you want to cook a frog you don't immerse him immediately into a pot of boiling water because he'll jump right out. The trick is to put him in cool water and then gradually raise the temperature until the unsuspecting frog becomes so comfortable in the hot water that he's willing to stick around and be boiled to death. Many teachers and administrators are like that frog. They've been reading the professional publications and listening to the consultants and professors for so long that they don't realize they are in desperate straits. Just like the frog, they're going to be boiled to death before they know it.

I'd even add one semiprofessional group to this mix, the National PTA. Unfortunately, this organization founded to represent parents has been co-opted by the NEA and has lost its independent voice. In many local districts, the PTA is merely a giant group of cheerleaders and fundraisers for the administration.

Education would like to blame parents for declining achievement. We don't spend enough time with our children. We don't have high expectations. We don't read aloud to them enough. Our children are at-risk, and we're to blame. Parents make a convenient scapegoat whenever test scores drop. But it's time for educators to bear their share of the responsibility and recognize that skipping down the primrose path of progressivism has brought them to a dead-end.

We all are to blame, however, for standing idly by and

letting it happen. The majority of us blindly trust the judgment of professionals; we are apathetic and indifferent; or we're too willing to let other parents get excited about the schools but not us. It's time for us all to get involved. In chapters 4 and 5 we will examine the two academic areas in which politics, professors, profits, and professional organizations have done the most damage to our schools and to our children: reading and mathematics.

Notes

1. William G. Durden, "Where Is the Middle Ground? When Educational Either/Ors Hold Sway, Judgment Can Yield to Advocacy," *Education Week* 4 October 1995: 48.

2. Ibid.

3. Horace Mann quoted in Rousas J. Rushdoony, *The Messianic Character of American Education* (Nutley, NJ: Craig Press, 1972) 29.

4. John Swett, *Biennial Report of the California State Superintendent of Education* 1964, quoted in Zach Montgomery, *Poison Drops in the Federal Senate: The School Question from a Parental and Non-Sectarian Stand-Point.* (1889; New York: Arno Press, 1972) 102-3.

5. Ibid.

6. National Education Association, *Report of the Committee on Secondary School Studies Appointed at the Meeting of the National Education Association 9 July 1892* (Washington, D.C.: National Education Association, 1893) 8-11, 16-17, 34-47, 51-55.

7. Quoted in Rushdoony 34.

8. John Dewey, *Democracy and Education* (New York: Macmillan, 1916) 231.

9. Samuel Tenenbaum, *William Heard Kilpatrick: Trail Blazer in Education* (New York: Harper, 1951) 141, 185. William Heard Kilpatrick, *Foundations of Method* (New York: The Macmillan Company, 1925) 278.

10. Edward Thorndike and Arthur Gates, *Elementary Principles of Education* (New York: Macmillan, 1929) 311.

11. George Counts, *Dare the School Build a New Social Order?* (1932; Carbondale, IL: Southern Ill. Univ. Press, 1978) 58.

12. Charles Beard, *The Unique Function of Education in American Democracy* (Washington, DC: National Education Association, 1937) 82.

13. Boyd H. Bode, *Progressive Education at the Crossroads* (New York: Newson & Company, 1938) 9.

14. United States Office of Education, *Life Adjustment for Every*

Youth (Washington, DC: U.S. Office of Education, 1945) 17.

15. Mortimer Smith, *And Madly Teach: A Layman Looks at Public School Education* (Chicago: Henry Regnery, 1949) 7, 21-24, 42, 59-60, 92-93.

16. Kenneth Benne, "Democratic Ethics in Social Engineering," *Progressive Education* 26.7 (May 1949): 201.

17. A. H. Lauchner, "How Can the Junior High Curriculum Be Improved?" *Bulletin of the National Association of Secondary School Principals* 35.177 (March 1951).

18. David Tyack and Larry Cuban, *Tinkering toward Utopia: A Century of Public School Reform* (Cambridge, MA: Harvard Univ. Press) 18.

19. Albert Lynd, *Quackery in the Public Schools* (Boston: Little, Brown and Company, 1953) 37.

20. Arthur Bestor, *Educational Wastelands: The Retreat from Learning in Our Public Schools* (Urbana: Univ. of Illlinois Press, 1953) 10.

21. A. S. Neil, *Summerhill: A Radical Approach to Child Rearing* (New York: Hart Publishing, 1960) 4, 25.

22. Max Rafferty, *What Are They Doing to Your Children?* (New York: New American Library, 1963) 43.

23. John Holt, *The Underachieving School* (New York: Pitman Publishing Corporation, 1969) 3.

24. Robert Kagan, "A Relic of the New Age: The National Education Association," *American Spectator* February 1982: 14-18.

25. John Holt, *Escape from Childhood* (New York: E. P. Dutton, 1974) 240.

26. William Hedges and Marian Martinello, "What Schools Might Do: Some Alternatives for the Here and Now," *Valuing and the Art of Growing: Insights into the Affective Feeling*, ed. Louise Berman and Jessie Roderick (Washington, DC: Association for Supervision and Curriculum Development, 1977) 235.

27. Benjamin Bloom, *All Our Children Learning: A Primer for Parents, Teachers, and Other Educators* (New York: McGraw-Hill, 1981) 180.

28. National Commission on Excellence in Education, *A Nation at Risk: The Imperative for Educational Reform* (Washington, DC: Government Printing Office, 1983) 4, 11.

29. Thomas Shannon, editorial, *American School Board Journal* July 1983: 43.

30. Biobhan Morissey, "A Cartoonist Can't Worry about the Good of the Country," *Washington Post* 14 July 1985: B3.

31. Allan Bloom, *The Closing of the American Mind* (New York: Simon and Schuster, 1987) 141.

32. William Raspberry, "'Reform' or Good Traditional Education?" *Washington Post* 23 March 1990: A23.

33. David C. Berliner and Bruce J. Biddle, *The Manufactured Crisis: Myths, Fraud, and the Attack on America's Public Schools* (Reading, MA: Addison-Wesley, 1995) xi, 13-63.

34. E. D. Hirsch, *The Schools We Need and Why We Don't Have Them* (New York: Doubleday, 1996) 66.

35. Ibid.

36. Public Agenda, "How Teachers of Teachers View Public Education," online, 1997. Available: http://www.public agenda.org/aboutpa/aboutpa3:html#press

37. Ibid.

TALES FROM THE TRENCHES

If You Can Read This, Thank a Teacher

Jeanne Nugent
Cofounder, TAPIS
Parent
Education Activist

The setting is a middle school in an affluent suburb in the Chicago area. Households in the attendance area have an average income of $107,000 per year. Two-parent families with at-home mothers are the norm. The neighborhood is stable with a mobility level far below the state average. The children who attend are involved and stimulated through a variety of extracurricular activities. The stay-at-home moms who chauffeur their offspring to soccer and music lessons are so enthusiastic in their commitment to volunteerism that feeder elementary schools often have fifteen or twenty individuals signed up to be room mothers.

The school has superior facilities. It is only three years old, outfitted with modern technology and furnishings. Everything is clean, cheerful, and orderly. One would be hard-pressed to find fault with such a learning environment. All parts of this equation point toward children who are poised to conquer the world. Everything that has been written about successful education in the '90s stresses the variables that are found in this school and community.

Yet, something is wrong with this picture. At a recent back-to-school night one teacher informed the eager parents who were crowded into the standing-room-only classroom that their seventh graders were "almost illiterate." They were having a difficult time reading novels more suitable for third and fourth graders.

With all of the marvelous educational advantages available to the children in this affluent community, illiteracy shouldn't happen. "If you can read this, thank a teacher," the bumper sticker proclaims. To whom should our children offer thanks if they can't?

Why Can't My Child Read?

4 The Reading Wars

> Some books are to be tasted, others to be swallowed, and some few to be chewed and digested; that is, some books are to be read only in parts; others to be read but not curiously; and some few to be read wholly, and with diligence and attention.
>
> —*Francis Bacon*

When my first child went off to kindergarten, I experienced all of the usual emotions. Not only was she leaving the nest, but in those new surroundings she would be instructed, examined, and evaluated. Would she measure up? Would she have fun? Would she like school? And most important to me, would she learn to read? I already knew my daughter liked books. I read aloud to her daily. I also knew that she understood and remembered a great deal of what we read together. But I had no idea if she could or even would learn to read with ease. My earlier attempts at teaching her had not been notable. Consequently, I didn't even attempt to teach her to read. I decided the joyful experience we shared together with books was too special to risk turning it into a battle.

She went off to kindergarten with anticipation and was not disappointed. One day in early October, she arrived home to announce, "I learned to read today." I couldn't believe what I was hearing. Perhaps she had confused writing letters on paper with reading. "Can you read for me?" I asked her with barely contained excitement. To this point she had never read a single word aloud to me.

Eagerly I pulled out a library book she had never seen before. She promptly began reading aloud with fluency and expression as if this were something we had been doing regularly.

In actuality, reading aloud was something we had been doing regularly. Only now the roles were reversed. My child was reading to me. And, I realized, in her mind she had learned to read in one day at school. She was not yet aware that the preparation for this moment when she was actually reading had been going on since she was an infant. The preparation for this moment had been five years of continuing conversation, incessant questions, endless repetitions of nursery rhymes and poems, and the reading aloud of hundreds of her favorite picture books. I believe reading aloud is the single most important thing that parents can do to ensure school success for their children. But, is it the way all, or even most children, learn to read? Absolutely not, as my second child's experience will indicate.

I fully expected my daughter's story to repeat itself when I sent my son off to kindergarten two years later. After all, he was going to the same school, had the same teacher, and had experienced five years of the same reading-rich environment. There was absolutely no reason to think that his experiences with reading would be any different than his sister's. He wasn't an "at-risk" child. He was a bright and eager learner. October came and went, however, and he didn't come home to tell me he had learned to read. He learned his sounds and began to blend simple words, but he never read aloud to me with fluency as his sister had done. In first grade he completed a phonics program as part of the basal reading series. We continued to read aloud every night. He read to me from simple readers, slowly and haltingly at first. He sounded out each word carefully but experienced success every step of the way.

In second grade, all of the pieces of the reading puzzle fell into place for him, and he truly began to read, over 1,000 books actually. By spring he was reading full-length novels by E. B. White and Beverly Cleary. How did he get to that point? Teachers that recognized his academic needs and met them and a curriculum that skillfully integrated a variety of learning materials and approaches but was built on a strong phonics foundation. What could account for the difference in how my children learned to read? Their gender? Perhaps. Their developmental readiness? Maybe. Differences in learning style? An idea worth considering. But who cares now? They are both successful university graduates.

Might the scenario have been different if my son had not experienced "phonics first"? Might my daughter's delight in reading everything she could get her hands on have been destroyed if teachers had not recognized her reading precocity and nurtured it? I'm certain of it. If my children were attending the same elementary school today that they attended in the mid-70s, my son may well have become a "retarded reader" because phonics is now out and whole-language is in.

What is the point of this personal story? Simply this. Many educators have done a terrible disservice to students by failing to recognize the importance to reading of *phonemic awareness* (the ability to recognize individual sounds in words) and *phonics* (the ability to blend those sounds in the reading of words). They have permitted reading to become a political football rather than an educational issue and we are all losing. Well-intentioned but uninformed educators have bought into the preposterous claims of the whole-language proponents that "children will learn to read naturally, just as they learned to talk." If this statement were true, illiteracy would not be a problem in this country. Everyone would learn to read, if not sooner, then later. For millions of Americans, however, time has run out. The statistics with respect to national illiteracy are frightening, particularly when one considers that those young people who do not have the ability to read are likely to end up unemployed, on welfare, or in the criminal justice system.[1] Consider these deplorable findings:

◆ Project READ, a national program to improve the reading skills of juveniles in correctional facilities, assessed 2,670 juvenile offenders and although the average age of the students tested was 15 years, 6 months of age, the average reading level was fourth grade. Thirty-eight percent of the students tested scored below fourth grade.[2]

◆ A U.S. Department of Justice study concluded that "low reading levels tend to predict the likelihood of the onset of serious delinquency. Longitudinally, poor reading achievement and delinquency appear to mutually influence each other. Prior reading level predicted later subsequent delinquency . . . [moreover] poor reading achievement increased the chances of serious delinquency persisting over time.[3]

◆ Though Americans have paid over $500 billion (in 1996 dollars) for Head Start and Chapter I classes since 1965 and for special education programs since 1975, nearly 25 percent of Americans over age sixteen can't read, and another 15 percent can't read very well.[4]

◆ Scores on 70 million academic tests given by the U.S. Departments of War, Defense, HEW, Labor, and Education show that over 60 million normal students have reached the fourth grade unable to read fourth-grade materials since 1945. Over two-thirds of those classified as unable to read grade-level material never learned to read at all.[5]

Sylvia Farnham-Diggory, director of the reading clinic at the University of Delaware, describes this tragedy.

> One of the most heartbreaking sights in American schools today is that of children—once so eager to read—discovering that they are not learning how. There comes over those sparkling eyes a glaze of listless despair. We are not talking about a few children and scattered schools. We are talking about millions of children and every school in the nation. And the toll in young spirits is the least of it. The toll in the learning and thinking potential of our citizenry is beyond measure.[6]

The "reading wars" or "the great debate," as the controversy between whole-language and phonics proponents has come to be known, is a mystery to most parents. Why do we continue to use a methodology that doesn't work? How did something so elemental to the entire schooling process—how students learn to read—become so controversial? How can intelligent educators commit malpractice by refusing to give students the tools they need to read the printed word?

> **Poor reading achievement increases the chances of serious delinquency persisting over time.**

Even "down under," the phonics/whole-language debate goes on. Dr. Kevin Donnelly, a high school and university English teacher in Australia, relates his family's experience with their second child, Amelia. Although their first child, James, received a "phonics first" approach in school, Amelia was not as fortunate.

> As with James, Julia and I spent time talking and reading to Amelia. Once again, we plodded through picture stories, books like *The Magic Faraway Tree,* and

the nonsense rhymes of Edmund Lear. Once again, we pointed out the names of everyday objects and corrected her when she made a mistake.

At first, all appeared to be going well. Amelia spent time reading books at home and her writing, while not as neat or correct as James's writing at the same stage, was developing from relatively simple ideas to more abstract concepts. We only found out that she could not read at the start of Year 4 (age 10) when I asked her to read aloud a book she had brought home from school. Those words that she knew well she could read and understand. Unfortunately, she was unable to decipher those words that she had not encountered before. Like trying to read a foreign language without a key, Amelia was forced to guess what words might be and what they might mean. At times, she could guess correctly because of the accompanying picture or because she knew what might happen next. Most of the time, she was lost.

Why hadn't we realized that Amelia could not read before Year 4? Firstly, like many children of her age, Amelia had taught herself how to disguise her reading problem. Secondly, at parent-teacher interviews we had been told that, yes, she was behind the other children in her year level, but don't be concerned. The teacher assured us that reading is a "developmental process" and that children learn at different rates. Rather than being overly anxious, which might harm Amelia's self-esteem, we were assured that she would eventually "grow" into literacy when she was ready.

Unfortunately, this did not happen. Over the year we realized that Amelia was not progressing and that, unlike her brother, reading was something that she increasingly saw as a chore. The reality was that the "look and guess" approach associated with whole-language failed to give our daughter the skills and understanding so vital for literacy success.

Luckily, as we were both teachers, we were able to help. The solution was to teach Amelia that words are made up of letter sounds and combinations of letter sounds. In practice, this meant that we no longer allowed Amelia to simply "look and guess" when she came across an unknown word. Hours were spent reading with her and correcting her when she made a mistake. Over time her confidence grew as she realized that she had the word attack skills so necessary for independent reading.

> "The 'look and guess' approach failed to give our daughter the skills and understanding so vital for literacy."

The change to our daughter was immediate. Amelia realized that her inability to read was not her fault and that she was actually capable of achieving a good deal. Whether it was sitting in the bath, lying in bed or curled up with a book on the couch, reading became exciting and challenging, and a whole new world of fables, adventures and characters was opened up.

James and Amelia are now at secondary school and both, by anyone's definition, are literate. James has mastered the arcane rites of Latin declension, and Amelia recently finished reading Tolkien's *Lord of the Rings*.

Amelia's story has a happy ending. Her parents taught her to read. But millions of children don't have trained teachers for parents, or even parents who know enough to question the ostensible "experts." For, despite the evidence both experimental and anecdotal to the contrary, countless teachers and administrators reject phonics and cling to whole-language with a tenacity that is remarkable. In a moment, we'll see why.

But first, a homework assignment—some vocabulary

study and a bit of history are in order. This is essential information for understanding the best way to teach reading.

Key Words to Know

Developmental: natural, something that will happen gradually over time as a child matures and cannot be taught; in the reading literature, the opposite of "learned." Talking and walking are developmental. You don't "teach" them in the strictest sense of the word, although parents certainly do a lot of encouraging, modeling, and correcting along the way.

Decoding: the ability to look at the printed page and translate it into language; an essential prerequisite to the ability to decode is phonemic awareness.[7]

Direct instruction: refers to a style of teaching in which the teacher is "in charge" and has carefully structured the presentation as well as the responses desired from students. Whole-language proponents find any kind of direct instruction to be anathema. In a whole-language classroom, the child is in charge!

Fluency: automaticity and flow in the act of reading. The act of repetitive decoding (sounding out) of a particular word that helps to establish the spelling patterns of that word in memory. The most effective way for students to become fluent with a specific word is for them to consciously process both the letter patterns and the sounds of the word the first few times it is read.[8] Since whole-language proponents encourage strategies like guessing and using context clues, students never get a chance to develop fluency. Uncertainty is the most consistent characteristic of a whole-language taught reader.

"Matthew effect": this phrase has its origins in the New Testament parable of the talents in which the rich get richer and the poor get poorer: "For to every one who has will more be given, and he will have abundance; but from him who has not, even what he has will be taken away" (Matthew 25:29, RSV). The term is used to describe the effect of reading deficits in phonemic awareness in kindergarten and first grade from which "poor" students almost never recover.[9] In other words, if a child doesn't learn to read the right way in the first place, he or she may never catch up. More recent research has shown that the "Matthew effect" is not only seen in the spiraling reading skills of successful early readers but also in their acquisition of knowledge and lifelong reading habits.[10]

Phoneme: the most basic element of the language system; a sound. Phonemes are very important on the reading scene today and much of the new research revolves around them.[11]

Phonemic awareness: the ability to recognize individual sounds in words (e.g., rhyming, blending spoken sounds into words, counting phonemes); a critical prerequisite to being able to learn to read. Lack of phonemic awareness in kindergarten or first grade is the single most reliable predictor of a future reading problem.[12] Whole-language proponents definitely qualify this definition: "ability to detect sounds in speech that *are supposed to be* [italics in the original] represented by the letters of the alphabet.[13]

Phonics: a term that has become a code word or rallying cry for those who support teaching basic skills in a direct and sequential way. Parents even label schools as "phonics schools" or "whole-language schools," even though phonics instruction at its very best will consume no more than half of the language arts activities in kindergarten and/or first grade. Phonics, stripped of its political baggage, is an instructional method for teaching students to sound out words rather than read them as a "whole" or "guessing" what they might be on the basis of context. Frank Smith, a whole-language proponent, defines phonics as "reading instruction based on the *assumption* [italics in the original] that reading is decoding to sound and requires learning spelling-to-sound correspondences."[14]

Reading: a process in which information from the text

and the knowledge possessed by the reader act together to produce meaning.[15]

Sight words: words that students have memorized and can "read" on sight.

Whole-language: Ken Goodman, a proponent of whole-language, describes it this way: "A pedagogy, or a way that teachers think about teaching; a bringing together [of] everything we've learned about how language works in terms of learning [and] how learning to read and write is an extension of oral language."[16] Frank Smith, also a proponent, defines whole-language as "an educational movement based on the belief that language learning takes place most effectively when learners are engaged collaboratively in meaningful and purposeful uses of language, as opposed to exercises, drills, and tests. Sometimes referred to as the naturalistic approach or (misleadingly) as child-centered learning, and known in Britain as real books. Frequently contrasted with direct instruction."[17] Some critics charge that whole-language is only the most recent incarnation of other methods such as "look-and-say," "sight method," and "whole word." Others call it the "guesswork" approach to reading.

Whole-language versus Phonics: A Timeline

The ugly battle between the whole-language proponents and the phonics folk has been raging on and off for a couple of hundred years. The terminology that is used, the protagonists in the debate, and the sophistication of the research have all changed, but the basic conflict still boils down to the question of how children best learn to read. If you did your homework in chapter 3, you will begin to recognize some similarities between the progressivist-traditionalist conflict and the phonics/whole-language debate. Here's a brief timeline of how this conflict has evolved and where we are today.

1500-146 B.C.

The Phoenicians invent the alphabet, and reading is taught by memorizing the sounds of syllables and blending them together to make words.[18]

1783

Noah Webster publishes his Blue-Backed Speller and has this to say about the competition:

> Among the defects and absurdities found in books of this kind hitherto published, we may rank the want of a thorough investigation of the sounds in the English language, and the powers of the several letters—the promiscuous arrangement of words in the same table. In attempting to correct these faults it was necessary to begin with the elements of the language and explain the powers of the letters.[19]

1791

German educator, Professor Friedrich Gedike, director of the Kölnische Gymnasium in Berlin, publishes the first look-and-say primer.[20]

1837

Horace Mann, educational reformer and secretary of the Massachusetts Board of Education, denounces the letters of the alphabet as "bloodless, ghostly apparitions that [are] responsible for steeping children's faculties in lethargy."[21]

1908

Edmund Burke Huey writes in *The Psychology and Pedagogy of Reading* that "the technique of reading should not appear in the early years, and the very little early work that should be tolerated in phonics should be entirely distinct from reading."[22]

1930s-1950s

The consensus in beginning reading instruction as reflected in textbooks for teachers and published series for students emphasizes recognition of sight words.[23] Drill and practice in phonics in isolation is not recommended: "The child should not isolate sounds and blend them to form words. Instead he should identify unknown words through a process of visual analysis and substitution."[24]

1955

Why Johnny Can't Read by Rudolph Flesch explodes onto the best-seller lists with a scathing critique of reading instruction in the United States:

> I say, therefore, that the word method [look-say/whole-language], is gradually destroying democracy in this country; it returns to the upper middle class the privileges that public education was supposed to distribute evenly among the people. The American Dream is, essentially, equal opportunity through free education for all. This dream is beginning to vanish in a country where the public schools are falling down on the job.[25]

1957

Romalda Spalding presents a comprehensive method for teaching children to read using phonics in *The Writing Road to Reading:*

> It is safe to say that most school officials now assert that their schools teach all methods [both phonics and whole-word]. Unfortunately however, very, very few teachers today know enough about phonics to teach it accurately. Very few teachers' colleges in the country give a separate, full course in phonics. One reading of this book [*The Writing Road to Reading*] will

make clear that a teacher does need to study and learn phonics thoroughly before teaching it.[26]

1965
Louise Gurren and Ann Hughes conclude after reviewing thirty-six studies that "rigorous controlled research clearly favors the teaching of all of the main sound-symbol relationships, both vowel and consonant, from the start of formal reading instruction."[27]

1975
The basal reading series used in American classrooms becomes more eclectic, including systematic instruction in spelling-to-sound correspondences along with stories and exercises to develop and reinforce comprehension skills.[28]

1985
Frank Smith, apologist for whole-language, weighs in with his view of how children learn to read: "Children cannot be taught to read. A teacher's responsibility is not to teach children to read but to make it possible for them to learn to read."[29]

1985
Becoming a Nation of Readers: The Report of the Commission on Reading is released by the National Institute of Education. Although the report recommends that children spend less time completing workbooks and skill sheets and more time in independent reading, it also includes this recommendation relative to phonics instruction: "The issue is no longer, as it was several decades ago, whether children should be taught phonics. The issues now are specific ones of just how it should be done."[30]

1986
Ken Goodman explains how he believes phonics instruction actually makes things worse rather than better:

Many school traditions seem to have actually hindered language development. In our zeal to make it easy, we've made it hard. How? Primarily by breaking whole (natural) language up into bite-size, but abstract little pieces. It seemed so logical to think that little children could best learn simple little things. We took apart the language and turned it into words, syllables, and isolated sounds. Unfortunately, we also postponed its natural purpose, the communication of meaning, and turned it into a set of abstractions, unrelated to the needs and experiences of the children we sought to help.[31]

1987

A survey of forty-three texts used to train teachers of reading finds that none advocate systematic phonics instruction and only nine even mention that there is a debate on the issue.[32]

1988

California mandates the exclusive use of literature-based instruction (whole-language) for teaching beginning reading.[33]

1990

In a comprehensive review of the reading instruction literature, researcher Marilyn Jager Adams concludes that "before children will learn to read, they must learn to recognize individual letters. They must become aware of the structure of language, from sentences and words to phonemes. And, most important, they must develop a basic understanding of the forms and functions of text and of its personal value to their own lives."[34]

1994

Frank Smith in the fifth edition of his reading text, *Under-*

standing Reading: A Psycholinguistic Analysis of Reading and Learning to Read, asserts that

> the difficulty many children experience in learning phonics rules, or indeed in making sense of them, has led to the notion that such children lack "phonological awareness," that is, the ability to deconstruct the sounds of spoken words. It is taken for granted that the tenuous relationship between letters and sounds must be of central importance to readers of alphabetic writing systems (compared with readers of non-alphabetic systems like Chinese)—why else have an alphabet? The alternative point of view, which may be slowly gaining ground, is that the alphabet primarily serves writing and should make no substantial difference to reading."[35]

1995

Reid Lyon, director of research for the National Institute of Child Health and Human Development, testifies before a Senate subcommittee that "most reading disabilities stem from a deficit in the most basic level of the language system—the phoneme."[36]

1995

The American Federation of Teachers (AFT) casts its vote in favor of phonics first. *American Educator* editor Elizabeth McPeek writes: "The Whole Language movement has brought to the forefront many complex and legitimate issues about the nature of teaching and learning and the goals of education, and it has brought fresh life to many classrooms. But to the extent that it has reduced decoding to an incidental place in the reading curriculum, it has done a terrible disservice to the children whose lives depend on mastery of that skill.[37]

1995
California passes the ABC law (Assembly Bill 170) requiring state officials to make sure that adopted materials give adequate attention to systematic explicit phonics, spelling, and computational skills.[38]

1997
The National Institute of Child Health and Human Development releases a study by Barbara Foorman concluding that "direct phonics instruction should be the first in a sequence of methods used to teach some students to read."[39]

1997
In a *Time* magazine cover story, the author concludes: "After reviewing the arguments mustered by the phonics and whole-language proponents, can we make a judgment as to who is right? Yes. The value of explicit, systematic phonics instruction has been well established."[40]

Why Doesn't Every School Use Phonics?

Although more and more of the reading instruction literature is beginning to include terms like "balanced," "eclectic," "integrated," and "contextual" when referring to the relationship of phonics and whole-language in reading instruction, this does not mean that systematic phonics is being taught. Huge numbers of educators refuse to even discuss the matter. Consider Anne Thompson's* experience with her son's first-grade teacher.

> I discussed the whole-language approach with my son's teacher and she shut me up right away by informing me she is a proponent of whole-language and will never teach explicit phonics again. She didn't have any answers for my concerns that she was undoing my efforts to break my son of the nasty habit of sight reading and guessing. It makes it very frustrating when I

have to tell him not to do at home what the teacher tells him to do. I wish I was in a position to pull him out and home-school him or send him to a private school [that teaches phonics].

Our school children are paying the price for this kind of confusion and closed-mindedness with poor reading achievement. Based on my personal experiences as a parent and an educator and after an extensive review of the literature, I must agree with Reid Lyon who states: "There is no debate. At a certain stage of reading, phonics is necessary. Then children need literature to read. Why we polarize it is a mystery to me."[41] It's no mystery to me. The same politicians, professors, profits, and professional organizations who have steered our schools into progressivism have steered them away from phonics.

Where Does Your School or Teacher Stand?

Do you know exactly where your school district (or your child's teacher) stands on reading instruction? Perhaps you need to do a little research. I would caution you against asking the question in too direct a way. Educators have grown wary of frontal attacks and will often get defensive if confronted. Or they will assure you that they do teach phonics—in the context of whole-language—which means that your child is still being taught to "guess" at words and whatever phonics is being taught may be totally useless.

If you really want to know how educators feel, use this agree/disagree quiz developed by Patrick Groff,[42] professor emeritus of education at San Diego State University. Perhaps you can cleverly work these questions into your next parent-teacher conference. Teachers who are totally committed to whole-language will agree with every single one of these statements. Teachers who really understand how children learn to read will disagree with all of them. In reality, many teachers today have been so poorly trained in college about how to teach reading that they don't know what they believe. They are blindly following directives from their principals, the central office administration, or some state department of education.

Reading Quiz

Do you agree or disagree with the following statements about how children learn to read?

- Children learn to read best the same way they learned to speak.
- Children can teach themselves to read. Formal instruction is unnecessary.
- Children should not learn reading subskills in any type of instructional sequence or "hierarchical" order.
- Children should guess at written words, using sentence context cues.
- Children should be taught to recognize words by sight as wholes.
- The length and complexity of words is of little consequence in beginning reading instruction.
- The intensive systematic teaching of phonics hinders reading comprehension.
- Intensive phonics makes it more difficult for children to recognize words.
- No workbooks or worksheets should ever be used.
- English is spelled too unpredictably for phonics to work.[43]

Unfortunately for the children who are currently experiencing whole-language instruction, "none of the whole-language principles [as stated above] are supported by any evidence, not by the historical record, not by 'structural linguistics' which made it possible to decipher writing systems and understand how they work, and not by any scientific research on how children actually learn to read."[44]

What Does a Good Reading Program Look Like?

There are three essential components in an effective reading program: 1) giving students direct, systematic instruction in phonemic awareness and phonics in kindergarten and first grade while also exposing students to the best in fiction and nonfiction read-alouds with comprehension instruction; 2) expecting students to read a great deal of challenging and excellent material as soon as they have acquired independent reading skills; and 3) teaching students to use comprehension strategies to help them to understand and remember what they read.

Direct Systematic Instruction in a Print-Rich Environment

The Council on Exceptional Children contends:

> Research makes clear that children do not learn to read the way they learn to talk. Speech is a natural human capacity, and learning to talk requires little more than exposure and opportunity. In contrast, written language is an artifact, a human invention, and reading is not a skill that can be acquired through immersion alone. Beginning readers benefit from instruction that helps them understand that the words they speak and hear can be represented by written symbols—and that letters and sounds associated with them, when combined and recombined, form words—just as they benefit from experiences that make reading fun.[45]

Even if teachers introduce phonics in the context of a whole-language pedagogy, the desired results still won't be achieved because of two heavily used strategies in the whole-language methodology: guessing at unknown words and using of reader-selected material that may be far too difficult for the student to read independently. A classroom teacher using a phonics-first approach discourages children from guessing at words by assigning stories composed of decodable words selected to provide practice to the students in applying their previously learned phonics knowledge. Decodable texts contain carefully controlled vocabulary for which the student has been fully prepared ahead of time through explicit phonics instruction so that he or she can correctly sound out all of the letters.

Here are the things that *all* teachers of beginning reading should be doing:

1. Make children aware of the characteristics of print. Print awareness includes knowing the purpose of reading, the structure of written text, how stories work, what a word is, how words are composed of letters, what spaces signify, and directionality (i.e., the ability to scan left to right and then sweep diagonally left and one line down).[46]

2. Begin teaching phonemic awareness (i.e., the conscious understanding that a spoken word is made up of a sequence of speech sounds) directly and explicitly at an early age (kindergarten). Children must be trained to hear the individual sounds (phonemes) of their language. They must be able to disconnect or "unglue" sounds in words in order to use an alphabetic writing system.[47] All or even most children do not develop this awareness naturally; they must be taught. This skill is absolutely essential in learning to read and spell. The lack of phonemic awareness is the most powerful determinant of the likelihood of failure to learn to read. If children cannot hear and manipulate the sounds in spoken words, they will have an extremely difficult time learning how to map those sounds to letters and letter patterns—the essence of decoding.[48] Phonemic awareness instruction should begin before instruction in sound-spelling relationships and should be continued throughout the teaching of sound-spelling relationships.

3. Teach each sound-spelling correspondence explicitly. The key word in this statement is *explicitly*. It is not adequate for teachers to introduce these correspondences in the context of a story and expect a child to figure them out on his or her own. This important aspect of reading instruction cannot be left to chance. The phonemes must be separated from the words for instruction. This can only happen if the teacher isolates each phoneme for the student. This is an intense listening experience that is best done without the use of key words or pictures. A brief daily lesson that includes the introduction of a new phoneme with practice of those learned earlier is accompanied by the reading of words and stories that use only the letter-phoneme relationships the children know.

4. Systematically teach frequent, highly regular sound-spelling relationships. The key word in this statement is *systematically*. Most sound-spelling programs teach about forty to fifty relationships, but I am most familiar with the Lindamood and Phono-Graphix methods (see appendix B). These programs teach the one-to-one correspondences (i.e., one sound to one letter) first and when these are mastered move on to one-to-many correspondence (one sound to several letters) and then to the "code overlaps" (i.e., those letters that have several different phonemes, i.e., sounds).

5. Show children exactly how to sound out words through blending the sounds. After children have learned several sound-spelling correspondences, they should then be taught how to blend those sounds into words. They must be shown how to move sequentially from left to right through spellings as they "sound out," or say the sound for each spelling. Daily practice sessions should include the blending of only the sound-spelling relationships the children have learned to that point. This skill must be "over-learned" so that it becomes highly accurate and automatic.

6. Use code-based readers rather than ordinary literature during early instruction. This statement does not mean that children's literature should not be a daily part of the instructional program at preschool, kindergarten, and first grade. Rather, it means that children should not use ordinary literature for their own reading experiences.

A curriculum that encourages guessing may actually hinder reading development. Although prediction is a valuable comprehension skill for predicting the next event or an outcome of the story, research indicates that it is not useful in word recognition. Children need connected, decodable text to practice the spelling relationships they have learned. The integration of phonics and reading can only occur with the use of decodable text. Children can begin reading decodable text relatively quickly, since learning just a few sound-spelling correspondences will enable the reading of dozens of words.

7. Correct oral reading errors. Whole-language instruction discourages teachers from correcting students who make errors, but children benefit when they receive corrective feedback, regardless of whether the errors influence the meaning of the passage.

8. Use interesting stories, picture books, poetry, and literature of all kinds to develop knowledge and comprehension. The use of a phonics instructional system does not rule out using all types of literature in the classroom. Only the use of these stories as *reading material* for early readers is ruled out. Teacher- and parent-read stories play a critical role in building children's oral language comprehension, which ultimately affects their reading comprehension. These story-based activities should be structured to build comprehension and vocabulary skills, not decoding skills. Teachers should read aloud to students several times during the school day and use these opportunities for discussion about text organization (fiction, nonfiction, poetry), vocabulary development, as well as general knowledge building.

9. Do both, but don't mix. Teachers must teach both phonics and reading comprehension, but in the beginning they should not be done together. A common misconception held by many educators is that if they are teaching sound-spelling relationships in the context of real stories, they are teaching phonics. Mixing decoding and comprehension instruction in the same instructional activity is clearly less effective, even when the decoding instruction is fairly structured. When phonics instruction is embedded it does not have the same effect as when it is taught purely and separately.[49]

10. Do phonics right. There are hundreds of published phonics programs, and now that the state of California and others have passed legislation regarding phonics instruction there will be hundreds more. The "great debate" has polarized the issue and could lead one to mistakenly conclude that "phonics is phonics." To the extent that most phonics programs teach the names and sounds of letters, that is true. They begin with the twenty-six letters and teach children the sounds that go with them. But there are forty-four sounds and many teachers (and programs) end up confusing kids rather than actually teaching them how to decode (and spell).

Children learn to read most efficiently when they start with the speech sounds (forty-four of them) and then learn which letter(s) stand for those sounds rather than learning the letter names first and then attaching sounds to them.[50] Since the alphabetic code (letters) was developed to match the sounds of language, it only makes sense to start with the sounds first. It would certainly have been handy if each of the forty-four English sounds had only one corresponding symbol. But our alphabet has twenty-six letters (four of which are wasted) and instead of making up new letters for the left-over sounds, the old letters were reused in some interesting and often inconsistent combinations.[51]

Immersion in Challenging and Excellent Material

The second important component of an effective reading program is reading! That statement may seem obvious to the layperson, but when one can visit classrooms regularly and seldom see children actually reading (particularly in first and second grade classrooms), it needs to be said. Turning the pages and looking at pictures doesn't count.

Students must become voracious readers in order to become fluent and competent readers. Once students have acquired the ability to decode, the single most important activity in which they can engage is reading. "Reading a lot" is one of the most powerful methods of increasing fluency, vocabulary, and comprehension, and becoming educated about the world.[52] Educators and parents must do whatever they can to encourage students to read a variety of materials. Literature-based classrooms are wonderful to a point, but unless a student intends to major in comparative literature or become a book reviewer for the *New York Times*, the current overemphasis on fiction is misplaced. To be sure, it's fun to read fiction. I have a stack of novels on my bedside table and dip into one each night before bed. But I also need to be able to read and comprehend nonfiction to work. Most jobs require all nonfiction reading (e.g., documentation, reports, specifications, and policies).

There are two main reasons that *reading a lot* is important: 1) the more students read the better they comprehend because the number of words they recognize and understand increases by leaps and bounds; and 2) the more students read, the more knowledge they acquire. This in turn helps students to understand even more the next time they read. To that end, students must be required to read a specific number of books each year. The upward spiraling of the "Matthew effect" to which we referred earlier is one of the most powerful forces that can be unleashed both at home and school.[53] The more kids read, the better they get at it.

Students must read challenging and well-written materials. At some point students have to move beyond Goosebumps and Babysitters' Club books. Although these genres serve a purpose in getting the reluctant reader "hooked on books," we must raise our expectations for what all students read and guide them to the best.

Students must be engaged in rigorous discussions of the structure, meaning, and interpretation of the text.

Teaching the structure of the text includes practices like pointing out the differences among fiction, nonfiction, and poetry; describing the elements of a story; and guiding students to examine the organization of an expository text while taking notes. In addition to learning about the structure of text, students must be expected to personally react and respond to what they read as well as determining what the author's message might be.

Guided discussion and interpretation are especially critical for late elementary and middle school students, and reading and writing around a variety of issues and themes should be taking place on a daily basis. A favorite classroom technique these days is cooperative learning, in which the students conduct their own discussions. In a whole-language classroom the teacher wouldn't presume to tell the students what a selection might mean; after all, each student brings his own meaning to reading. Students who have been led to believe that there are no right answers have a very difficult time choosing one when the standardized tests or state assessments are given. Perhaps that is one reason why so many reading scores are dropping and the use of performance assessments with fewer "right" answers is on the rise.

Instruction in Vocabulary, Comprehension, and Cognitive Strategies

This third important aspect of reading instruction deals with strategies. As adults we have each developed and used strategies in our own school life. We know the steps involved in writing a research paper, how to remember information needed to pass an exam, and how to understand and summarize a selection we have read. Each of these projects requires a set of different steps and tasks. Over time students should be taught and should learn these strategies—ways of approaching an intellectual task that help them organize, understand, and remember information.

101

What Can You Do?

What can you do to make a difference in the life of your child, your community, and our country with regard to reading? Here are my suggestions.

- Find out if your child is reading at an age-appropriate grade level. The *Reading Competency Test* available from the National Right to Read Foundation is designed to help parents and teachers evaluate how well a student has learned to apply letter/sound relationships to reading. It is simple, inexpensive, and given one-on-one orally, so one test works for an entire class or family.[54]

- If you are curious about your child's general knowledge in the areas of history, geography, mathematics, science, and the arts, visit the Core Knowledge Home Page (http://www.coreknowledge.org), which contains a planned progression of specific knowledge covering these subjects for each grade level. You can also consult the Core Knowledge books, one for each grade level, that contain a comprehensive list of things your child should know.[55]

- Your own children are your first priority. If they are in the early primary grades and are not being taught to read properly, either do it yourself or find someone who can. You cannot afford to wait. See appendix B for a complete list of phonemic awareness and phonics programs.

- Read all that you can read about this problem. Appendix C contains a suggested bibliography to help you become informed. If you prefer obtaining your information online, there are dozens of wonderful websites (listed in appendix D) with up-to-date research and links to parent groups that are working to effect change across the country.

- Use your knowledge to make a difference. Julie Anders of Cypress, California, became alarmed when she discovered that her third-grade granddaughter didn't know how to read. In the course of teaching her to read, she became aware of the National Right to Read Foundation and now she's the director for the state of California.[56] In response to what he saw as a lack of any phonics instruction in the public schools of surrounding communities, Dave Ziffer, a systems analyst in Batavia, Illinois, developed an after-school reading instruction program to be offered through park districts and day-care centers.[57]

Reading is not the only area of instruction in which schools are failing our children. Mathematics is also under close scrutiny by parent activists across the country. Chapter 5 describes the current state of affairs.

Notes

1. Michael S. Brunner, *Retarding America: The Imprisonment of Potential* (Portland, OR: Halcyon House, 1993).

2. Project READ, *To Make a Difference* (Silver Spring, MD: READ, Inc., 1978) 27.

3. David Huizinga et al., "Program of Research on the Causes and Correlates of Delinquency, Urban Delinquency and Substance Abuse," Office of Juvenile Justice and Delinquency Prevention (Washington, D.C.: U.S. Department of Justice, 1991), chap. 18: 17.

4. Information on the National Right to Read Foundation can be located at http://www.jwor.com/nrrf.htm

5. Regna Lee Wood, "20th Century American Illiteracy," Briefing 1 (The Plains, VA: National Right to Read Foundation, 1997).

6. Sylvia Farnham-Diggory, quoted in Romalda Bishop Spalding and Walter T. Spalding, *The Writing Road to Reading: The Spalding Method of Phonics for Teaching Speech, Writing and Reading*, 4th ed. (New York: William Morrow, 1990) 10.

7. Keith Stanovich, "Does Reading Make You Smarter? Literacy and the Development of Verbal Intelligence," *Advances in Child Development and Behavior*, ed. Hayne W. Reese, vol. 25 (San Diego: Academic Press, 1993) 133-80.

8. David L. Share, "Phonological Recoding and Self-Teaching: Sine qua non of Reading Acquisition," *Cognition: International Journal of Cognitive Science*, 55 (1995): 151-218.

9. Keith E. Stanovich, "Matthew Effects in Reading: Some Consequences of Individual Differences in the Acquistion of Literacy," *Reading Research Quarterly* 21 (1986) 360-407.

10. Anne E. Cunningham and Keith E. Stanovich, "Early Reading Acquisition and Its Relation to Reading Experience and Ability 10 Years Later," *Developmental Psychology* 33.6 (Nov. 1997): 934-45.

11. Bonnie Grossen, "30 Years of Research: What We Now Know about How Children Learn to Read," online (Santa

Cruz: Center for the Future of Teaching and Learning, n.d.). Available: http: //www.cftl.org/reading.html

12. Ibid.

13. Frank Smith, *Understanding Reading: A Psycholinguistic Analysis of Reading and Learning to Read,* 5th ed. (Hillsdale, NJ: Lawrence Erlbaum, 1994) 312.

14. Ibid.

15. National Academy of Education, *Becoming a Nation of Readers: The Report of the Commission on Reading* Washington, DC: National Academy of Education, 1995) 8.

16. Pila Martinez, "Universities' Reading Ethos Shuns Extremes," *Arizona Daily Star* 16 February 1997, A11.

17. Smith, *Understanding Reading* 313.

18. "Phoenicia," *Random House Encyclopedia,* 1977 ed.

19. Rudolph Flesch, *Why Johnny Can't Read* (New York: Harper and Row, 1955) 45.

20. Mitford McLeod Mathews, *Teaching to Read: Historically Considered* (Chicago: Univ. of Chicago Press, 1966) 15.

21. Art Levine, "The Great Debate Revisited," *Atlantic Monthly* December 1994: 40.

22. Edmund Burke Huey, *The Psychology and Pedagogy of Reading* (New York: Macmillan, 1908) 21.

23. Jeanne Chall, *Learning to Read: The Great Debate* (New York: McGraw-Hill, 1967) 14-15.

24. William S. Gray, *On Their Own in Reading,* 2nd ed. (Chicago: Scott, Foresman, 1960).

25. Flesch, *Why Johnny* 132.

26. Spalding, *Writing Road to Reading* 18.

27. Louise Gurren and Ann Hughes, "Intensive Phonics vs. Gradual Phonics in Beginning Reading," *A Review Journal of Educational Research* 58: 339-46.

28. Helen M. Popp, "Current Practices in the Teaching of Beginning Reading," *Toward a Literate Society: The Report of the Committee on Reading of the National Academy of Education,* ed. John B. Carroll and Jeanne S. Chall (New York: McGraw-Hill, 1975).

29. Frank Smith, *Reading without Nonsense* (New York: Teachers College Press, 1985) 7.

30. National Academy of Education, *Becoming a Nation of Readers* 36.

31. Ken Goodman, *What's Whole in Whole Language?* (Exeter, NH: Heinemann, 1986) 7.

32. Levine, "Great Debate" 41.

33. Karen Diegmueller, "California Plotting New Tack on Language Arts," *Education Week,* online, 14 June 1995. Available in the archives: http://www.edweek.org

34. Marilyn Adams, *Beginning to Read: Thinking and Learning about Print* (Cambridge: MIT Press, 1990) 422.

35. Frank Smith, *Understanding Reading* 148.

36. Karen Diegmueller, "The Best of Both Worlds," *Education Week* 20 March 1996: 33.

37. Elizabeth McPike, "Learning to Read: Schooling's First Mission," *American Educator* Summer 1995: 6.

38. Kathleen Manzo, "California Text Adoption Puts Emphasis on Phonics," *Education Week,* online, 15 January 1997. Available in the archives: http://www.edweek.org

39. Kathleen Manzo, "Study Stresses Role of Early Phonics Instruction," *Education Week* 12 March 1997: 1.

40. James Collins, "How Johnny Should Read," *Time* 27 October 1997: 78-81.

41. Kathy Lally and Debbie M. Price, "The Brain Reads Sound by Sound," *Baltimore Sun* 3 November 1997, online. Available at http://www.readingb9.com/

42. Patrick Groff, "Teachers' Opinions of the Whole Language Approach to Reading Instruction," *Annals of Dyslexia* 41 (1991): 83-95.

43. See appendix A for the original sources from which these statements were adapted.

44. Diane McGuinness, *Why Our Children Can't Read and What We Can Do about It: A Scientific Revolution in Reading* (New York: Free Press, 1997) 55.

45. Council for Exceptional Children, "Principles for Learning to Read," online, 1996. Available: http://www.cec.sped/ericec/principle.htm

46. Marie Clay, *Becoming Literate: The Construction of Inner Control* (Portsmouth, NH: Heinemann, 1991) 141-54.

47. McGuinness, *Why Our Children Can't Read* xiii.

48. Marilyn Adams, *Beginning to Read*.

49. Barbara Foorman et al., "The Role of Instruction in Learning to Read: Preventing Reading Failure in At-Risk Children," *Journal of Educational Psychology* 90: 37-55.

50. Phyllis Lindamood and Nanci Bell, "Sensory-cognitive Factors in the Controversy over Reading Instruction," *Journal of Developmental and Learning Disorders* 1 (1997): 143-82; and McGuinness, *Why Our Children Can't Read*.

51. McGuinness, *Why Our Children Can't Read* 80.

52. Stanovich, "Does Reading Make You Smarter?"

53. Stanovich, "Matthew Effects in Reading."

54. Patrick Groff, *Reading Competency Test* (The Plains, VA: National Right to Read Foundation, 1997). Available at (800) 468-8911.

55. E. D. Hirsch, *What Your Kindergartner Needs to Know: Fundamentals of a Good Kindergarten Education* (New York: Doubleday, 1996). Information on the rest of the books in the series can be found in the references or at the Core Knowledge website (see appendix D).

56. The Right to Read Foundation can be contacted at P.O. Box 490, The Plains, VA 20198 or at (540) 349-1614. To order materials, call (800) 468-8911. Their website can be found at http://www.jwor.com/nrrf.htm

57. The I Can Read website can be found at http://projectpro.com/icanread.htm

TALES FROM THE TRENCHES

A Condensed History of Math

Anonymous Quiz Writer
The Internet

1. Traditional Math (1960)
   A logger sells a truckload of lumber for $100. His cost of production is $\frac{4}{5}$ of the price.
   What is his profit?

2. New Math (1970)
   A logger exchanges set L of lumber for set M of money. The cardinality of set M is 100 and each element is worth $1. Make 100 dots representing the elements of set M. The set C of costs contains 20 fewer points than set M. Represent set C as a subset of set M, and answer the following question: What is the cardinality of the set P of profits?

3. General Math Concepts (1980)
   A logger sells a truckload of wood for $100. His cost of production is $80 and his profit is $20. Your assignment:
   Underline the 20.

4. Outcome-Based Education (1990)
   By cutting down a beautiful forest of trees a logger makes $20. What do you think of making a living this way? Topic for discussion:
   How do the forest birds and squirrels feel?

How Correct Answers Came into Disrepute

5 Is the New "New Math" Really Fuzzy?

Arithmetic is where numbers fly like pigeons in and out of your head.

—*Carl Sandburg, "Arithmetic"*

Are you ready for some high-speed, cross-country travel? The featured attraction on our tour today will be middle school math classrooms. The tour is focused on middle schools for two reasons: 1) you can observe the progress students have made thus far in their math education; and 2) you can judge for yourself how well this experience is preparing them for the rigors of high school math.

How long has it been since you sat in a math class? If it's been a few years, fasten your seat belt. What you are about to see will bear little, if any, resemblance to math as you knew it. The National Council of Teachers of Mathematics issued a new set of guidelines for math instruction in 1989, and math hasn't been the same since. To help you understand what you're seeing on the tour, I've included some explanatory comments.

Math Classes across the Country

The first stop is a classroom in California where seventh graders are working in cooperative groups. The students are taking turns reading aloud from a "scripted dialogue" in their math textbook. The imaginary students in the text are choosing appropriate containers in which to store phone books in connection with a recycling project. You'll discover that today's math textbooks never miss an opportunity to mix political, social, and environmental issues with math. Although the read-aloud dialogue does suggest that the students might measure the length and width of the bottom of the phone book and then multiply the two numbers to get the area, it says nothing about either the volume of the three-dimensional phone books or the three-dimensional container, nor does it discuss the critical question of how the books might need to be arranged within the container. Also not mentioned in the text is any discussion about the weight of the phone books or the strength of the container. No formulas for computing volume are introduced nor are there any entries in the glossary or index that could point the students in the right direction.[1]

One of your fellow tour group members mumbles to himself, "Are you sure this is a math class? It looks more like reading to me." In fact, math instruction today focuses far less on individual students' determining the correct answers to problems and far more on discussing problems in small groups and learning to work together in cooperative teams. The explanation often given for this emphasis is that the business world wants employees who know the meaning of teamwork.

The teacher is wandering about the classroom popping

in and out of each group, but he makes no attempt to clarify concepts for the students or ask any meaningful questions. Another tour group member wonders, "Does the teacher ever teach math up in front of the class?" Not usually. In today's math classrooms the teacher is no longer "the sage on the stage," but rather "the guide on the side." The teacher no longer directs, but instead facilitates.

The next stop is a sixth-grade classroom in the Midwest where the teacher is giving a timed multiplication test. This is an unusual occurrence in today's classrooms. Students used to be expected to master their multiplication facts in third and fourth grade, but timed tests are now frowned upon by modern math educators—too much pressure and competition. As in the teaching of phonics, arithmetic timed tests are often called "drill and kill."

The teacher, who is obviously frustrated and in conflict about her role, explains to the tour group that since her class is supposed to be working on multiplying decimals, she's trying to increase their skill level in multiplication. But she is not having much success, since once she collects the quiz the students have to get out large blue calculators so they can finish their decimal assignment. Of course, since the students can't independently calculate the answers, they also have no idea how to correctly place the decimal point when doing calculations on their own. Calculators are a common sight in today's classrooms. Students rarely master math operations, and one frequently sees finger counting even for operations as simple as addition.[2] The tour group is ready to move on.

> **Students are expected to figure out math concepts and operations using blocks and other objects.**

In the classroom next door the group observes middle school students using manipulatives. Manipulatives, what used to be called blocks, are widely used even in middle school classrooms. Students are expected to figure out math concepts and operations using the blocks and other objects. Class is already in progress, and the students and teacher are correcting an assignment together. The assignment directed the students to write a fraction for each block pattern pictured on a worksheet. Alas, the teacher is not a mathematician, so when the students begin to shout out equivalent fractions rather than ones that exactly match the block patterns, he flounders. The teacher does not panic, however, and tells the students, "There are no wrong answers. There are many right answers that are different." This surprising phrase has become the mantra of "fuzzy-math," one that is most distressing to parents and critics.

Some of the patterns that the teacher agrees are correct, however, simply are not. Conversely, he nails a student for an incorrect answer that is right. Fortunately, she sticks to her guns ($\frac{1}{7}$ does equal $\frac{2}{14}$), and the teacher gives in. One of the other students is overheard to say, "Can you believe he's our math teacher?" Unfortunately, math teachers often have had more educational methods courses than math classes and are distressingly ill prepared to teach their subject matter, especially in the higher grades.

The teacher then passes out the manipulatives and some of the students immediately begin to build towers and toss the blocks around. The teacher is in a losing battle to focus their attention on the lesson's objective—"discovering" a way to divide fractions using the blocks. At this point the class disintegrates. The frustration is palpable, and the students start to misbehave in earnest. As the group leaves the classroom, one tour group member takes a peek at a student's paper. Trying to cover his paper, the student says with some embarrassment, "Don't look at my paper because I can't do any of this math. I don't understand anything in this class." One of his classmates reassures him and adds, "Neither do I."[3]

If you think this tour is fiction, think again. What you've just read is based on actual classroom observations. If you're worried about what you've seen, you're in good company. In fact, many of the parents who are most concerned about the distressing state of math instruction and achievement also happen to be mathematics professors. These worried academics aren't "teachers of teachers," but rather specialists in mathematics and science who cannot teach their subject matter as they once did because the students sitting in their university classrooms don't have the prerequisite skills to handle the rigor. Among the most enraged at this pathetic state of affairs are mathematicians and scientists in California. They have formed organizations like Mathematically Correct[4] in San Diego and HOLD (Honest Open Logical Debate)[5] in Palo Alto to illuminate the current problems in math instruction for the parents and educators of their state. Those of us who live in states where textbook adoptions are not openly debated in the state legislature or discussed daily on the op-ed pages of newspapers can be grateful for the vigorous public debate that has been raging since the early '90s in the West. We will all be the benefactors of their activism.

> **Students guess and estimate about numbers just as in whole-language students guess about word meanings.**

What's Going On in Our Math Classrooms?

Perhaps you've been oblivious to the math crisis. Maybe you're unaware of what's being assigned to kids at the K-12 level. Here's a sampling:

- ◆ Fuzzy-math: a term coined in Palo Alto, California, referring to math texts that de-emphasize getting the correct answers in math.
- ◆ New "new math": a term for distinguishing the current math practices from the innovation of the '60s, called new-math, that emphasized set theory.

That older innovation has nothing to do with the changes in math education today.

- ◆ "Whole-math": whole-math is a lot like the whole-language pedagogy that you read about in chapter 4. Instructional methodologies focus on group discussions and answers; the students guess and estimate about numbers just as in whole-language students guess about word meanings.

- ◆ "MTV Math and Rainforest Algebra": one parent's characterization of her daughter's algebra textbook with its "poetry, pictures of Bill Clinton, and little insights from Tabuk and Esteban—youngsters chosen to enlighten students about the cultural differences in slope."[6]

- ◆ "Algebra Lite": a tongue-in-cheek description of a highly debated high school math program called, ironically enough, *College Prep Math*.

- ◆ "Placebo Math": a label given to the current brand of math instruction by the biomedical research community. Instead of getting "real math," so they'll be able to "do math," our children are getting "placebo math"—the experimental treatment that has no effect.

Although the terms are humorous and provide wonderful material for columnists, comedians, and talk-show hosts, the real tragedy is that our kids can't do math. The reminders hit us in the face daily. I stood in line at a fast-food restaurant recently and watched a young woman stare at a twenty dollar bill for what must have been a full thirty seconds. Her computer wasn't working, and she didn't know how to make change. She finally had to consult the manager who thankfully went to a school where they didn't believe in calculators and estimating. There are far worse things than not knowing how to make change, but this dismal state of affairs is only the tip of the iceberg. Does *your* fourth-grade son still count on his fingers? Does *your* seventh-grade daughter need a calculator to divide

612 by 3? Check out the math textbooks or program your child is using. Look for:

- dumbed down material that expects students to do less
- a reduced role for the teacher as an information provider (the "guide on the side" rather than the "sage on the stage")
- lots of writing about math at the expense of doing math
- less need for accuracy and mastery in the parts of math that actually do get done
- almost no practice and drills so basic skills don't become automatic
- dependence on the use of calculators.

Better yet, give your middle-grade student (9-12 years old) this problem and see what happens. No paper or calculators are allowed. "Pretend you're working at a flea market selling T-shirts. The T-shirts cost 3 for $10.00 or $4.00 for one. The first customer buys 7 T-shirts and pays for them with a fifty dollar bill. How much do the shirts cost and what is the correct change?"

Lauren Scheffers, an Illinois parent, is painfully aware of what fuzzy-math is all about now but believes it's almost too late for her daughter to overcome its impact. Lauren was shocked to discover that her formerly "gifted" daughter, who tested at the 99th percentile in math when she transferred into the district in fourth grade, had turned into a remedial student by seventh grade. She blames the decline of her math abilities on incompetent instruction. Lauren explains how fuzzy-math can destroy a child's ability:

> A question on the sixth-grade state math assessment went something like this: "One in five students prefer hot dogs to hamburgers. There are 100 students. How many students prefer hot dogs?"

Most of us would immediately think, "One-fifth of 100 is 20." But not my daughter. She drew 100 dots in groups of five, circled one in each group, and counted to 20. By current math standards my daughter showed great problem-solving ability, right? Aside from the fact that taking that amount of time on a timed test has a tremendously negative impact on results, it proved my child was totally mathematically illiterate. By the end of sixth grade she didn't know that "1 in 5" could be expressed as a fraction or ratio, or that $\frac{1}{5}$ of 100 was multiplication by a fraction, or the commonly known math concept that $\frac{1}{5}$ of 100 is 20. Personally, I don't need to hear any more pet theories about the benefits of constructivist math, given the incredible, possibly irreversible damage done to my child by well-meaning teachers.

Debby Arnold of Atascadero, California, sent her son Joey off to college confident he would do well after receiving As and Bs in high school math. Instead, he was put into a remedial program. Alarmed, Debby pulled her daughter out of the high school Interactive Mathematics Program that failed her son. She took her daughter to a tutoring center where she was diagnosed with second-grade math skills. She could not accurately and with reasonable speed add single digits.[7]

> "By the end of sixth grade she didn't know that '1 in 5' could be expressed as a fraction."

These horror stories related by angry parents are confirmed by international assessments that compare the mathematics achievement of students in the United States to their counterparts around the world. On the Third International Math and Science Study (TIMSS), U.S. middle-schoolers scored in the second lowest group. Are you surprised after what you observed on our guided tour? War-torn countries such as the Czech Republic, Slovak Republic, Slovenia, and Bulgaria all scored signigicantly higher than our students in grades 5-8. The top three countries, Singapore, South Korea, and Japan, all scored more than 20 percent higher than the United States. Singapore left us in the dust, scoring almost 30 percent higher. The report noted that "U.S. math instruction is a mile wide and an inch deep." Although our fourth-grade students did a little better than the middle-schoolers, scoring above the international average, they were still out-scored by seven of the twenty-five countries that participated in the study. The United States is the only country in the study where students' math achievement declined from above the average at fourth-grade to below average at eighth grade. The findings parallel Lauren Scheffers' experience with her daughter.

Here are the reasons for this abysmal performance:

1) The U.S. expects less of its middle school students than do high-performing nations;

2) U.S. mathematics classes require students to engage in less high-level mathematical thought and solve fewer multistep problems than classes in Germany and Japan; and

3) 40 percent of U.S. eighth-grade mathematics lessons included arithmetic topics, whereas only 13 percent of Germany's and none of Japan's lessons at the eighth-grade level included these topics.

The high school test results aren't much better. The twelfth-grade scores from the Third International Mathematics and Science Study (TIMSS) were released in February 1998, and U.S. high schoolers' performance "was among the lowest of the participating countries in mathematics and science general knowledge, physics and advanced mathematics."[8]

Maybe you're wondering what all the fuss is about. After all, reading is a much more important skill than math, and

> **Internationally, U.S. high schoolers' performance was among the lowest in math, science, physics, and general knowledge.**

if you're not going to be a rocket scientist, who needs it? My fourth-grade son certainly said that when I insisted he master his multiplication and division facts so he could recite them at the speed of sound. Neither was he keen on my dictum that he must take algebra in eighth grade plus complete four years of high school math, including AP calculus. Now about to receive his master's degree in economics from Stanford along the way to earning his Ph.D. in education, he has the good sense to thank his mother. I knew a few things he didn't:

♦ Students who take rigorous mathematics and science courses are much more likely to go to college than those who don't.

♦ Algebra is the "gateway" to advanced mathematics and science in high school.

♦ The benefits of taking rigorous mathematics and science courses extend to students heading into the job market and to both two- and four-year colleges.

♦ Two-year colleges often require all students to gain an understanding of intermediate algebra prior to graduation, regardless of their course of study.

♦ Four-year colleges and universities typically require more high school mathematics preparation for admission.

♦ In the job market, workers who have strong mathematics and science backgrounds in high school are more likely to be employed and generally earn more, even if they have not gone on to college, than workers with fewer math and science courses.[9]

If math is so important, why aren't we doing a better job of teaching it?

Who's to Blame for the Math Crisis?

The answer to this question is very simple: The National Council of Teachers of Mathematics (NCTM), to whom teachers, curriculum developers, and administrators have always looked for expert advice, has betrayed us. This organization published a set of standards in 1989 that would dramatically change the landscape of mathematics instruction in the United States.[10]

I trusted the NCTM standards when I was an assistant superintendent of education. I didn't get bamboozled quite as badly as some of my colleagues; our district soundly rejected several well-known NCTM-based programs because they just didn't make sense to our math committee. On the other hand, we spent thousands of dollars on math manipulatives because there were a number of primary teachers on the committee who liked the idea of discovering math concepts through play. I blush with embarrassment when I think about how much money we spent on calculators. It's not easy to admit you made a mistake. But it's clear to me now that I made a big one.

> The NCTM published a set of standards in 1989 that would dramatically change the landscape of mathematics instruction.

Even those at the very top were convinced by the NCTM standards. Chester Finn, assistant secretary of education in the Bush administration, was taken in by them. He courageously admitted his mistake in his January 21, 1998, testimony to the National Assessment Governing Board's hearing on the proposed voluntary mathematics test: "I need to begin with a big mea culpa. Much of what I'm about to tell you is a problem that can fairly be said to have begun on my watch, as a member of this Board for eight years." Finn goes on to explain how the NCTM stepped into a vacuum (no one else volunteered to do the job) and began to dictate that the structure of the National Assessment of Educational Progress in Mathematics (a test to measure the math achievement of our children) would be based on the NCTM's view of what was important. Emphasis was to be placed on open-response test items, calculator use, and conceptual understanding. Finn explains:

> NCTM was riding high as the arbiter of K-12 math for the U.S., perhaps even for the world. Its standards were held up as a model that other subjects might aspire to. Never mind that they [the NCTM standards] never included actual student performance levels or benchmarks. Nor, prior to their universal dissemination, were NCTM's standards subjected to field tests or clinical trials to ascertain whether they actually boost student performance. (The Food and Drug Administration would never allow a medical device or procedure to reach the open market under such circumstances. Nor would responsible physicians use it without solid data arising from large experiments.)"[11]

Exactly how did the NCTM standards come to be? One important thing to remember is that most of the people who wrote the standards are not mathematicians, but rather math educators, actually *progressive* math educators. The same philosophy that brought you whole-language, where kids guess at words and the teacher facilitates instead of teaches, is also at the root of the current math crisis. Progressive education has progressively taken the content out of education.

In the early 1900s, teachers in training attended specialized teacher-training institutions. These schools were primarily concerned with whether or not prospective teachers had actually mastered the subjects they were planning to teach: Reading teachers knew reading, history teachers knew history, and so on. Content was primary and teaching methods were secondary. Gradually, however, as teacher-training institutions or "normal schools" were absorbed into universities, they lost most of the responsibility for content. The math departments now taught math. That left the departments of education to teach methods. In order to justify their existence and pump up their faculties and budgets, the educationists began to downgrade the importance of content [facts]. American schools of education now preach content-independent methods and general skills. They denounce traditional knowledge transmission and the building of remembered knowledge based on discipline-specific facts and skills.

> **The educators who wrote the NCTM standards were trained to value process and methods over content.**

The educators who wrote the NCTM standards were trained to value process and methods over content. Therefore, it's not surprising that the NCTM standards currently driving math instruction are apparently driving it right into the ground. Do you know what *your* kids are learning in math?

What's Hot and What's Not?

What's Hot? "Social goals," "psychological considerations," and "content-independent skills."

What's Not? Focused, specific, basic, teachable, and measurable math content.

What's Hot? "Intuitively" acquiring factual knowledge through "real-world experiences and higher-order thinking skills."

What's Not? Direct, systematic, and sequential instruction by the teacher.

What's Hot? "Numerous and varied experiences related to

the cultural, historical, and scientific evolution of mathematics so [students] can appreciate the role of mathematics in the development of our contemporary society."[12]

What's Not? Math content.

What's Hot? Calculators and computers. (Note that Japanese and Chinese teachers do not use calculators or computers in mathematics classes because they want students to understand the concepts and operations necessary for the solution of problems. Only at the high school level, after students have had a clear understanding of the mathematical concepts, are East Asian students given the opportunity to use a calculator as a tool in solving mathematics problems.)[13]

What's Not? Paper, pencil, and memorization.

What's Hot? Problems generated by students and solved by trial and error, guess and check, and "acting out."

What's Not? Specific math knowledge used to solve problems provided by the teacher or the textbook.

What's Hot? Writing about math.

What's Not? Communicating in the symbols and language of mathematics, i.e., numbers and variables.

What's Hot? Political correctness. Here's an example:

> Students might like mathematics but not display the kinds of attitudes and thoughts identified by this standard. For example, students might like mathematics yet believe that problem solving is always finding the one correct answer using the right way. These beliefs, in turn, influence their actions when they are faced with solving a problem. Although such students have a positive attitude toward mathematics, they are not exhibiting essential aspects of what we have termed mathematical disposition.[14]

What's Not? Marking an answer wrong.

What's Hot? Informal (use of manipulatives) and inductive (generalizing from multiple observations) reasoning.
   What's Not? Deductive reasoning.

What's Hot? Estimation.
   What's Not? Figuring out an exact answer.

The Good News and the Bad News

There's good and bad news on the horizon. First, the good news. California, the first state to fully implement the NCTM standards, is making a change. In December 1997 the California Board of Education approved a set of standards for the state's public school students that emphasizes mastery of basic computational skills over the ability to write about math. Multiplication tables must be memorized by the end of third grade, long division mastered by the end of fourth, and the Pythagorean theorem of geometry by the end of tenth grade. Algebra is now recommended for eighth graders, a year earlier than most students study it now.[15] Unfortunately, it will take about thirty months for all the dust to settle on this latest action, and by that time hundreds of thousands more children will have missed out on rigorous math instruction.

The bad news is that the math disaster that quaked at California's epicenter is still sending aftershocks throughout thousands of communities around the country where the NCTM standards are the only game in town. Its recommendations pervade the teaching, textbooks, and tests in big cities and tiny hamlets around the country. Forty states have adopted NCTM standards-based math programs with performance-based assessments to follow; the National Science Foundation

> NCTM recommendations pervade the teaching, textbooks, and tests around the country.

spends $10 million a year on developing instructional materials based on the NCTM standards, and math programs like Mathland, Everyday Math, and Integrated Math are being adopted in districts even as you read this paragraph. In 1991, the National Science Foundation gave $10 million to the Montana Council of Teachers of Mathematics to overhaul that state's program. It's hard to believe that conservative Montanans would buy into this, but they're practical enough not to turn down $10 million. That's about $11.37 for every resident of the state. And if you divide the money by the number of school children, it's a bonanza.

The public debate over math in California hardly caused a ripple in a suburban Illinois school district where the superintendent, curriculum director, and a hand-picked math committee facilitated the adoption of a fuzzy-math series despite an undercurrent of protest. Parents were led to believe that the teachers supported the series, and the teachers who opposed the move were intimidated into remaining silent about their opposition. The waters remained calm through tight information control and spin at the administrative level. Parent activist Barbara Shafer attended meetings, provided information to the math committee, and brought in an independent math consultant to present an alternate point of view, but to no avail.

The district brought in Steven Leinwand, a member of the committee overseeing President Clinton's proposed national mathematics exam, to persuade reluctant parents to climb aboard. This is the same Steven Leinwand who wrote an essay explaining why it is "downright dangerous to teach students things like six times seven is 42, put down two and carry four. Such instruction sorts people out, anointing the few who master these procedures and casting out the many." He further stated that "there might once have been an excuse for such undemocratic goings-on, but we can now, because of technology, throw off the discriminatory shackles of computational algorithms [formulas]."[16] Educators and parents swallowed Leinwand's fuzzy-math testimony hook, line, and sinker.

Teaching, Textbooks, and Tests

Math instruction in the United States is currently in the stranglehold of the teaching, textbooks, and tests that have been prescribed by the National Council of Teachers of Mathematics. The NCTM standards have had more than ten years to influence education.

The *teachers* are well-meaning and dedicated but poorly prepared, inadequately supported, and often puppets in the hands of the "experts" who purport to know best. Most teachers never learned to teach math in their education courses, and many elementary school teachers are actually math-phobic, having taken the bare minimum of math in high school. Their abilities to organize instruction for the teaching of complex math skills such as long division or subtraction with borrowing is sadly lacking. They need assistance with effective teaching practices and the support of good materials. It's hard to find either of these on the math scene right now.

> "I still don't quite grasp the necessity for political correctness in an algebra textbook."

Textbooks are an even bigger obstacle on the road to math reform. Senator Robert Byrd, Democrat from West Virginia, recently held forth on the Senate floor on the topic of math texts. Having read Marianne Jennings's column in which she dubbed her daughter's math book, "Rain-Forest Algebra," Byrd obtained a copy of the book, titled *Secondary Math: An Integrated Approach: Focus on Algebra*.[17] Byrd described it as "wacko math." He explained on the Senate floor what he had found:

> This textbook written by a conglomerate of authors lists 5 so-called "algebra authors," but it boasts 20

"other series authors" and 4 "multicultural reviewers." We are talking algebra now. Why we need multicultural review of an algebra textbook is a question which I would like to hear someone answer, and the fact that there are 4 times as many "other series authors" as "algebra authors" in this book made me suspect that this really was not an algebra textbook at all. The odd amalgam of math, geography and language masquerading as an algebra textbook goes on to intersperse each chapter with helpful comments and photos of children named Tabuk, Esteban, and Minh. Although I don't know what happened to Dick and Jane, I do understand now why there are four multicultural reviewers for this book. However, I still don't quite grasp the necessity for political correctness in an algebra textbook. Nor do I understand the inclusion of the United Nations Universal Declaration of Human Rights in three languages, or a section on the language of algebra which defines such mathematically significant phrases as, "the lion's share," "the boondocks," and "not worth his salt."

After a further discussion of this fuzzy-math masterpiece, Senator Byrd concludes:

I was thoroughly dazed and unsure of whether I was looking at a science book, a language book, a sociology book, or a geography book. In fact, of course, that is the crux of the problem. I was looking at all of the above. This textbook tries to be all things to all students in all subjects and the result is a mush of multiculturalism, environmental and political correctness, and various disjointed discussions on a multitude of topics which certainly is bound to confuse the students trying to learn and the teachers trying to teach from such unfocused nonsense.[18]

This diatribe might be amusing if our children weren't paying the price with substandard math skills.

The final and most formidable obstacles to ousting fuzzy-math are the *tests*—the new glitzy, performance-based kind that are popping up everywhere (see chapter 6 for a more complete description). These tests can be found in your local school district, at the state level, and scariest of all, at the national level. As this book is being written, debate regarding the merits of a voluntary national mathematics test is going on. This sounds like a terrific idea, doesn't it? Well, only if the test actually measures something worthwhile.

The traditional, nationally normed, standardized tests are scary for the new-math gurus because they provide a yearly, reliable, standardized reference point by which to measure how groups of students (and individuals) are achieving. But fuzzy-math instruction doesn't produce high standardized test scores. Consider what happened in Ames, Iowa, a middle-class community where many of the parents work at Iowa State University. In 1985, Ames introduced an NCTM standards-based "math in context" program. Rote memorization was out, while calculators and solving real-world problems were in. In 1985-86 every grade level in Ames (third through eighth) was at the 90th percentile or above in mathematics achievement (actually every grade level except sixth was above the 95th percentile, and sixth was at the 90th). After ten years of fuzzy-math, the students in Ames were in most cases well below average. Third graders were at the 47th percentile, fourth at the 31st, fifth at the 26th, sixth at the 37th, seventh at the 21st, and eighth graders scored at the 24th percentile.[19]

> After ten years of fuzzy-math, the students in Ames were in most cases well below average.

It takes a fuzzy test to measure fuzzy-math! And fuzzy tests are on their way if the NCTM has anything to say about it. There are courageous educators out there who are lobbying tirelessly for a meaningful national test. Mary

Damer testified at a hearing in Chicago held to enable educators and parents to share their opinions about a national test. Here's a brief synopsis of what she told the committee.

As a college educator who trains special education teachers, a former principal, and a parent of children in elementary school, I initially welcomed the announcement of a new rigorous national test which would assess high standards in math and reading. I believed that high-stakes testing would provide citizen consumers with the quality information they have been seeking related to the effectiveness of their local schools. I hoped that improved testing in math and reading would provide objective information that might help stem the decline in math and reading literacy that I have witnessed these past twenty-five years.

After reading and analyzing the test specification for the proposed Voluntary National Test in Mathematics, I was disappointed to see that the proposed math assessment reflects the NCTM-based standards which are currently so controversial. Many of my concerns arise because the proposed math test is based on what skeptics are calling fuzzy-math curriculum, a curriculum which does not yet have any longitudinally based research support.

My own community of St. Charles, Illinois, implemented an NCTM-based math program, The University of Chicago "Everyday Mathematics Program," four years ago. Since then, education consumers in our community have become so concerned about a perceived "dumbing down" of the math curriculum, that we have tracked achievement test scores for the past three years. Our observation reveals math scores which have steadily decreased. Barrington, one of the first suburbs in Illinois to adopt the same NCTM program, recently returned to a more traditional math curriculum, because after several years their students' math skills were sinking.

Mary's testimony goes on to describe the limitations of a mathematics performance-based assessment that asks students to write about math:

> In one sample question for the proposed test a student, in order to receive full credit, must provide an explanation for why the answer is correct. In addition to mathematically solving the problem, the student must also exhibit language skills (usually in writing). Any child who has poor fine motor skills, who is a slow writer, who is a slow or inadequate speller, or who has indecipherable/sloppy writing might receive a lower score on the math assessment. School officials and parents analyzing the student scores will be unable to ascertain whether the lower performance is a result of poor writing ability or of inadequate math skills.

Barrington, Illinois, recently returned to a more traditional math curriculum because students' math skills were sinking.

If NCTM test makers have their way, your children may be facing questions like this sample test item from an early California math framework which suggests that teachers use mathematics to illuminate the mathematical side of social issues: "The 20 percent of California families with the lowest annual earnings pay an average of 14.1 percent in state and local taxes, and the middle 20 percent pay only 8.8 percent. What does the difference mean? Do you think it is fair? What additional questions do you have?" The framework then goes on to enthuse: "Such problems take percents, one of the most prosaic workhorses in mathematics, and open them up, breathing new life into them by introducing questions about reporting, statistics, and social justice."[20]

A letter to President Clinton, written by Mike McKeown of Mathematically Correct and signed by 235 mathematicians, educators, parents, and community activists (including such folk as Jaimé Escalante of *Stand and Deliver* fame, E. D. Hirsch, and many of the parents whose stories you have read in this book) also objected to the proposed performance-based math assessment. "We and many others across the country feel strongly that use of the 1989 NCTM Standards as a guiding document is a serious error which will undermine the credibility and usefulness of the national test." A second problem identified in the letter had to do with the people who would write the test. "Nearly all of its [the test preparation committee's] members are strong advocates of the NCTM Standards and of programs that repute to be aligned with the NCTM Standards . . . [and] are actively involved in the writing or promotion of particular mathematics curricula." Finally, the letter concluded that "the exam itself, at least as represented in the examination plan, is not at all adequate."[21]

What Can You Do?

What can you do to make a difference in the life of your child, your community, and our country with regard to math? Here are my suggestions.

Be Informed

Review the first and second reports of the American Mathematical Society Committee to Comment on the NCTM Standards (find it at http://www.ams.org/govern ment/nctm2000.html). These documents will give you a summary of what professional mathematicians have to say about the standards that are currently driving mathematics instruction in the United States.

Investigate Your District

Obtain a copy of the mathematics learning goals (or standards) for your school district and/or your state. Compare what you find in your school or district to either the Mathematics Standards of Learning developed by Mathematically Correct,[22] the Mathematics Standards for San Diego, California,[23] or the Core Knowledge series of books titled *What Your 5th Grader Needs to Know: Fundamentals of a Good Fifth Grade Education* (there's a book for every grade level that contains sections on mathematics; language arts; geography, world history, and American civilization; fine arts; and natural sciences).[24]

Turn on Your Fuzz Alert

Watch for fuzzy outcomes or goals that focus on social and behavioral issues rather than students' academic performance. The American Federation of Teachers has developed a set of Criteria for High-Quality Standards[25] that includes these requirements:

1) Standards must focus on academics
2) Standards must be grounded in core disciplines
3) Standards must be specific enough to assure the development of a common core curriculum
4) Standards must be rigorous and world class
5) Standards must include performance requirements

University of Michigan researcher Dr. Harold Stevenson has analyzed math education in Eastern Asia and the United States for fifteen years and has this to say about the NCTM standards:

> In our view the NCTM standards present a very vague, somewhat grandiose, readily misinterpreted view of what American children should learn in mathematics. Moreover, the view fails to meet what we would consider to be the meaning of "standards."

Standards should involve a progression of accomplishment or competencies that are to be demonstrated at defined times in the child's schooling. The NCTM Standards give no indication (beyond four year intervals) of the sequence with which the content is to be presented and are not helpful to the classroom teacher in designing lessons that meet the standards.[26]

> I have seen textbooks in which the content is so sparse or inaccurate that even the best teachers are hard-pressed to teach from them.

Find Out What's in Your Child's Textbooks

Check out the textbooks or math program your child is using. Even if you're fortunate enough to find a good set of standards of learning for mathematics in your state and/or district, the poor quality of the textbooks actually being used may make it impossible for the teacher to teach and your child to learn what is required. I have seen textbooks in which the content is so sparse or inaccurate that even the best teachers are hard-pressed to teach from them. In fact, many teachers engage in "clandestine teaching from old texts" to preserve their academic standards and integrity.

Check Out Your Child's Knowledge

Find out if your child has mastered the learning goals. Visit http://www.japanese-online.com/math/index.htm and check out some math problems translated from Japan's junior high school math placement test given to twelve year olds. The 225 problems are logic based and consist of about twenty different types of story problem. This site is designed to provide American students with quality math content based on world standards. See how your twelve- to sixteen-year-old child measures up to these challenges. You might also use the diagnostic math test that appears on the

Saxon Publishers website (http://www.saxonpub.com) designed for students from fourth to eighth grade.[27]

Help Your Child and Others Meet the Goals

If your child is deficient in math achievement, take steps to make sure the learning goals are met. You may need to become a tutor yourself, volunteer your services in the classroom (if permitted) to help your child along with other students, hire an outside tutor, enroll your child in an outside class like Kumon or a learning center, or even choose another schooling option for your child. Once you've identified the learning goals, monitor your children's progress. Watch them while they work problems. Give your children problems to solve from time to time to check on their understanding.

Be a Smart Listener

Don't be fooled by the promises of "easy math" that current educators are dishing out. Don't pay any attention to the warnings about "drill and kill" (the answer teachers give you when you complain that your child doesn't know math facts).

> Every successful program for teaching math to young people follows these three cardinal rules for early mathematics education: 1) practice, 2) practice, 3) practice. . . . Well-meaning persons who want to protect the joy of the childhood years wrongly fear that practice in mathematics portends a soul-killing approach to schooling. Nothing could be further from the truth. . . . The destroyer of joy in mathematics is not practice but anxiety that results from training that has denied them systematic familiarity with the vocabulary, grammar, and spelling of mathematics.[28]

"Practice, practice, practice."

Barry Simon, chairman of the math department at Cal

Tech, laments the passing of the rigorous theorem/proof courses that characterized his high school education at James Madison High School in Brooklyn:

> Why do I mourn the loss of what was a core part of education for centuries? While the geometric intuition that comes from the classical high school geometry courses is significant, what is really important is the exposure to clear and rigorous arguments. The trend away from theorem/proof geometry seems to be based on the following reasoning by the educational establishment. Some high school students are just unable to get this theorem/proof stuff. If we place them in a separate track, they'll wind up with a low self-image. So to prevent some students from having a low self-image, we won't ask anyone to understand it.[29]

Look for These Values in Your Math Program

Even if you're not a mathematical genius, you can look for these ten suggestions, or commandments, which Mathematically Correct recommends be a part of math instruction in every classroom in America:

- Honor the correct answer more than the guess.
- Do not eschew the value of repeated practice.
- Give good grades only for good work.
- Spare the calculator and spare the child.
- Teach proofs in high school.
- Ensure the math competence of the math teacher.
- Avoid vague objectives.
- Use objective tests to judge student achievement.
- Teach to mastery.
- Value knowing and honor the knowledgeable.[30]

I know that these commandments work. As an elementary school principal I inherited a school of 425 students most of whom scored at the 20th percentile in math on the standardized test we gave every spring. We began following the commandments. I got rid of teachers who couldn't teach and hired competent ones. We gave good grades for good work and instituted an honor roll. (It was called the A-team, and students who made it received T-shirts.) Every child in our school knew the math facts, backward and forward and upside down. We even beat the pants off a school in a nearby city with a Math Facts Super Bowl.

Can you imagine what would happen to some principal who tried to do today what I did fifteen years ago? We stopped spending the first half of every year reviewing what students were supposed to have learned the year before and started with brand-new material. We wrote our own mathematics learning outcomes for every grade level (the teachers hashed them out in heated discussions after school) and distributed them to our parents so everyone knew what was expected. Teachers were accountable for achievement and pulled out all the stops for the pupils who needed extra help. Very soon, the students we sent on to the junior high school qualified for the top math classes. The math department chair who in the past had automatically slotted all of our graduates for the remedial classes had to create more upper-level courses. Our standardized test scores were above the 60th percentile with many children scoring in the 90th percentile and above. In our school, where many of the students could have been considered "at-risk" because of their limited English proficiency and socioeconomic status, we had better achievement at some grade levels than more affluent schools in the district. It wasn't hard. We just obeyed the commandments!

> The junior high math department chair who in the past had slotted all of our students for remedial classes now had to create more upper-level courses.

Reading and math are just two of the major trouble spots in American classrooms, but by no means the only ones. In chapter 6 we'll examine some of what I call the virulent viruses that have invaded our schools—innovations that educators have promised would reform and improve our schools, but in reality have made a patient in crisis almost terminal.

Notes

1. *Interactive Mathematics: Activities and Investigations* Book II (New York: Glencoe-McGraw-Hill, 1995), Units 7-12: 76-77.

2. This classroom observation was reported by a midwestern university professor who regularly observes in classrooms around her state. She wishes to remain anonymous.

3. These observations are adapted from the already cited anonymous observer.

4. The Mathematically Correct website is a valuable source of information about the current state of mathematics instruction both in California and around the country. Find it at http://www.mathematicallycorrect.com

5. Peter West, "Palo Alto Parents Square Off Over Math Curriculum," *Education Week* 7 June 1995: 7. The reaction to the introduction of fuzzy-math in Palo Alto, California, is documented on the HOLD website at http://www.rahul.net/dehnbase/hold/

6. Marianne M. Jennings, "MTV Math Doesn't Add Up," *Wall Street Journal* 17 Dec. 1996: A22. A copy of this article has been reprinted by permission of the author on the Mathematically Correct website and can be found at http://www.mathematicallycorrect.com

7. Lynne V. Cheney, "The Latest Education Disaster: Whole Math," *The Weekly Standard* 4 Aug. 1997: 25-29.

8. U.S. Dept. of Education, "Pursuing Excellence: A Study of U.S. 12th Grade Mathematics & Science Achievement in International Context," online, 14 Feb. 1998. Available: http://nces.ed.gove/timss/

9. United States Deparment of Education, "Mathematics Equals Opportunity," online, 10 Oct. 1997. Available: http://www.ed.gov/pubs/math/

10. National Council of Teachers of Mathematics, *Curriculum and Evaluation Standards* (Reston, VA: National Council of Teachers of Mathematics, 1989).

11. Chester Finn, "Testimony to the National Assessment Governing Board," online. Available: http://www.mathematicallycorrect.com

12. National Council of Teachers of Mathematics, *Curriculum* Introduction.

13. Posting on the Education Consumers ClearingHouse by Dr. Harold Stevenson, Univ. of Michigan researcher and author of *The Learning Gap* who has analyzed math education in Eastern Asia and the United States for 15 years, 22 Dec. 1997.

14. National Council of Teachers of Mathematics, *Curriculum* Introduction.

15. Millicent Lawson, "Calif. Education Officials Approve Back to Basics Standards in Math," *Education Week* online, 14 Jan. 1998. Available: http://www.edweek.org

16. Steven Leinwand, "It's Time to Abandon Computational Algorithms," *Education Week* online, 9 Feb. 1994. Available: http://www.edweek.org

17. Addison-Wesley, *Secondary Math: An Integrated Approach: Focus on Algebra* (Reading, MA: Addison-Wesley, 1997).

18. Senator Robert Byrd, *Cong. Rec.* 9 June 1997: S5393.

19. Douglas Burns, "Ames Parents Angry over Drop in Basic Math Skills," *The Daily Tribune* [Ames, IA] 21 Feb. 1995: A1.

20. California State Board of Education, *Math Frameworks* (Sacramento, CA: State Board of Education, 1992). Meg Sommerfeld, "Calif. Parents Target Math Frameworks," *Education Week* online, 24 April 1996. Available: http://www.edweek.org

21. Mike McKeown, "Letter to President Clinton" online, Aug. 26 1997. Available: http://www.mathematicallycorrect.com

22. "Mathematically Correct," online. Available: http://www.mathematicallycorrect.com

23. "Mathematics Standards for San Diego Public Schools," online. Available: http://www.sdcs.k12.ca.us/standards/

24. Consult the references for a complete listing of the Core Knowledge series of books.

25. American Federation of Teachers, "True Standards that Parents Can Use," online, 6 Oct. 1996. Available: http://www.mathematicallycorrect.com

26. Harold W. Stevenson and James W. Stigler, *The Learning*

Gap: Why Our Schools Are Failing and What We Can Learn from Japanese and Chinese Education (New York: Summit Books, 1992).

27. You can obtain a copy of the Saxon Catalog for Home Schoolers by calling (800) 284-7019.

28. American Federation of Teachers, "True Standards."

29. Barry Simon, "Modern Mathematicians Have Lost Value of Proofs," *Binghamton Sunday Press and Sun Bulletin* [NY] 17 February 1998: E4.

30. "Mathematically Correct" website can be accessed at http://www.mathematicallycorrect.com

TALES FROM THE TRENCHES

The Four Stages of Outcome-Based Education Awareness

Ed Coleman*
Parent
Education Activist

Stage One: Complete OBE Ignorance
The parent is entirely unaware that anything is wrong. He sends his kids off to school with the expectation that they will receive something resembling a traditional education, much like the one he received as a child.

Stage Two: OBE Awareness
The parent is still unaware of OBE but notices that there is definitely something wrong at school. At this point, he either joins the majority of the public and rationalizes things or begins investigating and moves on to the next stage.

Stage Three: OBE Dissatisfaction
The parent starts mounting efforts to combat specific elements of OBE, believing them to be a series of unrelated and misguided programs being implemented randomly by his local authorities. He writes letters to school board members and politicians, and starts organizing local citizens to combat specific issues. He then puts his kids in a private school or starts home-schooling.

Stage Four: OBE Outrage
The parent realizes that OBE is a systemic program designed to destroy every last vestige of academic education. Realizing that if he were to try to alert his neighbors to the reality of this program, they would respond by labeling him a lunatic, he determines that others must be led down the same gradual path that he followed.

6 Other Educational Viruses in Schools

How to Tell If Your School Is Sick

> Tune your ears to wisdom, and concentrate on understanding. Cry out for insight and understanding. Search for them as you would for lost money or hidden treasure. . . . Then you will understand what is right, just, and fair, and you will know how to find the right course of action every time. For wisdom will enter your heart, and knowledge will fill you with joy. Wise planning will watch over you. Understanding will keep you safe.
>
> *Proverbs 2:2-4, 9-11, NLT*

There are a multitude of virulent educational viruses that have been incubating and mutating in our schools for decades. During the past fifteen years these viruses have gone on a rampage, and the damage they have done to a generation of children is incalculable. Educational viruses are similar to those that invade the human body. A healthy person abounds with viruses, much as a school or district will always have a few quirky ideas or far-out teachers hanging around the fringes. In order for a virus to do any harm in your body, however, it needs to interact

141

with the body's healthy cells. It does this in very clever ways, tricking the host cells into thinking it's something that it's not. The host cell then innocently provides the virus cell with nourishment and a warm place to live, and the virus begins to grow and multiply. A virus has several interesting characteristics that can also be found in educational innovations:

- ◆ It cannot say no to itself.
- ◆ It has no boundary, respects no boundary.
- ◆ It has no ability to learn from its experiences.
- ◆ It cannot sacrifice itself for the sake of other cells.
- ◆ It is an intracellular parasite with no life of its own.[1]

For educational innovations to do serious damage in the schools of your community, they need to find "host cells"—individuals who eagerly embrace change without taking the time to investigate the long-term ramifications and who are quick to jump on any bandwagon. In the absence of strong leadership from an individual or group to confront the innovators, ask the difficult questions, and bring critical issues to light, educational innovation viruses can be fatal.[2]

> **The distinguishing characteristic of these achieving schools is their belief that academics must invariably receive priority.**

The achievement declines detailed in chapter 1 are a direct result of these viral attacks. There are still schools, albeit an increasingly smaller number, that have resisted the viruses and where achievement has remained unchanged or even increased; the distinguishing characteristic of these achieving schools is their belief that academics must invariably receive priority over every other activity.[3] These schools offer no mini-courses and electives; whole-language and fuzzy-math are not allowed; neither are cooperative grouping and de-tracking. The virulent viruses have not been permitted to take hold.

The viruses I have selected to include in chapter 6 are arranged in alphabetical order, much like an encyclopedia or dictionary. Some entries contain only a brief definition and some are cross-referenced to other entries. The key entries include 1) a brief description of the innovation; 2) some of the ways the innovation might affect you and your child personally; 3) a quote from an expert, a first-person experience, or a relevant news report of the effects of the innovation in schools today; and 4) resources you can consult if you want to further educate yourself (e.g., websites, books, organizations).

Alternative Assessment

(*See* Performance-Based Assessment)

America 2000

(*See* Goals 2000)

Authentic Assessment

(*See also* Performance-Based Assessments)

Authentic assessment takes place in the regular classroom and measures not only students' ability to think and do but their attitudes as well. The testing situations are designed to replicate "real life" and involve group projects and demonstrations as opposed to traditional paper and pencil tests. Authentic assessment in the form of homework assignments, posters, and dramatic performances can enliven a class period and help teachers to see how well knowledge has been connected. The major difficulty with relying solely on authentic assessments is their subjectivity as well as their lack of reliability and validity.

Block Scheduling

Block scheduling (also called "semestering") is an organizational innovation that reallocates the time available in the typical high school or middle school schedule, ostensibly to offer more educational opportunities for students. In reality, academics usually receive short shrift as more electives like family living and career awareness are added to the schedule.

There are two major types of block schedules. The first, sometimes called 8 by 8, has classes scheduled for longer blocks of time (usually ninety minutes) every other day instead of meeting for the traditional fifty- to sixty-minute period on five consecutive days. The other major form of block schedule is sometimes called 4 by 4. This block schedule requires that a year-long class be compressed into one semester, and students take four such classes per semester. This results in students' taking year one of a foreign language or math class during the first semester of one year and year two of that subject in the first or second semester of the next year.

> **The downside to block scheduling is that it reduces the overall amount of time spent in academic classes.**

The adoption of block scheduling in a school or district is always made for so-called educational reasons and is often touted as a means of better meeting the needs of at-risk students. The proponents of block scheduling promise a format that encourages the use of instructional methods that are more motivating for the less interested and uninvolved student; tightens up delivery of instruction (more taught in less time); provides more time for complicated science labs that used to be crammed into fifty minutes; gives students the opportunity for interdisciplinary projects and group work. All of these are laudable goals.

The downside to block scheduling, however, is that it

reduces the overall amount of time spent in individual academic classes (sometimes by as much as 10 to 15 percent; e.g., two fifty-five minute classes become one ninety-minute class) and *forces* teachers into planning more hands-on projects to fill what can seem like an endless ninety-minute class period. Block scheduling is particularly disadvantageous for subjects that require frequent drill and repetition, such as math, music, or foreign language. It also shortchanges the very students for whom it is supposedly being implemented: the at-risk and unmotivated students who typically have shorter attention spans and are rarely well-organized. Giving these students longer class periods in which to be bored and more days between classes to forget what they've learned and lose their homework assignments are questionable practices if the goal is to increase achievement.

Those whose schools are considering block scheduling or already use it should check out two very comprehensive websites dealing with it: "The Case Against Block Scheduling" and "Block Scheduling Sources and Connections" (see appendix D for site locations). These websites detail the changes wrought by block scheduling and have in-depth reports of schools that are already using it or that tried it and abandoned it.

Careers

(*See* School-to-Work)

Certificate of Advanced Mastery or CAM

(*See also* Outcome-Based Education and School-to-Work)

The Certificate of Advanced Mastery (CAM) was established by School-to-Work legislation and is granted to students in some states when they complete the course requirements of job mentoring and community service, usually at age eighteen or after the senior year of high school. The Certificate of Advanced Mastery certifies that the student has obtained the needed skills and training to apply for a job in his chosen career major. However, this certificate is not recognized by major colleges and universities, so it cannot lead to higher education.

Certificate of Initial Mastery or CIM

(*See also* Outcome-Based Education and School-to-Work)

The Certificate of Initial Mastery (CIM) is an Outcome-Based Education diploma that students receive after they have met the state's federally approved Outcome-Based Education standards. A student ideally receives his certificate of initial mastery at age sixteen or at the end of his tenth-grade year. Without a Certificate of Initial Mastery a student cannot go on to receive a Certificate of Advanced Mastery.

Child-Centered Classrooms

(*See* Developmentally Appropriate Practice)

Constructivism

(*See also* Paradigm Shift)

Constructivism is a contemporary version of progressivism. The following description of constructivism from the Association for Supervision and Curriculum Development (ASCD) is an example of educational "doublespeak" at its finest. Educators are urged to leave behind outmoded images and practices, described as "images of control, not learning," and to instead construct new images that are

> reflective of new practices . . . that portray the student as a thinker, a creator, and a constructor. Schools can become settings in which students are encouraged to

develop hypotheses, to test out their own and others' ideas, to make connections among "content" areas, to explore issues and problems of personal relevance (either existing or emerging), to work cooperatively with peers and adults in the pursuit of understanding, and to form the disposition to be life-long learners.[4]

Constructivism is progressivism in a new package.

Cooperative Learning

Cooperative learning is an instructional method in which small groups of students of varying abilities (usually one high achieving student, one low achieving student, and two to three average ability students) are expected to work together as a team to complete a daily assignment or a long-term project. In theory, each individual in the group is accountable for contributing to the end product. In reality, the work usually ends up falling on the shoulders of one or two more capable students whose sense of personal responsibility and motivation keep everyone else from failing. Cooperative learning is designed to stamp out competition and foster teamwork, a quality that employers are reportedly looking for in their employees. The social skills that can be taught in the context of cooperative learning groups are admirable, but the question remains: do our children have time day after day for process activities when they don't know how to read, write, or do math?

> Overused and mishandled by poorly trained teachers, cooperative learning constitutes nothing more than pooled ignorance.

One of the key aspects of cooperative learning that is often completely ignored is individual accountability. When used judiciously by well-trained teachers, cooperative learning has the potential to help students learn to work together more effectively. Overused and mishandled by poorly trained teachers, it constitutes nothing more than pooled ignorance.

How Might Cooperative Learning Affect Children?

1. Some very bright children may be forced to endure frustration or boredom while working with a group of students who are unable or unwilling to contribute to the group goal.

2. Other very bright children may shoulder the burden for the entire group project even though the task was intended to be shared equally.

3. Students with special learning needs might not receive direct instruction from a certified teacher. They could instead be wasting time as the group of children pool their ignorance about something the teacher should have taught them in the first place. Faster learners often react to their frustration by plowing ahead into new territory despite the slower learner's lack of understanding. Educators rationalize this behavior as acceptable since group grades do not reflect the slower learner's deficits.

4. A great deal of valuable instructional time can be wasted as students engage in contrived problem-solving activities and group tasks to learn the problem-solving and social skills they supposedly will use when they get around to learning subject matter in cooperative groups.

What Do Knowledgeable People Think about Cooperative Learning?

According to the *Wall Street Journal,* one family withdrew their gifted daughter from fourth grade when she was placed at a table with three children of slower achievement speeds and directed to work as a team on math problems. Then the teacher gave a collective grade to the table as a whole. David Stillman, the father, says, "I thought the collective grade was a message that [my daughter] will be penalized if [the other students] don't learn." The superintendent responded by reminding Mr. Stillman that "collaborative learning is used by every school system in the country to teach teamwork and respect for differences."[5]

Parents, however, do not care if "everybody's doing it." They don't like it. In the 1994 Public Agenda poll, "First Things First: What Americans Expect from the Public Schools," parents came down firmly on the side of "learning environments that vary according to individual ability." They want team goals to be balanced by the individual pursuit of knowledge.[6]

More Information about Cooperative Learning

Johnson, David, Roger Johnson, and Edythe Holubec. *Cooperation in the Classroom*. Edina, MN: Interaction Book Company, 1988. (7208 Cornelia Drive Edina, MN 55435). The Johnsons, along with Robert Slavin from Johns Hopkins University, are the major advocates of cooperative learning.

Kohn, Alfie. *No Contest: The Case Against Competition*. Boston: Houghton Mifflin Company, 1986. *Punished by Rewards: The Trouble with Gold Stars, Incentive Plans, A's, Praise and Other Bribes*. New York: Houghton Mifflin, 1993. Kohn has been a persistent critic of competition in the schools and was recently hired to give a day-long workshop at prestigious New Trier Township High School on Chicago's North Shore. He spent the day speaking to groups of students about the evils of competition.[7]

Singal, Daniel. "The Other Great Crisis in American Education." *Atlantic Monthly* Nov. 1991: 59-69.

De-Tracking

De-tracking is the practice of abolishing all homogeneous groups or classrooms made up of students of similar abilities and dismantling all accelerated and advanced programs (e.g. advanced placement and honors classes) that

Tales from the Trenches

Brave New Olympics

Lauren Scheffers
Parent
Education Activist
Data Processing Consultant
Former Teacher

Incensed at the anti-excellence mindset she was encountering in her local school system, Lauren Scheffers wrote this tongue-in-cheek description of how the Olympics would be structured if it adopted the approach to achievement that is currently in vogue in the schools.

> Dear Editor,
> I have been watching the Olympics lately and am concerned about the possible negative impact of the United States' participation in this event. In particular, I am concerned about the self-esteem of the athletes. What about the self-esteem of those who failed to qualify for the Olympic teams? What about the self-esteem of the athletes who ended up in tears

Continued →

permit gifted students to cover more material more quickly. De-tracking could also include a widespread movement called inclusive education, in which students who were formerly in self-contained special education classes are now included in the regular classroom regardless of the severity of their disability. The primary reason usually given for abolishing homogeneous groups and accelerated classes is that students of lower ability will gain merely by being exposed to more difficult material and because they failed to win an Olympic medal? What about the harmful effect of publicly posting the judges' scores for the whole world to see? Wouldn't it be less harmful if there were no scores and every participant received a medal for participating?

I don't think that it's fair that only some athletes get to compete. Since competition is inherently harmful, shouldn't all events be cooperative relays, rather than individual events, with heterogeneous groupings of athletes with a wide range of athletic abilities?

Another concern I have is that I think the Olympic coaches push the athletes too hard. Shouldn't the coaches simply be facilitators, encouraging the athletes to work together with their peers to determine what is best? In particular, shouldn't the athletes from each country have hands-on experiences to learn about the sports programs of each of the other countries, since the Olympics are a global event? For that matter, shouldn't the athletes from various countries be placed on intermixed teams, so that no country feels badly about how its athletes performed?

If these statements sound ludicrous for the sports arena, why are parents and taxpayers allowing these philosophies to be implemented in our schools?

---

higher-ability students. Even if lower-ability students are not learning the same material as their higher-ability classmates, the lower-ability students' self-esteem is thought to skyrocket when they become the social peers of smarter role models.

How Might De-Tracking Affect Students?

1. Children of higher ability might not have the opportunity to accelerate and enrich their learning under the

guidance of a teacher. The opportunity to gain college credits through taking advanced classes in high school may no longer be available.

2. Children with lower abilities or diagnosed disabilities might take part in every aspect of regular classroom instruction and have all special services delivered in the regular classroom. Whether such children make measurable academic progress will depend on the skill of the classroom teacher, the instructional aide, and the facilitating teacher, who coordinates their efforts and constantly modifies the regular curriculum to meet the child's specialized needs. The immediacy of a child's social and emotional needs in an inclusionary setting will take precedence over the long-term academic needs of that child.

3. A child with a disability may become overly dependent on his or her personal aide, who in the process of making constant academic accommodations for the child's needs may create a sense of dependency.

What Do Knowledgeable People Think about De-Tracking?

Joan Beck, editorial writer for the *Chicago Tribune* and long an advocate for gifted students, believes that "such proposals do irreparable injustice and harm to bright children, who are just as entitled as other youngsters to an education appropriate to their abilities. . . . They need the challenge of new ideas and new materials and opportunities to learn at the accelerated speed most comfortable for them. To expect them to sustain a love of learning while marking time waiting for slower students to catch up is like asking Michael Jordan to be challenged by playing basketball at a local 'Y.'"[8]

More Information about De-Tracking

Oakes, Jeannie. *Keeping Track: How Schools Structure Inequality*. New Haven, CT: Yale Univ. Press, 1985. This is the most frequently quoted book in support of de-tracking.

Kulik, James A., and Chen-Lin Kulik. *Research on Ability Grouping: Historical and Contemporary Perspective*. Ann Arbor: Univ. of Michigan Press, 1991. These researchers concluded after reviewing the total body of research on ability grouping that higher-aptitude students usually benefit from ability grouping and that de-tracking and heterogeneous grouping have only small effects on the self-esteem of slower students.

Craig, Susan, and Ann Haggart. *Inclusion: A Teacher's Guide*. Hampton, NH: AGH Associates, 1993 (Box 130, Hampton, NH 03842 [603] 926-1316). This book will give you an insider's view of inclusive education.

Inclusion Press at http://www.inclusion.com offers a variety of books and materials in support of inclusive education.

> **Higher-aptitude students usually benefit from ability grouping, whereas de-tracking has only small effects on the self-esteem of slower students.**

Developmentally Appropriate Practice (DAP)

Developmentally Appropriate Practice (DAP) is an environment for instruction that is being promulgated by state departments of education and the National Association for the Education of Young Children. Some of the practices or beliefs that you will find in a DAP or child-centered classroom are as follows:

1. Multi-age groupings—e.g., first- through third-grade students in the same classroom;
2. Whole-language and whole-math curricula;
3. Integrated/interdisciplinary curricula with instruction focused on themes rather than subjects (e.g. popular themes are apples, a fairy tale like Cinderella, or the rain-forest);
4. Elimination of all standardized testing;

5. Real-world projects completed in cooperative groups;

6. Classroom learning centers;

7. Teacher as facilitator; and

8. Emphasis on students constructing their own meaning from learning (*see also* Constructivism).

Although many of these practices are entirely appropriate and highly recommended for preschool classrooms, they are of untested and unproven value for achieving meaningful academic goals in elementary school.

Developmentally Appropriate Practice classrooms place social and attitudinal aims ahead of academic achievement, and teachers are taught that schooling which attempts to do otherwise is known to be harmful. What is now called DAP used to be called open education, which was also intended to produce positive social and attitudinal changes.

How Might Developmentally Appropriate Practice Affect Your Child?

1. You may never know that your child doesn't know how to read or do math because there will be no tests, grades, or expectations in the classroom. Your child will receive narrative report cards containing educational jargon about social adjustment, self-esteem, and excitement for learning but little hard data about achievement.

2. Your child may remain with the same teacher for three or even four years, and the teacher will reassure you that your child is doing very well and "not to worry."

3. Your child will have a great deal of fun in school with a variety of field trips and cooking activities, as well as building and painting projects.

4. Your child will not experience any teacher-directed phonics or math lessons but will rather explore and wait for reading and math to conceptually emerge. Your child will always feel good about himself or herself in spite of any academic deficiencies.

What Do Knowledgeable People Think about DAP?

Sandra Holliday's* daughter attended a DAP classroom through second grade. She shares her observations of the approach:

> I became alarmed about the developmentally appropriate program after my daughter didn't seem to be progressing in kindergarten and first grade. We knew that she didn't learn anything new in kindergarten, but we did expect a more rigorous program in first grade. Instead, it was just more of the same weak, watered-down content.
>
> Parents were concerned that most of our children's school days were spent on play, coloring, arts and crafts projects with little or no educational value. My husband continually asked me to explain what the school was doing with our child. As an educator, I felt totally at a loss to explain the program. We have since removed her from the DAP setting, but I feel as though she will forever be playing catch-up, as we are constantly finding weaknesses in her work habits and skills. The banner over my daughter's kindergarten classroom reads "An education is a journey, not a race." I, too, feel it is important for my daughter to be a lifelong learner, but I did not want it to take a lifetime to learn what she could have learned in twelve or thirteen years.

More Information about DAP

Brederkamp, Sue, ed. *Developmentally Appropriate Practice in Early Childhood Programs Serving Children from Birth through Age 8.* Washington, DC: National Association for the Education of Young Children, 1988 (1834 Connecticut Avenue, N.W., Washington, DC 20009-5786). This is a description of what children will experience in a DAP classroom.

Lipsey, Mark W., et al. "The Efficacy of Psychological, Educational, and Behavioral Treatment: Confirmation from Meta-analysis." *American Psychologist* 48.12 (1993): 1181-1209. This comparison of traditional versus open classrooms shows a negative effect on actual achievement as well as student motivation to achieve in open classrooms.

Discovery Learning

(*See* Developmentally Appropriate Practice)

Diversity Training

(*See* Multiculturalism)

Domains of the Brain

(*See* Multiple Intelligences)

Education to Work

(*See* School-to-Work)

Experiential Education

Experiential education focuses on learning by doing (*see also* Cooperative Learning, Integrated Thematic Units, and Developmentally Appropriate Practice). In reading instruction, for example, experiential education means reading real texts, as opposed to doing worksheets. In mathematics, it means manipulating objects and constructing patterns instead of mastering math facts or working problems. In social studies' classrooms, experiential education means role-playing famous historical events and re-enacting political debates instead of developing a sense of historical chronology.

Fuzzy Math

(*See* chapter 5)

Global Education

(*See* Multiculturalism)

Goals 2000

Goals 2000 was originally called America 2000/Educate America Act. America 2000 was conceived when Bill Clinton was chairman of the National Governors Association,[9] and it is America's version of the global education agenda established by the World Conference on Education for All.[10] The America 2000/Educate America Act was first introduced in Congress during the Bush administration but did not become law. During the Clinton administration, nearly identical legislation was named Goals 2000 and became law. The six national goals that comprise Goals 2000 sound very reasonable to parents:

- All children in America will start school ready to learn.
- The high school graduation rate will increase to at least 90 percent.
- American students will leave grades four, eight, and twelve having demonstrated competency in challenging subject matter including English, mathematics, science, history, and geography; and every school in America will ensure that all students learn to use their minds well, so they may be prepared for responsible citizenship, further learning, and productive employment in our modern economy.
- U.S. students will be first in the world in science and mathematics achievement.
- Every adult American will be literate and will possess the knowledge and skills necessary to compete in a global economy and exercise the rights and responsibilities of citizenship.

♦ Every school in America will be free of drugs and violence and will offer a disciplined environment conducive to learning.[11]

> **Goals 2000 was designed to completely remove all power for educational decision making from local school boards.**

These goals are excellent, but the massive federal plan designed to bring about the goals is seriously flawed. Designed to completely remove all power for educational decision making from local school boards, the bill was signed into law in April 1994. It has been called "a stealth takeover of education,"[12] and "one of the most unconstitutional bills to ever pass through Congress."[13] The money to fund Goals 2000 was already in the federal budget in the form of the Elementary and Secondary Education Act (ESEA). Originally passed in 1965 to help disadvantaged children, ESEA must be re-authorized by Congress every four years. In 1994, a re-authorization year, Clinton increased the monies already in the ESEA budget to $12.5 million per year, had the bill completely rewritten to eliminate most of the provisions for disadvantaged children, and then added several hundred pages of strict federal controls over states and local school boards. The bill sailed through Congress, and ESEA was reborn as "The Improving America's Schools Act of 1994" or HR6. The "carrot" is $12.5 million yearly over the four-year authorization period (1994-98). The "stick" is Goals 2000. States and schools must comply with all of the mandates of Goals 2000 in order to get any money. Individual states submit and have approved a state improvement plan (an Outcome-Based Education plan) and then the money starts flowing.

How Might Goals 2000 Affect You and Your Child?

◆ Your state could toss out all of your locally elected school board members and replace them with someone else if they refused to comply with the mandates of Goals 2000 that make your district eligible for the funds. This is a critical component to the success of Goals 2000 because "it is tremendously difficult to build national momentum behind a particular reform when 50 state legislatures, 50 state boards and more than 15,000 local school boards have veto power."[14]

◆ Someone from the school district might want to be your "equal partner" in the raising of your child.

◆ School-based clinics might be established in which your children might receive physical exams without your knowledge.

◆ You might be asked to participate in programs that will train you in parenting skills.

◆ Your child might receive certificates of mastery rather than diplomas (see Certificate of Initial Mastery, Certificate of Advanced Mastery, and Outcome-Based Education).

◆ Your child's education might be driven by outcomes that have nothing to do with education (see Outcome-Based Education).

◆ Your child might have a computer on his/her desk that is connected to the mainframe at the state Department of Education so that all of your child's authentic and performance-based assessments, questionnaires, and attitude surveys can be tracked.

What Do People-in-the-Know Think about Goals 2000?

Donna Garner, a Texas educator who has been in the forefront of curriculum reform[15] in her state, is deeply worried about increased governmental involvement in the education process.

Garner says:

> Unfortunately there is an education establishment who is either afraid to change, does not really want children to be successful because of the loss of jobs for educators, or has a desire to change the way the next generation thinks. This latter really worries me because it makes political pawns out of the children in our classrooms. It is not my place as a classroom teacher to force my students to implement my value system or the value system of some government agency. That responsibility has been given to their parents. I fear that there are those in high places who do not believe that children still belong to their parents and who would like to control the future by carefully grooming the next generation.

> **It is not my place as a classroom teacher to force my students to implement my value system or the value system of some government agency.**

More Information about Goals 2000

Patrick, James, ed. *America 2000/Goals 2000: Moving the Nation Educationally to a "New World Order."* Moline, IL: Citizens for Academic Excellence, 1994 (P. O. Box 1164, Moline IL 61265). This 800-page compendium of articles, actual documents, and commentaries traces the background and philosophical development of Goals 2000. It is not easy reading, but what you find will be very revealing.

Group Grades

(*See* Cooperative Learning)

Group Projects

(*See* Cooperative Learning)

Holistic Learning

(*See* Fuzzy-Math, Whole-Language, Integrated Thematic Instruction)

Integrated Thematic Instruction

(*See also* Interdisciplinary Instruction)

When teachers use integrated thematic instruction, subjects are no longer taught as self-contained units. Mathematics, reading, science, and history are taught simultaneously in the context of a central organizing theme (e.g., apples or teddy bears in the primary grades; the rain forest in the intermediate grades; Native Americans in middle school; or the feminist perspective in high school). Because subjects are not taught as self-contained units, basic skills are acquired more slowly and often not at all. Since abstract concepts are rarely acquired without systematic instruction, each child must "reinvent the wheel."

Interdisciplinary Instruction

(*See also* Integrated Thematic Instruction)

Interdisciplinary instruction is the middle and high school version of integrated thematic instruction. Block scheduling (*see* Block Scheduling) enables a school to do more interdisciplinary instruction because it creates large blocks of time in which teachers of different departments can organize such units. For an insightful commentary on interdisciplinary learning, read the Tales from the Trenches by history professor Stephen Kern in appendix E.

Learner-Centered Classrooms

(*See* Developmentally Appropriate Practice, Paradigm Shift)

Literature-Based Instruction

(*See* Whole-Language in chapter 4)

Mastery Learning

(*See also* Outcome-Based Education)

Mastery learning was conceived by Benjamin Bloom, an education professor at the University of Chicago. The concept, which asserts that all children can learn given enough time and help, held out a false hope to educators always desperate for a "quick-fix" program. Mastery learning, first incorporated into a reading program in the Chicago Public Schools, was such a massive failure that the word *mastery* fell into disrepute in educational circles. William Spady, one of the early pioneers and researchers in mastery learning, then advised educators to change the name to Outcome-Based Education. "I pleaded with the group not to use the name 'mastery learning' in the network's new name because the word 'mastery' had already been destroyed. I argued that we had about five years before they destroyed the term 'outcomes,' but at least we could get a start."[16]

In order to confuse people and cover the trail of heated battles in states like Pennsylvania and Virginia, the names have often been changed to protect the "guilty." Here are just a few of the pseudonyms under which mastery learning and Outcome-Based Education have been masquerading in the past ten years:[17]

Total Quality
  Management

Quality Schools

Results Oriented

Essential Schools

Transformational
  Education

Restructured Education

Competency-Based
  Education

Break the Mold 21st
    Century Schools

Mission 2000

Vision 2000

Exit-Based Teaching

High Standards

Skills 2000

Performance-Based
    Learning

High-Level Learning

Mastery Teaching

Results-Based Curriculum

Mastery learning in tutorial environments can be quite effective because of the small teacher-student ratios and the intensive direct instruction this permits. For example, Sylvan Learning Centers utilize mastery learning and achieve high success rates because the tutor can keep the child on task and moving forward as quickly as possible. In a traditional classroom of eighteen to thirty students, however, a teacher lacks the time necessary to effectively monitor the progress of so many students and keep all children moving forward to maximize their knowledge acquisition. Therein lies the difficulty of using mastery learning in public schooling: The structure of the class-room is in total conflict with how mastery must be monitored to make it work for anyone.

Multi-age Classrooms

(*See* Developmentally Appropriate Practice)

Multiculturalism

Multiculturalism is all about teaching tolerance, acceptance, respect, and appreciation for the world's diverse lifestyles, cultures, values, and belief systems. This goal sounds honest and worthy. What multiculturalism is really about, however, is being politically correct, i.e., tolerating, accepting, respecting, and appreciating agendas that have absolutely nothing to do with learning to read, write, do math, or understand history and science.

> **Multicultural-ism is really about accepting agendas that have nothing to do with learning.**

How Might Multiculturalism Affect Your Child?

1. Your child may be exposed to stories, lessons, group activities, questionnaires, and even assembly speakers who will espouse values, lifestyles, and belief systems that you and your family find objectionable. To object, however, is to appear narrow, provincial, and prejudiced. You and your child may be labeled as reactionary and right-wing.

2. Your child may be assigned textbooks featuring perspectives that are more politically correct than historically accurate.

3. Your child may be exposed to materials and points of view that are more global and pantheistic in nature than national and Judeo-Christian.

4. Your child may be trained to view himself or herself as a member of an overall world community rather than as an American citizen.

5. Your child's report card or performance-based assessments may reflect the opinions, beliefs, "prejudices," and attitudes of your child regarding issues of multiculturalism.

What Do People-in-the-Know Think about Multiculturalism?

In a textbook for teachers, Christine Bennett explains: "Multicultural education strives to integrate multi-ethnic and global perspectives." Its goal is not to teach factual history but to "challenge [the student's] cultural assumptions" and create in children "an emotional commitment to the fundamental unity of all humans."[18]

The arguments for multiculturalism sound plausible to the average educator and even to many parents, but what is not always evident in these harmless-sounding platitudes are the following ideological foundations:

◆ Multiculturalism is necessary to enable our students to

participate actively in the emerging global economy.

♦ An increasingly diverse population within the United States requires and demands education in a variety of cultures.

♦ Intergroup relations are better when people are introduced to each other's cultures in school.

♦ Education itself is better when presented from various perspectives and derived from culturally different social groups.[19]

Today when people disagree over issues, someone will inevitably suggest, "Just respect each other's views." That is certainly what multiculturalism is all about. But this attitude denies that there are some views that one should not respect. As one commentator writes, "We should certainly not respect the views of Hitler, or the views of criminals who believe they are justified in acting illegally against others." Today many children are being "expected" or in some cases "required" to respect and tolerate views that according to their religious faith or family values are "wrong."[20]

More Information about Multiculturalism

Bernstein, Richard. *The Dictatorship of Virtue: Multiculturalsim and the Battle for America's Future.* New York: Knopf, 1994. This book has an excellent chapter titled, "The Battle of Brookline and Other Struggles over Young Minds," which details the experiences of the Brookline, Massachusetts, community in dealing with creeping multiculturalism in their schools.

D'Souza, Dinesh. *Illiberal Education: The Politics of Race and Sex on Campus.* New York: The Free Press, 1991. This book will give you a sense of how the seemingly innocuous philosophies behind the multiculturalism curricula that are finding their way into K-12 schools are being played out on university campuses. The author's thesis is a controversial and interesting one: "The multicultural activists have split the university on moral grounds, producing not a truly diverse community, but balkanized, race-conscious tribal enclaves without shared commitment to the goals of liberal learning."

Lefkowitz, Mary. *Not Out of Africa: How Afrocentrism Became an Excuse to Teach Myth as History.* New York: BasicBooks, 1996. This author is a classicist who is incensed by the lack of respect for academic truth by those who teach history as a way of increasing the self-esteem of the disadvantaged.

Sommers, Christina Hoff. *Who Stole Feminism? How Women Have Betrayed Women.* New York: Simon & Schuster, 1994. This book is a chilling commentary on the transformation of curriculum along gender-equity lines. It also makes a compelling argument against the currently accepted wisdom that schools are biased against girls.

All of these books are disturbing to read, but they will help sensitize you to the subtleties of multiculturalism and global education. These authors are courageous and have braved censure from the academic community by speaking the truth as they see it.

Multiple Intelligences

The theory of multiple intelligences was conceived by Harvard psychologist Howard Gardner, and it has become a popular organizing structure for many classrooms and even entire schools (e.g., McWayne School in Batavia, Illinois). The idea was first introduced to parents and educators in Gardner's book, *Frames of Mind*. The author has now become a frequent speaker at educational conferences and a consultant to school districts. He believes that what he defines as the verbal and logical/mathematical intelligences, the ones generally tapped and developed in school, are far too narrow and that teachers must tap into spatial, bodily-kinesthetic, musical, interpersonal, and intrapersonal intelligences to most effectively educate students.

How Might Multiple Intelligences Affect You and Your Child?

1. Your child's school curriculum may not include reading, writing, and mathematics as separate and distinct disciplines of study but will instead be integrated, thematic, and interdisciplinary. The curriculum may attempt to tap into all of your child's ways of knowing the world: a) language; b) logical-mathematical analysis; c) spatial representation; d) musical thinking; e) the use of the body to solve problems and to make things; f) an understanding of other individuals; and g) an understanding of ourselves.[21]

2. Your child may spend an entire day (week, or month) learning in the context of an interdisciplinary unit. The unit might, for example, have as its goal the "appreciation of the perseverance, curiosity, and dedication of early aviators and inventors." Your child might become familiar with the achievements of Wilbur and Orville Wright, and in addition to understanding their work with kites, wind tunnels, wing warping, gliders and airplanes, will use a map to find places important in aviation history. Your child might then construct a model of the Wright brothers' airplane using plastic meat trays donated by a local market. Music will be an integral part of the study of airplanes. Using the melody of "Take Me Out to the Ball Game," your child could sing "Take Me Out to the Airfield," with words written by a Wright brothers' biographer. Your child will be encouraged to write new verses to the song, which ask or answer questions about airplanes.[22]

3. Instead of objective grades based upon percentages of content gained as knowledge, allowances are made for individual differences, and personal creative expressions are given equal credence to the understanding and mastery of academic content (in essence, the teacher creates an educational "handicap" much like those used in the

> **The teacher creates an educational "handicap" like those in golf.**

games of golf and bowling that are intended to level the playing field).

4. Your child's schooling will be based on a theory that is not well accepted in the scientific community (see quotes below).

What Do Knowledgeable People Think about Multiple Intelligences?

Howard Gardner, who conceived the theory of multiple intelligences and trains thousands of educators yearly, had this observation to make upon reading about the abysmal, near-the-bottom performance of our nation's twelfth grade students on the Third International Mathematics and Science Study (TIMSS): "We should resist the tendency to focus on increasing our students' scores on these tests. These tests don't measure whether students can think scientifically or mathematically; they just measure a kind of lowest common denominator of facts and skills. So getting students to do well on them doesn't necessarily mean much in the real world."[23]

Denis Doyle, a senior fellow at the Hudson Institute, makes this observation:

> Watching schools implement untested theories about "kinesthetic," or other intelligences when they can't teach reading looks suspiciously like one more fad. The hard truth is that today's youngsters, as never before, must hone their academic skills. Knowledge pays and pays handsomely; ignorance costs more than we can afford, individually or socially. Schools may want to teach English, mathematics, or physics by using music, dance, or football, but they cannot be permitted to lose sight of their academic mission.[24]

Psychologist George Miller summarized the scientific consensus regarding the multiple intelligences theory:

Since none of the work has been done that would have to be done before a single-value assessment of intelligence could be replaced by a seven-value assessment, the discussion is all hunch and opinion. It is true that, if such profiles were available, an educator might be better able to match the materials and modes of instruction to an individual student. But since nobody knows whether the educator should play to the student's strengths or bolster the student's weaknesses (or both), the new psychometrics does not seem to advance practical matters much beyond present psychometrics.[25]

Where Was Multiple Intelligence First Promulgated?

Gardner, Howard. *Frames of Mind: The Theory of Multiple Intelligences.* New York: BasicBooks, 1983.

_____. *The Unschooled Mind: How Children Think and How Schools Should Teach Them.* New York: BasicBooks, 1991.

_____. *Multiple Intelligences: The Theory into Practice.* New York: BasicBooks, 1993.

Non-Graded Schools

(*See* Developmentally Appropriate Practice)

Outcome-Based Education

(*See also* School-to-Work, Goals 2000, and Mastery Learning)

Outcome-Based Education (OBE) has two main tenets: 1) the belief that all students can learn and learn well; and 2) the idea that equality should mean equality of outcomes rather than equality of opportunity, i.e., outcomes will be reduced to a lower common denominator to make sure that all can learn. These two tenets sound sensible and are very seductive and appealing to educators who are always frustrated when all of their students don't experience success. Once educators and parents have bought into the tenets of OBE, however, they will find that the methodology is suspect and that the outcomes (that all students will learn and learn well) have nothing to do with academic content or subject matter.

How Might Outcome-Based Education Affect Your Child?

1. The implementation of OBE in the classroom may drive a wedge between you and your child. Kids may be convinced that parents are out-of-step with the realities of the twenty-first century and cannot be trusted to have any knowledge or understanding about education.

2. Classroom academic content in K-12 may be reduced by as much as 50 to 75 percent as students study subjects in a thematic and integrated way, are responsible for being self-directed and choosing their own educational goals, and are focused on process rather than content.

> **Classroom academic content in K-12 may be reduced by as much as 50 to 75 percent.**

3. Your child's educational outcomes may be centered around societal problems such as abortion, saving the rain forest, alcoholism, etc. Your child's outcomes may be achieved and assessed through various projects, normally done in groups for group grades. The projects are usually real-world related, and they may be designed to elicit personal information about the child and his or her family.

4. Your child's education may no longer be time based, and your child could move along through all the grades with no awareness that outcomes are not being met until suddenly at age sixteen your child may be invited to attend an alternate school in order to meet the outcomes he has not yet mastered.

What Do People-in-the-Know Think about Outcome-Based Education?

The most dramatic story of Outcome-Based Education and its effects on one family comes out of Cottage Grove, Oregon. Barbara Tennsion, who with her husband, Bob, have become well-known critics of OBE, tells her story here:

Shortly after Oregon's Education Act for the Twenty-first Century was passed into law in 1991, South Lane School District won a grant to implement Outcome-Based Education at Cottage Grove High School. We were one of six pilot schools, each implementing a different part of the reform program.

Prior to the beginning of the 1992-93 school year, informational meetings were held at our high school. People and community members were invited to these meetings for the purpose of developing the district's goals and vision for schools of the twenty-first century. When asked where the program came from, our local and state school officials told us that the table was bare and that we could develop our program from the ground floor up.

Our students, we were told, would be on the cutting edge and all eyes would be on them as they began the program that would have more rigorous academics and world class standards. The students were told they would be the envy of other students as they traveled down this road toward the twenty-first century.

But it was all a lie. The table was not bare; the goals, mission statement and vision that teachers and other community members had worked so hard developing was not their own. As the story unfolded, we learned that some of our teachers and administrators had attended an OBE conference and they, along with our superintendent, sold the program to our school board.

I only discovered all of this after my son had been in the program for two years. During that time Jay tried to tell his father and me that he wasn't learning, and that his teachers weren't teaching him. He said he was supposed to be a "self-directed learner" who was responsible for his own learning. Bob and I did not believe him; we defended the teachers. Bob and I thought Jay was just being lazy and making excuses because the course work had gotten harder and he couldn't do it.

As I began to ask questions and attend parent and school board meetings, I found that my son was receiving only one quarter of the previous traditional academic content. I discovered that the new OBE program was not about more rigorous academics but about changing his values and behavior. It was about teaching him how to get a job, not preparing him for college. It was about the school becoming the "parent" and "best friend" of my son, replacing my husband and me.

> "I found that my son was receiving only one quarter of the previous traditional academic content."

To say that I was angry is probably a very mild statement. As I talked to other people, I discovered that many of them had caught on much earlier than I. In joining this group, I found comfort in the fact that I was not alone. I also discovered that people were being told by administrators that they were the only ones complaining or that our children were not telling the truth about what was happening in classrooms.

The discovery that not only were our kids telling us the truth but that teachers and administrators whom we had trusted for years could look us in the eye and tell us lies was shattering. We no longer knew who could be trusted.

What we also discovered in the summer of 1994 was even more upsetting. The chairperson of the high school site council recommended to the administration that any teacher who did not "get on board" should be shown the door. Our curriculum director said they would get on board or they could get out. It dawned on us for the first time that our teachers were afraid to speak out for fear of losing their jobs.

Our school board refused to see the truth. They would not look at any of the research or documentation that people brought before them. Members of the community who supported the school board openly referred to us as right-wing religious fanatics and kooks—too stupid to know what was best for our kids. We were told that if we would only compromise, things would be all right.

The statistics from that very first class to begin their high school career under OBE tell the story. The graduating class of 1996 began their ninth-grade year with 299 students. At the end of four years only 137 students remained to graduate. *CGHS lost 162 students in four years.* The high school continues to lose between 75 and 100 students a year.

Where Can I Find More Information?

Blumenfeld, Samuel. *The Whole Language/OBE Fraud: The Shocking Story of How America Is Being Dumbed Down by Its Own Education System.* Boise, ID: Paradigm Company, 1996. This book provides a comprehensive overview of OBE by a traditionalist.

Boschee, Floyd, and Mark A. Baron. *Outcome-Based Education: Developing Programs through Strategic Planning.* Lancaster, PA: Technomic Publishing Co., Inc., 1993. This book will give you an insider's look at the entire OBE process.

"The Challenge of Outcome-Based Education." *Educational Leadership* March 1994. The entire issue is devoted to articles about OBE. *Educational Leadership* is published by the progressive Association for Supervision and Curriculum Development.

Concerned Women for America. *Outcome-Based Education: Remaking Your Children through Radical Educational Reform.* 370 L'Enfant Promenade S.W., Suite 800, Washington, DC 20024. (202) 488-7000. An excellent summary of the down side of OBE.

Holland, Robert. *Not with My Child You Don't: A Citizens' Guide to OBE and Restoring Education.* Richmond, VA: Chesapeake Capital Services, 1996. Here you can read about how a variety of ordinary citizens across the country have fought OBE.

Glasser, William. *Schools without Failure.* New York: Harper & Row, 1969. Glasser is a chief spokesman for OBE.

Sunseri, Ron. *Outcome Based Education: Understanding the Truth about Educational Reform.* Sisters, OR: Questar Publishing, 1994. A succinct summary of the dangers inherent in OBE.

Tennison, Barbara and Bob. Consult the website of the Tennisons, who tell the complete story of their children's experience with OBE in Oregon: http://www.rstenison.com

Paradigm Shift

A paradigm is a worldview or a mental framework for thinking and organizing information. The paradigm shift in educational circles is a massive change in thinking that occurs to educators after they have attended an OBE, TQM, School Restructuring, or Quality Schools workshop. Educators will return to their schools and districts armed with stacks of handouts and plans for enlightening everyone else about how to experience this same paradigm shift (see Barbara Tennison's story of OBE implementation in

Cottage Grove, Oregon, in the Outcome-Based Education entry).

These shifting paradigms occur in nine major areas of school life: grouping, competition/cooperation, assessment, grading, recognition/rewards/incentives, student input, approaches to the curriculum, academic tasks, and remediation. Notice as you read through the following comparisons between the old and new paradigms (as presented at an OBE workshop) how unattractive, old-fashioned, and controlling the old paradigm is made to appear. OBE workshops never offer any research showing how the implementation of the new paradigm will improve student learning. "Just trust us" is the slogan.

> **OBE workshops never offer research showing how the implementation of the new paradigm will improve student learning.**

If parents ask, "Can you prove that restructuring [implementation of a paradigm shift], will improve student achievement?" they are most likely to get this kind of answer:

> Not conclusively. Right now we don't have reliable ways to measure students' improvements in learning. Traditional standardized achievement tests are inadequate measures of thinking skills, problem-solving abilities, creativity, communication skills, and teamwork. We need new tests and demonstrations of applied knowledge and learned skills to complement these traditional measures.[26]

Comparison of Old and New Paradigms

Grouping. Old Paradigm: grouping by ability for efficient information delivery, use of standardized tests for accountability

New Paradigm: grouping by topic, interest, student choice; frequent reformation of groups

Competition/Cooperation. Old Paradigm: competition between students; contests with limited winners

New Paradigm: cooperative teaming

Assessment. Old Paradigm: using test data as a basis for comparison

New Paradigm: using test data for diagnosis; using alternatives to tests such as portfolios

Grading. Old Paradigm: normative grading; public display of grades

New Paradigm: grading for progress; involvement of students in determining their grades

Recognition/Rewards/Incentives. Old Paradigm: recognition for relative performance; honor rolls for high grades; overuse of praise, especially for the completion of short, easy tasks

New Paradigm: recognition of progress; an emphasis on learning for its own sake

Student Input. Old Paradigm: decisions made exclusively by administrators and teachers

New Paradigm: opportunities for choice; student decision making, self-scheduling, self-regulation

Curriculum. Old Paradigm: departmentalized approach to curriculum

New Paradigm: thematic approaches/interdisciplinary focus; viewing mistakes as part of learning; allowing students to redo work; encouraging students to take academic risks

Academic Tasks. Old Paradigm: rote learning and memorization; overuse of worksheets and textbooks; decontextualized facts

New Paradigm: providing challenges and complex work to students; giving homework that is enriching and challenging; encouraging problem solving and comprehension

Remediation. Old Paradigm: pull-out programs; remediation

New Paradigm: cross-age and peer tutoring; enrichment

Undoubtedly you have begun to see some recurring themes in various entries throughout the book; this is not accidental. The old paradigm stressed knowledge, content, teacher direction, accountability, rewards for achievement, and competition as a motivational tool. The new paradigm emphasizes feelings, self-esteem, process, teachers as facilitators and friends, rewards for "punching the clock," and no winners or losers.

Progressive education can remind one of the junk food aisle at the convenience store. There are lots of different colored packages and many different brand names, but they all basically offer the same empty content. Progressive education is being packaged in many different ways and is being sold under many labels, but the contents are basically the same: education that is "progressively" losing all of its academic focus.

Performance-Based Assessments

Performance-based assessments rely on open-ended answers, writing about subjects like math and science, role-playing, and drawing pictures instead of objectively assessing knowledge gained. The assessments are suspect for a number of reasons:

◆ They include fewer questions and thus sample a smaller portion of what a student knows than a standardized test, which takes the same amount of time to complete.

◆ They are significantly more expensive than standardized tests (estimates range from 5 to 30 times) because they require trained scorers who spend large amounts of time rating students' work.

◆ They introduce more bias because they call for a greater degree of subjective judgment than traditional testing methods.[27]

How Might This Affect You and Your Child?
1. Your child may be evaluated for a diploma or certifi-

cate on the basis of a poorly designed test and biased scoring.

2. Your child's mathematics or science ability may be judged more on the basis of his writing and reading ability than on his knowledge of subject matter.

What Do People Think about Performance-Based Assessments?

Richard Innes of Villa Hills, Kentucky, has been following the KIRIS (Kentucky Instructional Results Information System) performance-based assessments since early 1994. Although he has only been able to examine a brief sampling of questions from the test, he has found poor test design, errors in printing, and unreliable scoring, all problems encountered when using performance-based assessments on a statewide scale. "Assuming that the samples I have seen are a fair, random sample," Innes says, "then the total number of bad questions on the test would be of considerable concern."

> **Your child may be evaluated for a diploma or certificate on the basis of a poorly designed test and biased scoring.**

He points out that too many subject matter questions (e.g,. in science) have degenerated into nothing more than politically correct creative writing assignments. What's more, he notes, what "science" is present is too often wrong. He illustrates for us:

One of my favorite examples is an eleventh-grade open response KIRIS question that asks students to consider the problem of sucking water up a long straw while standing on an eight-meter cliff. Students are to discuss various factors that would make the job easier or harder.

Things degenerate in a hurry when you examine the scoring guide. It says it is easier to suck liquid up a thinner straw. If you have ever compared the task of sucking liquid up a thin bar straw to doing the same job with a big straw from a local fast food restaurant, you have enough scientific experience to know the scoring guide is totally incorrect. But the situation gets even worse when the sample student answers are examined!

The student who receives a top score of 4 on this question gets credit for saying it is easier to suck liquid up a wider straw. That is correct, but it totally disagrees with the scoring guide. Now, here's the best part. The student who gets a 3 also receives credit in the example; *but* this time it's for saying a thinner straw makes the task easier!

Don't think the 4 student is really "science smart." He also says that a water faucet "sucks" water out of the plumbing system! He got credit for that, too! So, at least for this question, science is out the window, the scoring guide is ignored (perhaps the graders knew it was worthless), and creative writing is the name of the game. Just get the correct buzzwords on paper—no matter if they are connected together with totally wrong ideas.

More Information

Maeroff, Gene. "Assessing Alternative Assessments." *Phi Delta Kappan* 73.4 (1991): 273-81.

Marzano, Robert J., Debra Pickering, and Jay McTighe. *Assessing Student Outcomes: Performance Assessment Using the Dimensions of Learning Model.* Alexandria, VA: Association for Supervision and Curriculum Development, 1993. This book will turn you into a walking encyclopedia of information about performance-based assessments. It contains some scoring rubrics that give insight into the "mind-bending" that goes on as part of Outcome-Based Education.

Shavelson, Richard J., et al. "Performance Assessments: Political Rhetoric and Measurement and Reality." *Educational Researcher* 21.4 (1992): 22-27.

Portfolios

A portfolio is a collection of student work that is assembled over a single year or even over the entire school career of a student. The collection is used to evaluate student performance. The portfolio may include art projects, written assignments, research reports, journals, and even videotapes or computer disks. Teachers have always kept portfolios of student work, usually to share with parents at a conference or open house, but the current practice in some schools of refusing to send work home with students because it needs to stay in the school portfolio has many parents alarmed because they want to review their child's progress.

Marlene Tobin, a school board member in a prestigious district in southwestern Pennsylvannia, is vigorously fighting the portfolio trend in her district. She describes how the system works there:

> Instead of keeping one or two examples of work, most teachers are now keeping all of their students' work at school. Of course, parents are allowed to view the work if they want to. The reality, however, is that parents are allowed to view their child's classroom work if they call the school first, make an appointment with each individual teacher, and then possibly take time off work. For middle or high school students, a parent might be asked to make five or six different trips to school to cover all teachers. If parents have more than one child, they'll make even more trips. And, keep in mind, if parents truly want to keep up with their children's work, they may need to do this on a weekly basis.

Marlene reports that "parents have been totally taken out of the loop."

In 1995 a panel of nationally known experts conducted a review of the use of portfolios in Kentucky's statewide testing system (KIRIS). They concluded that the assessments based on portfolios were "inappropriate" and "too flawed" for use in their system of accountability.[28]

Reading Recovery

Reading Recovery is one of the most well-known and popular remediation programs in the United States. Although Reading Recovery itself is now copyrighted, and there is a carefully screened and very lengthy teacher training process, many variations on it have been developed by school districts that don't want to commit the time and money that the genuine RR program takes.

> Instead of keeping one or two examples of work, teachers are now keeping all of their students' work at school.

I have personal experience with one Reading Recovery clone that I used while I was an assistant superintendent for instruction. I made my decision based on the fact that this program was developed in New Zealand, where literacy was the highest of any developed nation in the world. *If everyone in New Zealand can read,* I reasoned, *this must be a fabulous program. We'd better have it right away.* I did not take the time to investigate the truth of the matter and accepted the enthusiastic recommendation of a colleague. I regretted my decision. I have since wised up, done my homework, and discovered that New Zealand's reputation for being the best is based on a 1970 international reading survey of fifteen countries in which New Zealand's fourteen- and eighteen-year-olds ranked top. Literacy rates in New Zealand today are plummeting, and there is national concern over the reasons. In a country of 3.4 million, close to 20 percent of the population is illiterate.[29] That's how Reading Recovery came about.

Reading Recovery, a tutoring program aimed at the bottom 10 to 20 percent of first graders, has been called a "huge ambulance at the bottom of the cliff" by New Zealand educator Tom Nicholson.[30] He wonders why the country isn't doing it right in the first place instead of waiting until children fail. Between 30 and 50 percent of the children in New Zealand are eligible for Reading Recovery at the end of first grade. The program was developed by reading expert Marie Clay in the early '70s, was exported to Ohio in 1984, and has also become well ensconced in the UK. The National Reading Recovery Center, located on the Ohio State University campus, is directed by education professors Carol Lyons, Gay Su Pinnell, and Diane DeFord. First-grade students are pulled out of their classrooms for half an hour of one-on-one tutoring.

Even if your district doesn't call the program they are using Reading Recovery, be on the lookout for the following program components, which are identical to the whole-language philosophy:

- Both approaches use only whole books.
- Skills are taught in the context of real reading and writing, not in isolation.
- The reader is viewed as orchestrating a variety of strategies to identify words instead of focusing on one strategy (e.g., phonics) to the detriment of others.
- Readers use predictable texts and invented spelling as integral parts of instruction.[31]

In spite of the glowing reports that have spread by word of mouth about Reading Recovery, unbiased analyses identify major questions and problems regarding both its effectiveness pedagogically and its cost effectiveness.[32] The bottom line is this: Reading Recovery is expensive and it might not work. Furthermore, if students were taught to read the right way first, they wouldn't need to be "recovered."

School-to-Work (STW)

The School-to-Work Opportunities Act was signed into law on May 4, 1994. It contained basically the same provisions as Oregon's Education for the Twenty-First Century legislation passed in July 1991. What has happened to education in Oregon in the '90s may soon be duplicated around the country. The vast majority of states have already initiated School-to-Work programs with federal funding, and all fifty states have received planning grants. The program goes by a variety of names; it is currently called Education Edge in Tennessee. Other names that signal a School-to-Work thrust are Career Fairs, Education to Careers, VoTech, and School-Business Partnerships. No matter what the program is called, it has the potential to substantially change education, particularly during the junior high and high school years.

Here are some of the big ideas associated with School-to-Work:

♦ Outcome-Based diplomas rather than traditional high school diplomas (see Certificate of Initial Mastery and Certificate of Advanced Mastery).

♦ A Bureau of Apprenticeship and Training (one might also watch for the merging of the Education Department and the Labor Department).

> **Your child may be forced to choose a career as early as eighth grade.**

♦ Career exploration and guidance counseling . . . in as early a grade as possible.

♦ Workplace mentoring: Students will be spending a good share of their time following someone in the workforce around during their final two years of high school.

♦ One-stop Career Centers where job training, counseling, remediation, and whatever else a student needs will be connected with and housed in schools.

♦ Creation of a labor market information system to guarantee that students are being trained according to the demands of the workforce.

How Might School-to-Work Affect Your Child?

1. Your child may no longer receive a traditional high school diploma but rather a Certificate of Initial Mastery (by the end of the sophomore year if he or she meets the required twelve outcomes). Then your child would be required to choose from one of six career directions. If a student doesn't meet the twelve outcomes (e.g., be an involved citizen, understand positive health habits, be a constructive thinker, and understand diversity), he or she could be moved to an "alternative learning site" to stay until the twelve outcomes are mastered. If your child can do and say all of the right things, he or she will move on to work on a Certificate of Advanced Mastery.

2. Your child may not be able to attend the college of choice because it does not accept the Certificates of Mastery.

3. If your child wants to attend a highly selective liberal arts college, he or she may have to acquire the necessary credits someplace else other than a public high school.

4. Your child will spend most of the school career getting ready to be an employee (trained) instead of gaining knowledge and understanding (educated).

5. Your child will spend more time in career counseling during his school career than most adults have in a lifetime.

6. Your child will lose the option that most of us have had to choose our own career path, muddled as it may have been. Your child may be "guided" into a career that seems to mesh with his attitudes and abilities as early as eighth grade and most certainly by age sixteen.

What Do People-in-the-Know Think about School-to-Work?

Marc S. Tucker, president of the National Center on Education and the Economy, recognized some of the concerns that the School-to-Work concept would generate for parents who want their children to attend college. In a letter to Hillary Clinton one week after the 1992 election, Tucker discussed the NCEE's vision for a labor-education partnership and described how the plan could dodge these parental concerns.

> Focus groups . . . show that parents everywhere want their kids to go to college, not be shunted aside into a non-college apprenticeship "vocational" program. By requiring these programs to be a combination of classroom instruction and structured on-the-job training, and creating a standard-setting board that includes employers and labor, all the objectives of the apprenticeship idea are achieved, while at the same time assuring much broader support for the idea, as well as a guarantee that the program [School-to-Work] will not become too narrowly focused on particular occupations.[33]

Barbara Tennison is working to make sure that School-to-Work will not continue to be a viable program in Oregon. She fears that the state reforms are designed to further the interests of business, not parents and children. She explains that "students participate in career or work lessons at the expense of academics."[34] Barbara filed a lawsuit against the Oregon school reforms, including the state's school-to-work plans. She lost in the lower court but has filed an appeal with the ninth U.S. Circuit Court of Appeals.

The directors of admissions of the University of Michigan, Vassar, Northwestern, Stanford, and Wellesley have all agreed that the CIM and CAM are worthless in terms of a college career.[35]

> **Admissions directors of five top universities have said that the CIM and CAM are worthless.**

Parents are conspicuously absent from the planning and implementation for School-to-Work initiatives. This is not surprising considering that parents want schools that focus on academics, teach traditional knowledge and skills (i.e., math facts, mental computation, phonics, grammar, and spelling), group students homogeneously (by grade and/or ability), and prepare them for college.[36] Nowhere in the School-to-Work legislation will you find any of the aforementioned items.

More Information about School-to-Work

Patterson, Chris. "School-to-Work: The Coming Collision." San Antonio: Texas Public Policy Foundation, 1998. This working paper is a must read for everyone concerned about School-to-Work. The document is heavily footnoted, making it easy for readers to locate the original sources. It can be found at the website of the Texas Education Consumers Association (http://www.fastlane.net/~eca/stwcollision.html). Also available at this same website is a collection of school-to-work anecdotes submitted by parents and educators from around the country (http://www.fastlane.net/~eca/stwanecdotes.html).

Olson, Lynn. *The School-to-Work Revolution: How Employers and Educators Are Joining Forces to Prepare Tomorrow's Skilled Workforce*. Reading, MA: Addison-Wesley, 1997. This book was written by an *Education Week* newspaper reporter who traveled around the country to visit School-to-Work sites. Although the author attempts to remain neutral, she is clearly impressed by the claims of School-to-Work proponents.

"The Tangled Web: A Cumulative Report Incorporating Research of Original Documents Concerning School-to-Work" is a website with more information than you'll be able to absorb in a single visit: http://www.ionet/~study/tang.htm

Thematic Instruction

(*See* Integrated Thematic Instruction)

Whole-Language

(*See* chapter 4)

TALES FROM THE TRENCHES

My Education Awakening

Gayle Cloud
Southern California
Parent
Education Activist

Although much has been written about the turmoil in education today, little has been written about how the fads and schemes of that system have affected individual families. My story, although troubling, is minor compared to the educational devastation suffered by thousands of American families. Even more disconcerting are the underlying problems evident in the fabric of our society that so little values academics—and children.

The problems don't just lie with reading fads, fuzzy-math, and teachers' unions; they are much more comprehensive. Most folk would simply not believe that money, power, and influence have replaced the classroom teacher, learning, and students as the motivation behind much of what happens in the bloated bureaucracy of education today.

Continued →

I began to have niggling doubts several years ago when our district adopted a whole-language reading program and several well-versed friends had concerns about the program's lack of phonics. My kids were learning to read, and I was too busy with my preschoolers to look beneath the surface of the program. I began to come out of my cocoon when we got a new principal a few years later. Not only did he promote whole-language and all of its underlying philosophy, but he did his best to squelch any dissent.

I learned that there was much more happening in education than just the curricular issues I had seen. And I learned to be an advocate for my children. I discovered that there were other parents at other schools who shared my concerns about the reading program. We met with school board members individually. We also met with district administrators, always telling them that the reading program wasn't working well enough to enable district children to read.

Most of the school board members listened politely. One woman, however, suggested that we should get back to "canning and playing tennis." Undeterred, we visited schools in southern California that used phonics programs. Their test scores were always higher than those in our district. One such visit was to Bennet-Kew in Inglewood, hardly the picture of an elite suburban school. The principal, Nancy Ichinaga, was a delightful maverick who was determined to ensure that her students learned. And they did—they read much better than students in comparable grades back in our hometown.

Our next visit was to our administration. We spoke different languages. They were concerned about all children. We had a narrow perspective. They looked at all the complexities involved in educating children today. We were simplistic. They believed reading was a whole process in which children learned to read in context. We had

Continued →

research which showed children learn systematically. They were experts. We were just parents. We hit a brick wall.

We decided to show our administration that the community supported a return to phonics. We gathered signatures for a couple of weekends at a neighborhood store where all the great minds congregated. We gathered several hundred, which we then presented to our board. They were unimpressed.

By this time, school board elections were looming, and I decided to try for a seat. Obviously others felt some changes were needed, since twelve candidates filed. The teachers' union got very involved and gave the three candidates they supported several thousand dollars. They won the three seats, but I came in fourth, first runner-up in a campaign run by moms. We were novices. We designed signs, held coffees, walked precincts. In the end, the three union candidates blitzed the media. And, of course, the union and board competitors labeled me a right-wing "stealth" candidate perched to take money from the Christian Coalition and work for the downfall of public education. Never mind that the Christian Coalition did not know me or ever offer me any money. Never mind that the system was doing a great job of self-destructing. Our group was actually attempting to save it.

The school board campaign was over, but the campaign to help our kids learn to read continued. Several former candidates and supporters met and formed a group, Citizens United for Education (CUE). We formulated by-laws, charged a membership fee, and distributed a monthly newsletter. We sorted through our accumulation of information and began to share our knowledge with other parents and legislators. We were surprised but happy to learn that we were not alone. We held monthly meetings and had speakers share expertise, legal knowledge, and political savvy.

When the big story about California's low NAEP [assess-

Continued →

ment test] scores broke, interest in what parents had been saying suddenly blossomed. The test scores proved that California's kids didn't read very well—we were tied for forty-ninth place with Arkansas. Now the national press and our legislators were interested. I was interviewed and quoted in *Newsweek, USA Today,* and the *Wall Street Journal.* Because of the widespread coverage of California's dismal reading scores and pressure from parents, legislators took action and passed a series of bills (known as the ABC bills) that required materials adopted in grades K-8 to include "systematic, explicit phonics, spelling, and basic computational skills."

I am heartened of late because there seem to be some signs that the tide is turning. The nature of reforms has recently come under scrutiny. California's State Board of Education has made some wonderful changes toward true academic reform. Newspapers are carrying stories on the real nature of education reform. And E. D. Hirsch, who has traced the nature of these problems in his book, *The Schools We Need and Why We Don't Have Them,* has received some small measure of acclaim. So, I press on . . .

The virulent viruses to which you have been introduced in this chapter are everywhere in today's schools. There are few elementary classrooms in the United States that have not been invaded by whole-language and fuzzy-math. Ask students around the country, and they will all have encountered cooperative learning and thematic units in their middle schools and high schools (many of them with block scheduling). Poll teachers about paradigm shifts, outcomes, and performance-based assessments. They've been there, done that! The only question that no one will be able to answer for you is this: Where is the research to show that these innovations will result in increased learning for students?

The parents you will meet in chapter 7 have been asking this hard question in their districts around the country. Their stories will intrigue and, I hope, inspire you.

Notes

1. Peter L. Steinke, *Healthy Congregations: A Systems Approach* (Washington, DC: Alban Institute, 1996) 56.

2. I have previously used the viral analogy to describe destructive communication patterns used by parents in my book for school administrators titled, *How to Deal with Parents Who Are Angry, Troubled, Afraid, or Just Plain Crazy* (Thousand Oaks, CA: Corwin Press, 1998). Permission to adapt the material for publication in this book is granted by Corwin Press.

3. Scott Thomson and Nancy DeLeonibus, *Guidelines for Improving SAT Scores* (Reston, VA: National Association of Secondary School Principals, 1978).

4. Jacqueline Brennan and Martin G. Brooks, *In Search of Understanding: The Case for Constructivist Classrooms* (Alexandria, VA: Association for Supervision and Curriculum Development, 1993).

5. Dennis Farney, "For Peggy McIntosh, 'Excellence Can Be a Dangerous Concept,'" *Wall Street Journal* 14 June 1997: A1, A3.

6. Public Agenda, *First Things First: What Americans Expect from Their Public Schools* (New York: Public Agenda, 1994).

7. Dennis Bryne, "No Winners—and No Losers," *Chicago Sun Times* 8 Feb. 1998: 35.

8. Joan Beck, "Let Bright Pupils Move Ahead, Even If It Seems Unfair," *Chicago Tribune*, 4 June 1990: A13.

9. John W. Donohue, "'Goals 2000: Educate America Act': Notes for a Chronicle" *America* 170.21 (18 June 1994) 61-63.

10. World Conference on Education for All, Jomtien, Thailand, 5-9 March 1990. Described in detail in James Patrick, ed., *America 2000/Goals 2000: Moving the Nation Educationally to a "New World Order"* (Moline, IL: Citizens

for Academic Excellence, n.d. (P.O. Box 1164, Moline, IL 61265.)

11. United States, Dept. of Education, *America 2000: An Education Strategy* (Washington, DC: Dept. of Ed., 1991) 3.

12. Robert Holland, "Stealth Takeover of Education?" *Washington Times* 8 Feb. 1994: A16.

13. An unnamed former U.S. Department of Education official is credited as the source for this quote in Brannon Howse, *Reclaiming a Nation at Risk: The Battle for Your Faith, Family, and Freedoms* (Chandler, AZ: Bridgestone Multimedia Group, 1995).

14. Thomas Toch, "The Perfect School," *U.S. News and World Report* 11 Jan. 1993: 46-59.

15. For more information about Donna Garner's work, visit the website of the "Texas Alternative Document," a language arts curriculum that she and her colleagues developed in opposition to what was being put forth by the Texas State Board of Education (http://www.htcomp.net/tad).

16. Ron Brandt, "On Outcome-Based Education: A Conversation with Bill Spady," *Educational Leadership* Dec. 1992/Jan. 1993: 68.

17. Howse, *Reclaiming a Nation at Risk* 31-32.

18. Christine Bennet, *Comprehensive Multicultural Education* (Boston: Allyn and Bacon, 1990) 12.

19. Thomas Sowell, *Inside American Education: The Decline, the Deception, the Dogmas* (New York: Free Press, 1993) 72.

20. Dennis Cuddy, "We Should Not Respect All Views," *Christian News* 11 April 1988. Reprinted in Dennis Cuddy, *An American Commentary* (Oklahoma City, OK: Hearthstone Publishing, 1993) 4.

21. Howard Gardner, *The Unschooled Mind: How Children Think and How Schools Should Teach* (New York: BasicBooks, 1991) 12.

22. Charlene Thomson-Myers, "Paper Airplanes Let Fifth-graders' Imaginations Soar," *Binghamton* [NY] *Press & Sun Bulletin* 19 Feb. 1998: B1.

23. Howard Gardner, "Low Scores Are No Disgrace," *New York Times* 2 March 1998: A19.

24. Denis Doyle, "Issue," *Update* (Association for Supervision and Curriculum Development) 36.8 (Oct. 1994).

25. George A. Miller, "Varieties of Intelligence," *New York Times Review of Books* 25 Dec. 1983, Sect. 7, 5:1.

26. Marjorie Ledell and Arleen Arnsparger, *How to Deal with Community Criticism of School Change* (Alexandria, VA: Association for Supervision and Curriculum Development, 1993) 20.

27. Mary Damer, "Testimony on Item and Test Specifications for the Voluntary Test in 4th Grade Reading," 27 Jan. 1998" Chicago, IL. Personal communication, 28 Jan. 1998. Mary's testimony is also available on the Mathematically Correct website: http://www.mathematic allycorrect.com

28. Ronald K. Hambleton, Richard M. Jaeger, Daniel Koretz, Robert L. Lin, Jason Millman, and Susan E. Phillips, "Review of the Measurement Quality of the Kentucky Instructional Results Information System" (Frankfort, KY: Office of Education Accountability [Capitol Annex, Frankfort, KY, 40601, 502-564-8167]) 6.

29. Jenny Chamberlain, "Our Illiteracy: Reading the Writing on the Wall," *North and South Magazine* [Auckland, New Zealand] June 1993: 67-76.

30. Quoted in Chamberlain, "Our Illiteracy" 69.

31. Steven Stahl, "Does Whole Language or Instruction Matched to Learning Styles Help Children Learn to Read?" *School Psychology Review* 24: 393-405.

32. B. Carpenter, ed., "Reading Recovery Task Force Report" (San Diego, CA: San Diego County Office of Education, 1996). Bonnie Grossen et al. "Reading Recovery: An Evaluation of Benefits and Costs," *Effective School Practices* 15.3: 6-24.

33. Marc S. Tucker, "Letter to Hillary Clinton," National Center on Education and the Economy, online, 11 November 1992. Available: http://www.sover.net/nbrook/ Hillary.html

34. Diane Dietz, "Students Get Real Work Lessons," *Eugene Register Guard* 29 Dec. 1997: 1C.

35. Letters from college and university admission directors

were introduced as public testimony during an Oregon state legislative session by State Representative Pattie Miline.

36. Public Agenda, *The Basics: Parents Talk about Reading, Writing, Arithmetic and the Schools* (New York: Public Agenda, 1996); and Public Agenda, *First Things First: What Americans Expect from the Public Schools* (New York: Public Agenda, 1994).

TALES FROM THE TRENCHES

Time to Step Up to the Plate

Dawn Earl
Parent
Former Public School Teacher and Principal
School Board Member

I remember reading an anecdotal account of how the late Sonny Bono became involved in politics. As a business owner in Palm Springs, he requested permission from the city to post a sign for his business. Bono's efforts to meet the city's requirements were summarily dismissed by the official in charge. In sheer frustration, Bono decided to run for mayor and fire the belligerent city official. Mayor Bono's subsequent tenure as mayor served as a lesson to less-than-responsive government employees.

Confronting the issue of public servants who fail to serve the public is what motivated me to run for school board. After trying to work with the administration and school for over three years with little success, I felt that gaining a seat on the school board was the last chance to effect any meaningful change to the district's weak curriculum. With five of the seven seats up for election and three incumbents declining to run, the climate seemed right.

The time and effort I had invested in understanding the system stood me in good stead. I was informed and up-to-date on both local district issues and state and national concerns. In addition, my master's degree in curriculum and supervision plus over fifteen years of teaching and administrative experience gave me an advantage.

We have no one to blame but ourselves if we don't step up to the plate when the opportunity arises. I have devoted my entire professional career to the education of children. I care too much about their future, and that of our country, to sit idly by and watch the deterioration.

7 Fifty Plus Things You Can Do

How to Make a Real Difference in Education Today

Wise people treasure knowledge, but the babbling of a fool invites trouble. . . . People who accept correction are on the pathway to life, but those who ignore it will lead others astray. . . . Don't talk too much, for it fosters sin. Be sensible and turn off the flow!

—*Proverbs 10:14, 17, 19, NLT*

There is both good and bad news regarding the prospects for containing the viral invasion that you have read about in chapter 6. First, the good news.

♦ The Annenberg Institute for School Reform at Brown University released findings of an eighteen-month study on public involvement in education. Calling this movement "a quiet revolution," the report investigated over 175 "public engagement activities" around the country. Titled "Reasons for Hope, Voice for Change," the study demonstrates the power of parents to help shape the direction of public education.[1]

◆ A new national panel is being formed at the behest of Congress to identify reliable and valid research into effective methods of teaching early reading to determine how they can be applied in the classroom; to disseminate the information to teachers and parents; and to discern where more research is needed.[2] Although the current reading wars may sidetrack the panel before they get to their assignment, the fact that Congress finds reading instruction to be important enough to warrant legislation is encouraging.

◆ A flurry of new legislation related to reading instruction has been either introduced or passed at the state level during the last two years. According to a report from the Southern Regional Education Board of The National Right to Read Foundation,

> this is a reflection of a growing sense of urgency about helping children who are having problems with reading. In several states, the legislation includes the need to provide direct instruction in phonics. It is also in response to the large and growing body of research showing that many children who fail to learn to read do so because they fail to master the building blocks of written language, specifically awareness of the alphabet and of the 44 phonemes—sounds formed by letters and combinations of letters—that make up the English language.[3]

◆ In 1997 the U.S. House of Representatives passed the "Reading Excellence Act" (HR 2614) by unanimous consent. This bill provides competitive grants to states for in-service training of teachers in Chapter I disadvantaged districts, based on reliable, replicable research in reading instruction. Tutorial Assistance Grants are available to parents whose children have not mastered the skill of reading. In 1998 U.S. Senator Paul Covedell from Georgia introduced S1586, the Senate version of the Reading Excellence Act.[4]

♦ Twelve of the nation's leading education groups have agreed to work together to improve the teaching of reading and mathematics. Designated as the Learning First Alliance, the group has agreed to focus on learning instead of lobbying. They have issued a summary report titled "Every Child Reading—An Action Plan," which recommends that reading instruction and policy be based on replicated research in reading instruction, phonemic awareness, formal instruction in well-sequenced systematic phonetic instruction early in first grade for all children, and reading practice using decodable text. If these groups can truly lay aside their special interests and look at empirical data, there may be progress.[5]

♦ Educators are finally beginning to realize that many of our real problems are rooted in the lack of adequate preservice preparation for teachers. Young educators don't know how to teach reading, writing, and mathematics. Many states are intervening to mandate more rigorous coursework in these areas.[6]

> "Many children who fail to learn to read do so because they fail to master the building blocks of written language."

Although promising, this good news isn't exactly overwhelming. The bad news continues to roll off the presses. The public schools are critically ill with the viruses of progressivism and reform, and they desperately need transfusions of clear thinking and courage. There has never been a more challenging time in which to become an activist for traditional education. There aren't nearly enough parents who are willing to speak out and get involved. Dan Connell concluded in a column in the *Kingsport* (TN) *Times-News* that "nothing will change until parents and taxpayers decide to take on the education bureaucracy, hold school boards responsible for quality education, and demand that schools respond to academic needs."[7] Although the conflict between the progressivists and traditionalists as described in chapter 3 is as divisive as ever, there is a growing body of parents who are beginning to discover what some parents have known for years: that the virulent viruses described in chapter 6 have invaded their schools. These parents are beginning to get involved. I hope you will join them.

J. E. Stone, founder of Education Consumers Clearing-House, observes a

> growing number of parents, school board members, lawmakers, taxpayers, and journalists who simply do not trust the public schooling community and its governmental affiliates to act in the public interest. As parents observe the educational progress of their children, as employers assess prospective employees, as policy makers look at reports of measured achievement, more and more people can see that they have been misled about that which is taking place in the schools. The nice words for it are *spin* and *public relations*. The not so nice word is *deception*. The simple truth is that there is a substantial and growing number of people who do not trust the schools.

James Davison Hunter, author of *Culture Wars: The Struggle to Define America*, agrees with Stone's perspective. He points out that although activists on either extreme of the educational philosophy continuum are in the minority (perhaps 20 percent on each end), the 60 percent of the population in the middle is increasingly dissatisfied with public education and is ready to join forces with the traditionalists.[8] Whether you're among those who are already actively involved in making a difference in the schools of your community or are one of the majority of parents who have just begun to realize that your school is "sick," this chapter has something for you. It contains more than fifty positive things that you can do to stem the rising tide of mediocrity and anti-intellectualism that is sweeping the schools of our country.

The suggestions here begin with the basic requirements of citizenship and good parenting and naturally progress to sophisticated activities that will consume your commitment and energies. The activities build upon one another. For example, I wouldn't recommend that you run for school board if you've never attended a meeting and aren't conversant with the issues. Or you wouldn't be advised to give workshops and seminars for other parents if you haven't done your own homework. Remember that before you try to reform the world, your first responsibility is to your own children's educational needs.

> "Nothing will change until parents and taxpayers decide to take on the education bureaucracy."

1) Vote

Voting is the very least you can do to make your voice heard regarding school governance in your community. Attend candidate forums, read newspaper articles, and talk to those who are knowledgeable about the issues. Even if your children are not enrolled in the public schools, the quality of education in your community affects your property values. Throughout the research for this book I have met many parents who are working tirelessly as community activists to improve the public schools while their children are being home or privately schooled. No citizen can afford to be apathetic about who sits on the school board. These officials are managing multimillion dollar budgets, and parents are providing the cash.

2) Attend Meetings and Public Hearings

Most school board meetings are pretty boring. I've spent some of the best years of my life attending them in my

TALES FROM THE TRENCHES

Seven Steps to Effective Education Activism

Barbara Shafer
Parent
Education Activist

Step 1: Don't Look Before You Leap

Theodore Roosevelt said, "The efficacy of leadership depends, to a large degree, on the leader's incognizance of the negative consequences of doing right." Education activism isn't going to win friends for you unless they are other education activists or close confidants.

Step 2: Don't Look Down, Look Up

If you spend too much time looking at where you are, you won't be focused on what will get you to the next step: looking up. Looking up information, looking up people in power, looking up history, and looking up details will lay the groundwork necessary to achieve your goals.

Step 3: Look Over

Look over your district's handbook before doing anything. There are channels for everything, and even though it is often a useless exercise for accomplishing change, always follow the proper channels. The purpose of following

Continued→

---

various administrative roles. I also know that board members sit up and take notice when the public attends. "A watched board is a careful board; its members know that the public feels what they do is important enough to monitor and that their actions must pass public scrutiny."[9] Don't expect to become an expert on school affairs by attending just one or two meetings. Sit through an entire channels is to disarm the establishment artillery, not to effect change.

Step 4: Look Over Here!

This step might be alternately titled, "Who's Afraid of the Big Bad Public Relations?" School administrators, that's who. The Letter to the Editor filled with truth, spoken in love, is your best friend as an education activist.

Step 5: Look Out!

Unfortunately, there is typically some fallout from doing the right thing if you're effective. By holding to a set of principles for yourself—(1) Is what I'm doing truthful? (2) Is what I'm doing necessary? and (3) Am I doing what I'm doing as nicely as possible?—you can eliminate your own doubts and take the high road in avoiding mud-slinging.

Step 6: Look to Others for Counsel

Activism is a lonely road. Network with other activists. They will be your encouragers.

Step 7: Look within Yourself

Your strength will need to come from within. A meaningful faith, a firmly established core of beliefs, a supportive family, and personal heroes who have blazed similar trails elsewhere will keep you strong.

---

yearly cycle to hear the full range of discussions about textbooks, hiring and firing of staff (although many discussions will take place in closed sessions, the decisions reached will be made public), suspension and expulsion of students, curriculum changes, special education programs, test results, bills to be approved for payment (looking at the bill list is an instructive activity for finding out just where and how much money is being spent), tax referenda, budget proposals, etc.

Beware of boards of education that do not publicly discuss or debate their decisions. Be suspicious of boards of education that allow few or no opportunities for parental input at their meetings. Boards of education that view themselves as "closed clubs" definitely have problems and bear even closer watching than the average board of education.

3) Become Informed

Read *Education Week, Educational Leadership,* and *Phi Delta Kappan.* These publications will inform you about what is happening in the real world of education. There is no substitute for having current information.

4) Read the Literature of Reform on Both Sides

Consult the recommended reading lists in appendix C and chapter 6. At first, the rhetoric and terminology will seem unfamiliar. Do not become discouraged. Eventually, you will understand how it all fits together.

5) Read to Understand the History of Education

Those who do not understand history are doomed to repeat it. Only by understanding the history of progressive education can you begin to grasp the depth of the issues facing our public schools. The first book to read without delay is *The Schools We Need and Why We Don't Have Them,* by E. D. Hirsch. This book will lead you to others. Nearly all of the parents who have shared stories for this book took the first step toward education activism through intensive study and learning.

6) Learn to Speak the Language

Don't be intimidated by educational jargon. Steve Underwood* understands the frustration of parents who are confused by educationese. He recommends learning the language immediately, however. "Not only is it possible," he advises, "but I believe it is critical for those people who wish to actively participate and make positive changes to learn about the issues and study the research."

Underwood believes that every concerned parent needs to take the responsibility for educating friends, family, and neighbors also. "This is an important part of the process," he suggests. "It's not enough to just parrot the words of others. We have to really know and understand the subject. I've discovered that when you know your subject well, you are no longer just a parent. People will listen when you can speak their language. When you can clearly and precisely state your position and back up those statements with research, you gain credibility."

7) Pay Attention to What Is Going On in Your Child's Classroom

Trust your instincts, and don't be reluctant to get involved. Sarah Phillips seems like the quintessential "soccer mom"—four children, two-story colonial, and a Chevy Suburban. The only thing that's missing is the dog. But don't let appearances deceive you. Sarah is an education activist—someone who attends meetings, does research, writes letters to the editor, and asks the difficult questions that many parents are afraid to ask. She didn't interview for the job and would rather be doing something else with her spare time. In fact, she and her husband moved to one of the best districts in suburban Chicago precisely so they wouldn't have to worry about the schools. But, unfortunately their high property tax investment was not paying the dividends they expected. So, Sarah became involved. Here's how it happened:

> It was not until my daughter had an excellent teacher for third grade that I realized what she and my

> **"My awareness of the huge discrepancies between classrooms in the same district became a watershed for me."**

seventh grade son had been missing throughout their school years. Oh, I had been having uneasy feelings about the lack of rigor and the fact that my son could consistently get *A*s with very little effort, but not being an educator I didn't have a clear picture of what was missing until I saw how Patty Reynolds* ran her classroom and organized her curriculum. In her classroom I saw the content, structure, and purpose that were not present in other classrooms in which my children had been students. My awareness of the huge discrepancies between classrooms in the same district became a watershed for me, and I began reading insatiably about educational issues. I read books and articles and documents that would normally have bored me to tears. I was riveted by the information because I realized that my four children, and ultimately our society, were going to be directly affected by the ideas underlying all the educational rhetoric.

I understood Abraham Lincoln's observation that the classroom philosophy in this generation will be the philosophy of the society in the next generation. It became very apparent to me that the move away from a knowledge-based curriculum in our district was part of a major philosophical shift that educational leaders were quietly imposing on students across the country.

By the time all of these revelations became clear to me, the district where my children attend school had already been implementing whole-language in its reading/language arts program for about five years. Because this district prides itself on not having a "prescribed" curriculum for its teachers to follow (i.e., there is just a philosophical framework with sketchy content and attitudinal expectations), many of the more experienced teachers continued to teach as they always had, thereby slowing down the overall decline on the district-wide standardized tests in reading comprehension.

As the more experienced teachers began to retire, however, the district adopted "Ventures in Excellence," a program for hiring facilitators rather than teachers. The scores on standardized reading/language arts tests increasingly began to reflect the gaping holes in our program, which was based on the whole-language philosophy. Amazingly, our administrators have appeared unruffled by falling reading scores, explaining that all the districts to which we compare ourselves are also experiencing falling reading scores, so there is nothing to worry about!

Up to this point, I had tried unsuccessfully to get results by working through the proper channels. I was concerned about my eighth-grade son sitting in a reading class day after day in which the teacher read books aloud that my son had read in third and fourth grade. I first went to the teacher, who informed me that this was the curriculum she was instructed to follow. So I went to the assistant principal, who sent me to the assistant superintendent for instruction, who directed me back to the teacher. No one seemed able or willing to answer my questions about why a student, who was labeled "advanced" in reading, was sitting bored in a class while a teacher read aloud from below-grade-level books, or why the teacher couldn't give my son assignments to be done at home, such as comparing and contrasting these books with other literary works.

I ended up in front of the school board in the fall of 1994, expressing my concerns about a lack of consistent, rigorous, academic curriculum throughout the district, and relaying the message that the teacher had given me—that if I wanted a rigorous academic curriculum for my children I would have to send them to private schools, because I would not find it in this district.

I obviously raised the ire of the superintendent by publicly making such a statement, and he asked that I meet with him to work this out. The meeting, in hindsight, seemed more for the purpose of figuring out what box I would best fit into. I saw no indication, beyond rhetoric, that there was a willingness to establish a more consistent, rigorous curriculum to which teachers would be held accountable to teach. Indeed, the philosophy that was being moved into the district was the antithesis of a rigorous, academic curriculum; they had no intention of offering options.

When the district moved to adopt an NCTM-based mathematics program, Sarah became a one woman "information central," alerting parents to the philosophical direction the school district was taking and encouraging them to take a close look at the materials for themselves. Her concerns began to be echoed on the sidelines of baseball diamonds and soccer fields that spring, and Sarah networked with a variety of parents who shared her concerns. During the summer of 1995, CARE (Citizens Advocating Responsible Education) was formed. CARE's mission was to be a clearing-house of information on educational issues for parents and to work with the district administration to implement options within the public school curriculum.

Sarah explains the benefits of a well organized group:

> It was our view that a group could serve to protect individuals from the derogatory labeling that inevitably occurred when anyone dared to question the administration on any issue. Granted, our group was immediately dismissively labeled by the administration, but as we had hoped, CARE served as a safe forum for many individuals to express concerns and

obtain information, without the administration knowing the identity of all those involved.

8) Find Out What Your Children Are Supposed to Know

Then take steps to find out if they actually know it. Don't trust that the good grades or favorable comments your children are receiving on their report cards actually mean they are learning to read, write, and do math. If your school does not administer standardized tests, you have no real way of knowing what your children know or don't know. There are

> The philosophy that was being moved into the district was the antithesis of a rigorous, academic curriculum.

two ways to find out: 1) Ask them to demonstrate their skills and judge for yourself; or 2) Take them to a learning or assessment center and have them tested by a professional. There are a wide variety of standardized tests that can be administered individually that will give you an accurate picture of your child's academic achievement. Chapters 4 and 5 contain information about how to assess your child's reading and mathematics achievement.

9) Make Sure Your Children Are Being Taught Properly

Don't lose focus on your children's welfare. If your children are not being taught what you believe they should know, find a way to make it happen. You can do it yourself or you can hire someone else to do it. Just do it!

10) Communicate with Your Child's Teacher

Do this in straightforward, honest, but positive ways. Use every opportunity you can to communicate to your child's teacher your views regarding teaching and learning. Jud Martinson* wrote this reply to the Math Learning Profile he received about his son, Lucas*, a first grader. He was concerned that the narrative gave no clear idea of what Lucas was expected to learn during the year.

> The math curriculum seems unsequenced and without focus. There is little commitment to mastery of sub-skills, no teaching of algorithms or logical progression of topic area, and only rare use of practice to complement conceptual understanding.
>
> If we are to judge from the Math Learning Profile, it seems as if the approach taken to math is to give Lucas problems marginally beyond his conceptual understanding and then let him struggle to find his own method by which to solve them, using you, the teacher, as his coach to guide his discovery of the necessary mathematical principles and skills. If this perception is accurate, then there is probably empirical data showing that this approach is effective at inducing children to develop the foundational mathematical skills. Do you have access to studies that show this method to be more effective than an approach using more direct means of explicit teaching?

Jud is quick to point out that the teacher can't be blamed totally for what is happening in the classroom and lets the teacher know that he is also forwarding his comments up through channels: "Because we realize our concerns are largely philosophical and as much relevant to questions of district policy as they are to your specific classroom practice, we are sending a copy of this response to the principal and superintendent, so that we might be able to begin a dialogue with them about these issues."

11) Communicate with School Officials

Instead of complaining over the back fence, bring your

concerns to someone who might be able to do something about the problem. Here is an excerpt from a letter Jeanne Nugent, an Illinois parent, wrote to the superintendent of her daughter's school district:

The intention in Everyday Math [the program used in her school district] is for the student to have fun, and to think math, to discuss math. Well, my daughter did think about math and found it utterly confusing. Fun was not what she had. My daughter's thinking was so muddled by the end of her second year in the program that she was unable to reason through any word problems and did not understand the simplest concepts.

Programs such as Everyday Math promise that kids will find their own way. Many do not, or they find some erroneous method of problem solution. For instance, my daughter spent nearly the whole school year subtracting numbers (where regrouping was necessary) incorrectly. She found her own way to do it, and it was wrong. The journal used for in-class work never comes home, so the parent has no indication as to whether the child understands the material. I became concerned when my daughter didn't have a clue about how to do math despite assurances from her teacher to the contrary. Imagine my surprise when I inspected this journal only to find out that not one mistake had been corrected. This journal/workbook comprised the majority of my child's math work.

When I pursued the matter, I was informed that children need to learn in a risk-free environment and that we adults are too hung up on right and wrong answers. I have yet to find one benefit for my daughter based on such philosophical musings. . . . I don't have the insight of a mathematician or of the academics who argue the pros and cons of different approaches to math instruction. I am simply a logical person who sees serious flaws in educational programs that expect kids to figure out critical concepts in math and other subjects where constructivist theory has been applied. Remember, these same children must be reminded daily to brush their teeth! We expect them to learn crucial skills on their own? Let us all be a bit more realistic.

12) Be Assertive

Barbara Tennison, who has been on the cutting edge of education activism in Oregon, believes that parents should never be shy or afraid that their children will "suffer" for their involvement.

> When I first became assertive, I went directly to the school principal, then on to the school board and the district superintendent. I made it very clear that I did not expect either of my sons to suffer in any way because of my views on education reform and what was happening in their classrooms. I respectfully let them know that I intended to be vigilant and very vocal. I put them on notice that they could expect to see a lot of me in the future. I also let them know that I intended to ask a lot of questions, and I expected their cooperation in getting the answers to me.

Barbara was always polite, smiled a lot, and never challenged their authority in any way. But she never gave up. "I fulfilled my promise to be vigilant and vocal," she reports. "My sons have never suffered because of my views on education, and I have thousands of documents supplied to me by our schools and school district office, all of which I used to discredit the education reform movement in our district."

Barbara laments the apathy of most parents.

As in most school districts, not many people attend

school board meetings, so they only know what the school board members and administrators tell them. That is why we need vigilant and assertive parents, grandparents, and other interested people to do the things we do. We do take a lot of heat for our troubles, but in the end it will all be worth the efforts we have made.

> Not many people attend school board meetings, so they only know what the administration tells them.

13) Articulate What You Believe a School Should Do

What do you believe the purpose of the public schools should be? Mortimer Smith, former chairman of the Council for Basic Education, suggests it's pretty simple:

- to teach children to read, write, and figure
- to transmit facts about the heritage and culture of the [human] race
- in the process of accomplishing (a) and (b), to train the intelligence and stimulate the pleasures of thought
- to provide an atmosphere of moral affirmation.[10]

Larry Cuban, professor of education at Stanford University, offers these criteria for determining whether a school is good:

- Are parents, staff, and students satisfied with what occurs in the school?
- Is the school achieving the specific goals it has set for itself?
- Are democratic behaviors, values, and attitudes evident in the students?[11]

Parents must be ready to articulate what they believe schools should do for their children as a benchmark against which to measure what schools are currently accomplishing.

An excellent source of information about this is a small booklet titled *Parents' Handbook for Successful Schools*. Written by Chris Patterson of the Texas Public Policy Foundation, it is furnished to help parents learn more about what is taking place in the schools their children attend and to help parents evaluate the effectiveness of a school's academic program. It offers tips for locating important information and identifies where assistance can be obtained. This handbook also recommends publications and websites for more information about educational issues. To receive a free copy, contact Texas Public Policy Foundation, P.O. Box 40519, 8122 Datapoint Drive, Suite 816, San Antonio, TX 78229.

14) Be Prepared for Diversionary Tactics

Some educators use these in both open meetings and individual appointments. Unless you understand the diversionary tactics used by educators, you will feel powerless every time you meet with one or more of them. When you encounter a group facilitator or administrator who is trying to shut you down, remember these helpful hints.

Smile and Be Courteous
Moderate your voice so as not to seem belligerent or aggressive.

Stay Focused
If at all possible, write your questions down to help you remain on the topic. When meeting facilitators or administrators are asked questions they don't want to answer, they often digress from the issue raised and manipulate the conversation to make the questioner appear foolish or aggressive. Do not fall for this tactic. Be charming, thus

deflecting any insinuation that may put you on the defensive. Always bring the facilitator back to your original question. If your question is rephrased into an accusatory statement simply state, "That is not what I asked. What I asked was . . . (repeat your question)."

Be Persistent

If putting you on the defensive doesn't work, facilitators often resort to long, drawn out dissertations on unrelated or vaguely related subjects. During that time, the group usually loses focus on the question asked (which is the intent). Let the facilitator finish with his or her dissertation. Then repeat the statements: "You didn't answer my question. My question was . . . (repeat your question.)" One parent has described this process as "gentle persuasion relentlessly pursued."

Do Not Become Angry

Anger directed at the facilitator or administrator will immediately make you the aggressor and cause the other group members to feel sympathy toward the facilitator. On the other hand, if you, the participant, become the victim, the facilitator may lose face and favor with the crowd.

Bring Others Along

Whether you're attending a large group meeting or a small conference at school, bring a friend or two along so you won't feel outnumbered and beleaguered.[12]

15) Attend Educational Seminars

Go to conferences offered by the education establishment to hear for yourself what is being taught. Tom White,* who is especially interested in gifted education (he and his wife have a gifted daughter), inquired about attending a one-day State Department of Education teacher training session for teachers of gifted students. He was invited to observe. He found the workshop to be valuable and well presented and the teachers to be genuinely concerned about children and pleasant company for a day away from work. He did worry a bit about the qualifications of some of the teachers selected for teaching the gifted, however. He relates the details of his experience:

> **The young teacher didn't know the number of feet in a mile.**
>
> In part of the session we divided into small groups and were doing various math challenges. One problem that was given went something like this: "If a car is traveling 55 miles per hour, how many feet will it go in 12 minutes?" I said to my group, "That's about 11 miles. 52,800 plus 5,280 is 58,080." The young teacher sitting next to me asked "Where does the 5,280 come from?" It turns out that she didn't know (and didn't recognize even in this context) the number of feet in a mile. If she were from another country, I could understand, but she was born and raised in Indiana. She seemed like a bright enough person, and I wouldn't want to judge her abilities by one bit of ignorance, but what kind of educational experience could she have had? What is she teaching to gifted children?

16) Start Surfing the Net

If you don't have a computer, begin saving right now. Then find an Internet provider and sign up for a monthly subscription. Perhaps you may find the Internet jargon incomprehensible initially, but with the patient tutoring and support of customer service representatives, you will be "surfing the net" with ease. The Internet is one of the most valuable resources an education activist can have. Within seconds you can be connected to websites offering research on reading instruction, details of the latest education legislation in Washington, or the archives of *Educa-*

tion Week. You can also be in direct communication with education activists around the country by e-mail. If you have a specific question about a program or textbook under consideration in your community, you can find out immediately about its implementation in other places and receive commentary on its effectiveness. If you are able to access the worldwide web, consult appendix D for a comprehensive list of websites devoted to all aspects of education and reform.

17) Join the Education Consumers ClearingHouse

The Education Consumers ClearingHouse is an Internet mailing list whose purpose is to empower education's consumers. It serves as a medium for communication and a source of consumer-friendly advice and expertise. Subscribers are able to ask questions, post information and opinion, or just listen. A nominal user fee is charged based on usage. The ClearingHouse is founded on the belief that education's consumers need access to information and opinion that is independent and sympathetic to their concerns and priorities. Subscribers are limited to parents, concerned citizens, employers, policy makers, taxpayers, and others who invest in and rely on the public schools. Individuals who are both consumers and professional educators (by training or occupation) are welcome but are asked to wear a consumer's hat while participating in the ClearingHouse. J. E. Stone, professor of educational psychology at East Tennessee State University, is the founder, moderator, and resident resource person. He aids subscribers by updating them on recent developments, interpreting educational jargon, responding to questions about educational issues, providing references to useful sources of information, offering analysis and opinion, and otherwise facilitating the flow of information. You can subscribe to the Education Consumers ClearingHouse by e-mailing a request to professor@tricon.net.

18) Join Your School Site Council

Not every school has a school site council. For those that do, the council is a governing group composed of parents, teachers, and community members. A school site council has officially sanctioned authority (usually from the board of education) and is typically very different from other parent-teacher organizations like the PTA. Some school site councils (e.g., those in the city of Chicago) actually hire and fire administrators. If your school has a school site council, consider becoming involved. Typical councils may do some or all of the following tasks.

- Collect and analyze information about conditions in the school
- Set priorities for school improvement
- Monitor implementation of planned activities
- Set up subcommittees to address schoolwide issues
- Make program and policy recommendations to the central office and board of education
- Evaluate achievements of the school and the council

19) Form a Community "Watch-dog" Organization

Carolyn Steinke is a California mother of seven who in 1987 formed PIE, Partners Involved in Education. From a single organization in her community, PIE has grown to become a nationwide oversight group that links grassroots chapters and provides information and lobbying. Individual cities with a core group of parents can join PIE and receive updates, alerts, education, and documentation to assist in their efforts to keep the public schools accountable to parents.

20) Publish a Community Newsletter

Mary Damer and Jeanne Nugent, co-founders of TAPIS

(Taxpayers for Academic Priorities in St. Charles Schools) publish a quarterly newsletter that gives district residents an alternative viewpoint about what is happening in the schools. The newsletter, twelve pages in length, has provided an in-depth analysis of test scores, informative articles on subjects like School-to-Work, whole-language, cooperative learning, and constructivism as well as answers to the questions most often asked by parents in the community. The newsletter is sent free to school board members, school administrators, media representatives, area politicians and community leaders, sympathetic teachers, and by subscription to an ever-increasing list of key parents in the district's schools. Although donations

> **The intrusion of Outcome-Based Education and psychological curricula has resulted in the parents' rights movement nationwide.**

trickle in, a core group of TAPIS members dig deep for mailing and printing costs. The newsletter is a labor of love in addition to a financial commitment, but the members find it to be worth every penny invested, gaining not only local attention from the *Chicago Tribune* and the *Chicago Sun Times* but from the national education newspaper, *Education Week.*[13]

21) Read Public Documents

Check out your state's Freedom of Information Act (FOIA) and be informed of your rights to obtain copies of public documents. Ask your public reference librarian for help in locating a copy of your state's School Code. Examples of materials you might obtain include lesson plans, standards and outcomes, minutes of curriculum meetings, grant applications, budgets, teacher/parent surveys, textbooks, and test results. Local policy may require that you pay for photocopying costs.

22) Write a Newspaper Column

Bruce Crawford turned into an education activist when his son complained about a problem his math teacher had marked wrong on a test. "He was sure he had the right answer," Bruce said. "And he was right. I told him to have the teacher check it the next day." Bruce dismissed the issue from his mind only to have his son return to announce that the teacher still insisted his answer was wrong. Bruce, a former instructor in Admiral Rickover's nuclear power program, put his pencil to the problem and solved it another way. His son's original answer still came up as the right one. The teacher then conceded that even if Bruce's son may have come up with the right answer, he hadn't solved it in the right way. Intrigued, Bruce solved the problem yet again, this time using the accepted method. He still came up with his son's original answer. His son returned to class once more to show the teacher his error.

"The teacher finally capitulated," said Bruce, "but then said he wasn't going to change my son's grade on the test. One, it wouldn't change his overall grade in the course, and two, if he marked my son's correct then he would have to go back and change the grades on all the other kids' tests." It turned out that the teachers' guide was wrong and even though the book had been in use for three years, this was the first time the error had been discovered.

Bruce started paying closer attention to what was happening in his children's classrooms after that and was dismayed to find that teachers were constantly making errors as they corrected papers. At that point he began reading about education. Lynne Cheney's *Telling the Truth* was the first book he read.[14] He followed that up with *The Closing of the American Mind* by Alan Bloom.[15] He began finding references to progressive education and especially to Rousseau's *Emile*[16] and read that one as well. The pieces in the puzzle began to fall into place for Bruce as he realized what progressive pedagogy was all about and how it was being manifested in his children's classrooms.

Bruce reports that

> all along I had known my kids weren't getting exposed to as much substance as I had (high school class of '63). I grew up outside of Memphis, Tennessee. Like California today, Tennessee was in the bottom five educationally then. Yet we had to know so much more. We had to take math tests that were orally administered. If you couldn't run the numbers in your head and had to resort to using a pencil or fingers, you would miss the next problem.

Bruce is frustrated by the educational establishment's denial of its failure. He says, "I've watched our assistant superintendent for instruction defend creative/inventive spelling. I've seen the Saxon math program shot down in review committee because it didn't have enough pretty pictures to keep the kids' interest." Bruce now writes regularly for the *Orange County* (CA) *Register*. One of his first published pieces humorously suggested a voluntary academic decathlon for teachers much like the one his district organized for students. He proposed that a substantial prize be given to the winners as an incentive for teachers to participate and study in preparation. Bruce has received anonymous hate mail and messages on his answering machine, but he has been undeterred. He continues to educate himself and write about what he's learning for other education consumers. Newspapers are a powerful forum for getting out the truth.

23) Determine Your Bottom Line

Know what you want to accomplish and where you are willing to compromise (if at all) when you set out to bring about change in your school district and community. Once educators begin to sense a growing power base, they *will* offer compromises. If you don't know what your bottom line is, you may be fooled by the easy promises of "working together for the betterment of our children and the community."

24) Understand the Mindset of Educators

Unfortunately, there are very few educators (i.e., educrats) who meet parents with an open mind. The minute you raise a question regarding curriculum or instructional practices, the red flags will go up and the labels will be affixed. These well-meaning but misguided educators will mentally be discounting everything you say while remembering in detail the advice they've received at workshops on how to deal with parental criticism (e.g., "Imagined grievances are as serious to the person who feels them as real ones" or "People are primarily emotional, not rational" or "Even those who have no justifiable beef are entitled to a diplomatic explanation of why they are in error"[17]).

If you understand this mindset from the outset, you won't be disappointed when you aren't able to "connect" immediately. It may take more effort and more time to communicate with educrats than it does to get your point across to ordinary mortals.

25) Join a School District Task Force

Becoming a member of a school district task force, curriculum council, or strategic planning committee can be a challenging experience, particularly if you hold a divergent or minority viewpoint. If you know what to expect from the experience and how to conduct yourself, you can make a real difference in bringing truth to the table. Anne Newman, director of the Texas Family Research Center in San Antonio, Texas, offers some excellent advice for those who are willing to become involved in what can be a frustrating, albeit rewarding, experience.

Why Join?

1) Task forces are usually formed to build consensus about what has already been decided. The key players know the agenda; the rest of the task force believes the table is clear. A trained facilitator is used to guide the task force to agreement using group processes, time limits, and strict rules to shut down open discussion.

> There are very few educrats who meet parents with an open mind.

2) Community leaders are invited to be a part of task forces for their name identification, contacts in the community, and leadership ability. If respectable people appear to be leading and making the decisions, then others will think they must be good decisions. Unless these specifically selected community leaders are the driving forces behind the agenda, they are likely to be provided only with limited and favorable information.

3) Although all sides will be invited to the table, those expected to disagree will usually be outnumbered. If differing members of the community refuse to join the task force, organizers can then say "we invited them, but they wouldn't come." If traditionalists do join the task force, their names can be used to document the diversity of the task force.

4) Organizers expect that those who don't agree will get angry and quit, which gives those behind the agenda an opportunity to say "we invited them, but they got mad and quit." When this happens, the organizers can portray their opposition as unreasonable and unwilling to work toward positive solutions.

How Can You Contribute?

Although you may not be optimistic about your chances

for making a positive difference on a school district task force, Anne has some advice for helping you to be successful.

1) Don't quit. In almost every case, those in the minority feel like quitting. Minority members tend to feel that the opposition is overwhelming, and they can't possibly do any good. When minority members don't quit, however, they are often able to turn the committee process around. Organizers may get frustrated when they are challenged and questioned or the real agenda may be exposed, and the minority view will prevail.

2) Insist on documented research to support a position. Be polite but assertive and relentless in your requests.

3) Ask what the purpose of the task force is, what the goals and objectives are, who has made decisions, who will approve the recommendations of the task force, and what measures have been taken to assure parental knowledge. Ask lots of questions such as, What is the origin of this concept? Does the district have to apply for a grant? Always ask for copies of the grant requirements. Don't take anything for granted. Ask for copies of policies, laws, and materials. Often when you speak up, others will begin to question things, too.

4) Insist that opposing views be heard.

5) Invite friends and supporters to observe the meeting. Almost any group appointed by an elected body is subject to open meeting laws (i.e., required to be open to the public). Even if the meeting isn't subject to open meeting laws, the organizers will be reluctant to throw out observers for fear of adverse public opinion.

6) Do your homework regarding the backgrounds and positions of quoted authors and consultants involved in the issues. If something strikes you as suspicious, check it out. Determine if goals, programs, and efforts are related to national efforts. Check out the affiliation of other task force members.

7) Keep a record of the activities of the task force, noting

dates, times, names, organizations, etc. If you have to document something later, your record will be invaluable.

8) If the process is unfair or if the task force is not balanced, address this with the appropriate authority, e.g., the school board if it appointed the committee.[18]

26) Create Your Own Website

Many parent activists have found the creation of a website on the Internet to be one of the fastest ways to distribute information to large numbers of people. If you haven't yet joined the "computer crowd," a website contains the home page of an organization or individual, as much information as they care to include for the perusal of all who visit there, and "links" or connections from that website to others that are related. One must have a computer, a modem, an Internet service provider, and special software to "browse" from one site to another. Your service provider will usually supply everything you need except the modem and the computer. Your local bookstore or public library will have dozens of books to help you learn about the Internet.

Jeanne Donovan, founder of the Texas Education Consumers Association, became an education activist when she realized that her daughters couldn't organize ideas, compose coherent sentences, or spell correctly. She discovered that teaching methods and practices had changed dramatically since her childhood. When she began networking with other parents, both locally and nationally, she found that others were having similar experiences.

> **Parents everywhere were being given the same response: "Your complaints are unique and therefore unfounded."**

She found that parents everywhere were being given the

same story when they questioned instructional practices: "Your complaints are unique and therefore unfounded." Educators then proceeded to extol the virtues of their practices, using unfamiliar jargon that left most parents feeling totally ignorant and confused. Jeanne determined that what parents needed most was help in translating the jargon into terms they could understand. The first thing she established on her website was a glossary of educational terms that every parent needs to know. She also posts information about many current educational issues.[19]

Steve Goss's website focuses on reading instruction and contains links to a variety of important sites explaining the current debate between phonics and whole language. Steve's organization, Arizona Parents for Traditional Education, provides educational news and an outstanding collection of reading research.[20] Since whole-language proponent Ken Goodman is based at the University of Arizona in Tucson, the site will give you an idea of what can happen when a major city goes for what Steve calls "whole language nitwittery."

Barbara and Bob Tennison created a website to share the story of their experiences with school reform in Oregon. Once you have visited the Tennisons' website complete with family pictures, you will feel like an old friend as you read about the battles they have won and lost in Cottage Grove, Oregon. The Tennisons also provide a forum for many education activists to publish their writings. Look for my favorite author, "Redyarrow," who will give you a birds-eye view of what is happening in today's classrooms.[21]

For an annotated list of web sites devoted to educational issues of all kinds, see appendix D.

27) Develop a Strong Emotional Support Group

If you are planning to become an education activist, you will need a strong emotional support group. Educators will not take kindly to your meddling. Many parents will be distressed that you are rocking the boat. They would prefer to remain blissfully ignorant. Surround yourself with friends who "speak your language" and support your efforts. Join an education network or form one yourself.

28) Run for School Board

Running for a seat on the school board is only the first step. Getting elected is the second. Step three, becoming an effective school board member who can actually make a difference, is the hardest one. Let's assume that your campaign was successful and now you're on board. The real work is just beginning. There are many lone rangers who ran with the idea of bringing a fresh perspective to the board. These eager beavers immediately discover that the educrats want nothing more than to keep them in their places. When David Anderson* was elected to the school board in the state of Washington in November 1995, he experienced what most new board members encounter after they are elected.

> I was told to run everything through the superinten-
> dent, rely on him as my sole source of information,
> discuss any questions or concerns with him in private,
> and not dissent at public meetings, he says. David got
> the advice that all new board members get: New
> board members should be seen and not heard. This
> is the conventional wisdom promulgated by the Na-
> tional Association of School Boards intended to si-
> lence new board members until they have been "in-
> doctrinated." But David broke all the rules from the
> very beginning.
>
> I went to the county treasurer and county assessor
> to find out how much money we owed on the con-
> struction bonds that were issued in 1978. We are a
> smaller district with about 2,000 students and a $14
> million annual budget. I found almost $800,000 ex-

cess sitting in a fund of which the superintendent and board president (a 14-year incumbent) were unaware. As a result of private discussions, followed by public discussions, we were able to pay off half of the remaining bonds early, saving interest costs. I pointed out at a public meeting that our enrollment figures were inflated beyond reasonable expectations. In other words, we were lying to the State of Washington. I pointed out publicly that there was between $400,000 and $700,000 hidden in our budget in addition to our budgeted reserves.

David started receiving supportive phone calls from community members who appreciated a board member who was doing his homework and taking a stand. But the experience hasn't been an easy one for him. He says,

It's hard not to take negative comments personally. But I keep reminding myself that I was elected to be an overseer on behalf of the citizens who own their public schools. I am not a representative of the school administrators or employees. I will not be dismissed. They know that I am serious and follow through. People need to believe in government again. I have an opportunity to restore their faith.

> **"I was elected to be an overseer on behalf of the citizens who own their public schools."**

Ann Mactier of Omaha, Nebraska, is winding up her fourth four-year term on the board of education in the Omaha Public Schools.

I started out seventeen years ago just hoping to get dialogue going about public school education that would include the viewpoint of ordinary people as well as those of educators. It seemed to me that the public was ill-informed about education, with their main source of information coming from the education establishment. I was amazed that I won my first time out. I think I can claim some success. Issues have been raised and are being discussed. Now I'm in my second year on the Nebraska State Board of Education. There is still a lot of work to be done.

29) Help with a School Board Campaign

Behind every successful school board candidate is a dedicated cadre of workers—folk who stuff envelopes, walk the neighborhoods, erect yard signs, and write letters to the editor. If your talents don't lie in making campaign speeches, you can make a difference behind the scenes by supporting candidates who will represent your views on the board of education.

30) Cultivate Newspaper Reporters

Most education reporters (particularly those on small-town newspapers) are recent journalism school graduates, babes-in-the wood with regard to educational issues. They need to be led by the hand and shown both sides of an issue. Do all you can to provide an alternative viewpoint to the one being provided by the school district's public relations manager. Invite the reporter to coffee and share some of your concerns. Provide well-written articles and press releases that need no editing. Raise thought-provoking questions that will arouse a young reporter's curiosity. Be known as an individual of integrity who provides quality information.

31) Lobby Your Elected Representatives

Anne Barbera, a Pennsylvannia activist, suggests the following steps when lobbying elected representatives:

a) Become very familiar with the bill under discussion. Sometimes you will know more about the bill than the legislative aides. Challenge them to read the bill for themselves rather than rely on agencies like the State Board of Education or the U.S. Department of Education.

b) Develop a packet of material to support your position that includes arguments in outline form and backup documentation.

c) Be brief and to the point whenever you meet with a legislator. Keep emotions under control and be polite.

d) Be sure to get the date, time, and contact person with whom you set up an appointment.

e) Remember that the majority of legislative staff are young, idealistic, and not particularly well informed about the real world.[22]

32) Debate Your Opponents

Challenge your opponents to debate. They won't always accept the invitation, but when you have the opportunity, be sure to stay calm and focus on substantive issues. Educators are more comfortable with jargon and educationese. Keep coming back to the issues and quote from specific sources to back up your assertions.

33) Persuade Your School District or School to Try a Pilot Program

Perhaps you won't be able to change everything overnight, but a clever way to get your foot in the door is to suggest a pilot program. John Saxon, the publisher of Saxon math books, frequently makes districts an offer they can't refuse: "Use my math books in one or two classrooms and compare the test results [to those scores obtained from students using a different text]."[23] Chuck Arthur, a teacher at Wilkes Elementary School in Gresham, Oregon, has convinced his administration to give him two years to prove that direct instruction in reading, math, and language will get superior results over other instructional methods. He has raised over $17,000 from local businesses and educational foundations to buy the materials for what he calls the Cornerstone Model Project. Arthur is using a program developed at the University of Oregon that has documented experimental research showing its effectiveness. Arthur is concerned that too many of his colleagues think their dedication and love for children is more important than what and how they teach. It's a tragedy that dedicated teachers like Chuck Arthur have to beg for money to teach the basics the right way. But people who care will get the job done no matter what it takes.[24]

34) Suggest Positive Alternatives

Be ready with a well-conceived plan of your own if you don't like the way business is currently being done. When school board members are able to see side-by-side comparisons, e.g., of an academically focused program compared to one majoring in vague generalities, you are more likely to achieve the goals you desire.

Donna Garner, an English teacher at Midway High School in Hewitt, Texas, was a member of the writing team charged with developing standards for language arts (reading and writing) in the state of Texas. She, along with a writing team of forty-five, spent three years and $9 million of the federal taxpayers' dollars to produce the document, Texas Essential Knowledge and Skills (TEKS). But she and a handful of teachers on the team found much to fault about the final product. It was based upon whole-language strategies instead of on current research that demonstrates that students must first be taught phonemic awareness and then decoding skills in conjunction with decodable texts. There was far too much "wiggle room" for teachers to freelance with reading instruction. The whole-language standbys of guessing and using context clues were emphasized.

So, this group of brave souls wrote their own standards,

known as the Texas Alternative Document (TAD) English, Language Arts, and Reading. The over-two-hundred-page document was produced without a penny of state funds and received excellent reviews from experts around the country. Garner and her husband, a football and track coach at the high school, converted the spare bedroom their grown sons had vacated into an office, bought a copy machine, and began churning out copies of the new document. Even though the state board of education did not adopt the TAD document but instead supported a revised version of TEKS, Donna Garner's efforts resulted in changes to the final TEKS draft. Her efforts have not gone unnoticed in other parts of the country. Requests are coming in for copies of the document which also drew praise from E. D. Hirsch. Kinko's, which distributes it, has received over five hundred telephone requests for a reprint of TAD. The National Right to Read Foundation has made TAD available upon request as one of its publications, and several national publications have featured stories about Garner and her work.[25]

Margaret Brown of Birmingham, a research analyst for the Eagle Forum of Alabama, has prepared a resource guide to help education activists develop positive alternatives to the paradigm shifts that are being recommended in many states and districts. Titled "Regaining Excellence in Education," the guide is divided into four parts: Producing Academic Excellence; Protecting Parents' and Students' Rights; Making School Systems Accountable to Local Citizens; and Getting the Dollars to the Classrooms.[26]

35) Become a Substitute Teacher

In many states one can obtain a substitute teaching certificate with a bachelor's degree in any field. If you really want to find out what is going on in classrooms today, sign up. Carl Ball, chairman emeritus of the Ball Seed Company in West Chicago, Illinois, wanted to find out more about what was happening in the schools that educated his future employees. When he officially retired at age seventy from his position at the seed company founded by his father in 1905, Ball obtained a substitute teaching certificate in DuPage County and rolled up the sleeves of his button-down oxford shirt to find out what was happening in the classrooms of the '80s. Today he has turned his commitment to education into activism at the Ball Foundation of Glen Ellyn, Illinois, which is opening charter schools in Arizona and Illinois.[27]

36) Become an Expert in One Aspect of the Curriculum

Richard Innes, a retired air force flight instructor with advanced degrees in electrical engineering, has become a walking encyclopedia about performance-based assessments since his daughter participated in the first KIRIS (Kentucky Instructional Results Information System) tests during her junior year in high school (1991-92). He has carefully followed the results of KERA (the Kentucky Education Reform Act) since its inception and produces consumer-oriented research and evaluation of the outcome-based reform. He has blown the whistle on the inflated claims of educational progress in Kentucky by comparing KIRIS scores to those of the National Assessment of Educational Progress (NAEP):

> The picture of Kentucky education painted by KIRIS is very different from the picture of Kentucky education painted by NAEP. While KIRIS identified very large 4th and 8th grade math score increases of 20.9 and 17.2 points respectively, on a 140 point scale, NAEP showed a very small increase at both grades of just 5 points on a much larger 500 point scale.[28]

37) Learn How to Evaluate Educational Research

Mary Damer, cofounder of Taxpayers for Academic

Priorities in St. Charles (IL), initially became active in raising concerns about her public schools after the district adopted the University of Chicago Everyday Mathematics Program. Together with others, she met with the school superintendent to ask why the district had chosen to sink so much of its time, money, and resources into a highly experimental math program. By return mail she received a snazzy packet entitled "Perspectives of Everyday Mathematics: Student Performance Data." Despite her background as a college instructor and former principal of a special education school, Mary was more intimidated by the five research studies contained in the document than she had been by the superintendent. She did what each of you should do when confronted with a daunting educational question—her homework. Armed with an article written by Bonnie Grossen on educational research[29] and her old statistics and research textbook, she went to work. After her assignment was completed, she asked a retired education professor to review her work. He concurred with her findings: the research was seriously flawed. The snazzy packet was "smoke and mirrors," and unfortunately lots of parents and educators were fooled. Mary submitted all of her findings to the superintendent, but as is frequently the case, the district preferred smoke and mirrors to empirical data.

> **Richard Innes has blown the whistle on the inflated claims of educational progress in Kentucky.**

38) Write Letters to the Editor

Writing a letter to the editor of your local newspaper is one of the easiest and quickest ways to alert parents to potential problems. Read some already published letters to get a feel for the best way to present your ideas and don't be disappointed if the editor condenses what you submit.

39) Call Radio Talk Shows

If your community has radio talk shows, call in with a question or concern. I am a regular guest on *Parent Talk* with hosts Kevin Leman and Randy Carlson as well as *Midday Connection* with hosts Wayne Shepherd and Andrea Fabry. I appreciate the parents who call with concerns and questions about their schools. When they are honest about what is happening in their school districts, they encourage other parents to speak up also.

40) Host a Conference or Seminar

Ask your church, school, or other community organization to host a seminar on educational issues. There are few opportunities for parents to engage in meaningful discussion about education other than on the sidelines of baseball and soccer games. Ernesto Cortes, Jr., suggests that

> when parents and community members are truly engaged, they are organized to act on their own values and visions for their children's futures. They do not just volunteer their time for school activities or drop their opinions in the suggestion box. They initiate action, collaborating with educators to implement ideas for reform. This kind of engagement can only happen through community institutions—public schools, churches, civic associations. These institutions provide the public space where people of different backgrounds connect with one another, listen to others' stories, share concerns; this is where they argue, debate, and deliberate.[30]

I can envision an educational conference for parents held at a large community church in which the keynote speaker is E. D. Hirsch. Parents will then move to breakout sessions where they can listen to activists like Jeanne Donovan, Barbara Tennison, and Barbara Shafer discuss what is happening in their communities around the country. Other workshop sessions will be held on how to evaluate educational research, write newsletters, and run for school board. The closing session would feature Robert Holland, education columnist and author, or perhaps Peg Lusik, the courageous crusader against Outcome-Based Education in Pennsylvannia.

41) Give a Workshop or Teach a Class

Gayle Cloud has accumulated lots of experience and battle scars shepherding her six children (ranging in age from a daughter about to enter medical school down to a second grader) through the Riverside, California, school district. Although she has teacher certification, she credits her ability to discuss curriculum, parents' rights, and School-to-Work issues to extensive personal research and networking with experts. She has needed every bit of experience and knowledge to make sure her children survived whole-language, fuzzy-math, new science, and every other California education fad. She was recently invited to speak to a group of doctoral students:

> A University of La Verne (CA) education professor contacted me and asked me to share my views on public education from a Christian perspective with a group of doctoral candidates in educational administration. That sounded intriguing! Usually I was in the position of listener rather than speaker, and I had a lot to say.
>
> The administrators were supposed to learn from me and my partner (a former pastor from central California) about the motivation and concerns of Christian parents. Some of the other groups of influence they heard from included gays, Hispanics, African Americans, and Asians. The purpose for the seminar was to dispel the stereotyping that often occcurs in dealing with parents and other groups.

Although I was happy to share my Christian values and faith, I feel the concerns I have about public education transcend my faith. As I have met other parents around the state and country, I have discovered that we have many of the same educational concerns even if we do not share religious or political convictions. These concerns, rather, stem from a lessening academic rigor and de-emphasis on parental rights. I had the opportunity to emphasize that truth with twenty students.

For the most part these were eager learners and genuinely nice folks. Since they were placed in our group, most had opposite life experiences from ours. One or two seemed genuinely surprised that Christians could be articulate and more concerned about getting rigorous education than prayer into the schools. Many genuinely believed that we Christians were out to destroy public schools and institutionalize our faith. We assured them that our concern was grounded in remaining a fair influence in the public schools and ensuring that our rights as parents were understood.

I truly enjoyed facilitating this group. I especially enjoyed the role-playing portion when the administrators in training had to act out their newfound "faith." I became the administrator and used the education jargon and trite phrases so often used to intimidate parents (i.e., "you're the only parent with this concern" or "I understand your concerns, but we care about all children"). I think the point was made.

I have come to realize that one person can make a difference. I began my educational journey by asking questions of my child's teachers, then his principal, then the administrators and state legislators. I even had the opportunity to stand (actually sit) before "governors and kings" at the National Education Goals Panel meeting and share my concerns with them. Because of the many parents and others who have begun sharing their stories, California's schools are heading back to common-sense education.

> "This is my child, and I'm not comfortable with what you're doing with my child in school."

Gayle also regularly shares her expertise with parents through workshops at her church. She has spoken at political gatherings and business groups as well. Her topics run the gamut: How Education Reform Will Affect Your Child; Choices in Education; and The Educated Decision. She recently taught a class of what she calls uninitiated parents, parents who are frustrated with administrators who "talk around them." Gayle calls it "drowning them in rhetoric." Her advice to these parents: "When all else fails, use this simple statement: 'This is my child and I'm not comfortable with what you're doing with my child in school.'"

Gayle finds that most parents simply do not have enough information to evaluate their children's education, and she is trying to help these confused parents acquire the "critical thinking skills" so in vogue in today's schools. She chuckles as she considers the irony. "I love that term because the truth is that most educators don't really like the critical thinkers they are supposedly training; they ask too many questions!"

This full-time mother has become a full-time activist. She's been quoted in the *Wall Street Journal*, *Newsweek*, and *USA Today*.

42) Deal Unemotionally with Emotional Subjects

Keep calm, rational, and in control at all times. Don't lose your temper or resort to name calling. Stick to verifiable facts and use original documents to prove your point whenever possible.

43) Educate Others

Once you have educated yourself, begin to educate others in your community. Develop an information dissemination system. Use every available avenue to get the word out to parents and others: word-of-mouth, newspapers, radio, cable television, flyers, and newsletters. Find the medium that suits you and use it.

44) Become Proactive about Legislation

Use your expertise to affect legislation at the local, state, or national level. Recently, education activists have been instrumental in the passage of reading legislation (or district mandates that specified the teaching of phonics in the school curriculum) in Ohio, California, North Carolina, Wisconsin, Texas, and Nebraska.[31] Steve Goss of Tucson, Arizona, began by questioning reading instruction practices in his son's classroom. Then he created a website to help parents like himself obtain information about reading instruction. Now he has turned his attention to lobbying for better reading instruction in the state capital.[32]

45) Document All You Say and Do

Whenever you choose to begin your educational process, start your filing system at the same time. Save articles, documents, research studies, and correspondence. Be able to show as well as tell people what you have discovered in your research. Be ready to provide citations, quotations, and research in support of your position. Whenever you have a conversation with a teacher, principal, superintendent, or board member, take notes, date them, and file them away for future reference. Sometimes it can be helpful to follow up your meeting with a memo or letter summarizing what took place (from your perspective). I

TALES FROM THE TRENCHES

Power to the Consumer

Marilyn Keller Rittmeyer
Parent
Public School Teacher
Ph.D. Candidate,
Northwestern University School of Education

Marilyn favors parental choice in its many forms: charter schools, home schooling, vouchers for private/parochial school, and neighborhood public schools. She hopes to become a principal of a Core Knowledge School of Choice.

> Private schools are controlled by consumer power, and public schools are controlled by producer power. I am deeply concerned about the amount of power that the producer interests have over the lives of children in public schools.
>
> Education's producers are well organized via the teacher unions, the American Association of School Administrators, the Association for Supervision and Curriculum Development, the National PTA, the

Continued→

have found in my years as an educator that there is no substitute for a complete and accurate paper trail.

46) Support Organizations That Lobby around Important Issues

Julie Anders is the California Division Director of the National Right to Read Foundation. She works as an

Council of State School Officers, the American Association of Colleges for Teacher Education, the Education Commission of the States, the National Associations of Elementary and Secondary School Principals, the National Association of School Business Managers, the National Association of State Boards of Education . . . need I name more?

By comparison, education's consumers have no organizational strength. Some public educators have stated to me that parents do not know enough to make a good educational choice for their children. I respectfully disagree. I don't have much depth of knowledge about medicine, but somehow I am able to choose a good doctor for my children. If parents were offered different educational options, I would trust them to make an informed decision. The state could retain some regulatory authority over schools that receive public monies—possibly by requiring accreditation and annually published standardized test scores.

The battle between David (education consumers) and Goliath (education producers) is not one for the fainthearted. Advocates of choice need to find a few politicians with the courage and determination to battle the giants.

---

unpaid volunteer and digs deep into her own pockets to make the truth about reading instruction available to all searchers. She works full-time in her volunteer position, which has become her mission and passion since rescuing her eldest grandchild, whom she describes as "a whole-language victim." The National Right to Read Foundation publishes a newsletter and offers an extensive list of resource materials about reading instruction.[33] It is only one of many organizations working to bring about change in education. Concerned Women for America, the Eagle Forum, Parents Involved in Education, and countless local organizations are all looking for volunteers to bring leadership, energy, and funds to their efforts.

47) Call and Write Your Elected Officials Regularly

Don't be shy about letting your elected officials know where you stand on educational issues, both state and national. A sincere letter or phone call from a constituent makes a difference. Don't fall into the trap of thinking that somebody else will do it. Take the initiative and responsibility to hold elected officials accountable. The most persuasive letters are those that share personal and poignant stories of your own children's educational experiences.

48) Ask Your School or District to Survey Parents

Many school districts don't want to know what their constituents think about what they're doing. They prefer following their own agenda. Direct the attention of these administrators to an article that appeared in the October 1, 1997, issue of *Education Week*, a widely read newspaper in educational circles. Written by Clifford B. Janey, superintendent of the Rochester City School District, it describes a nineteen-question parent survey the district is using to sample consumer satisfaction. Here are four of the survey items to which parents can respond by checking "usually," "sometimes," "rarely," "don't know," or "doesn't apply."

- The teacher makes clear what my child is expected to learn in this class.
- The teacher deals with me in a fair and respectful manner.
- As needed, the teacher and I develop a cooperative strategy to help my child.

- The teacher encourages my child to work hard to succeed.[34]

49) Appear on Radio Broadcasts

Dave Ziffer, Mary Damer, and Barbara Shafer, three out-spoken education activists in the suburban Chicago area, recently appeared as guests on *Extension 720,* a nightly WGN radio talk show devoted to contemporary topics of interest to the educational elite of the Chicago area. Their show generated a heavy volume of calls both from parents who shared their displeasure with what they see happening in public schools and educators eager to defend their practice and deride the activists for undermining public education. It takes a tough skin to be an activist.

50) Identify Potential Supporters in Congress

If you encounter state or federal legislators who express strong support for your position, make the most of this opportunity. Tell them you appreciate their vote. Ask them what they would be willing to do: give a speech on the floor? issue a press release? come to your community and give a speech? introduce a bill? Tell them what you're willing to do: stuff envelopes, make phone calls, hold re-election coffees.

51) Establish a Charter School

"Charter schools are public schools, financed by the same per-pupil funds that traditional public schools receive. Unlike traditional public schools, however, they are held accountable for achieving educational results."[35] Parents who are disenchanted with the academic excellence and accountability of their public schools are increasingly turn-ing to the charter alternative as a means of getting what they want for their children without turning to private or home-schooling options. Joe Nathan suggests that the charter school movement brings together four powerful ideas:

- Choice among public schools for families and their children
- Entrepreneurial opportunities for educators and parents to create the kinds of schools they believe make the most sense
- Explicit responsibility for improved achievement, as measured by standardized tests and other measures
- Carefully designed competition in public education[36]

Marilyn Keller Rittmeyer is an educator in the northwest suburbs of Chicago. She is writing her dissertation for her Ph.D. in school administration at Northwestern University. Dissatisfied with the kind of education her five children were receiving, Marilyn enrolled them in parochial schools and joined with others in her area to write a charter school proposal which featured the Core Knowledge Curriculum as its centerpoint. Although the proposal was rejected by Elk Grove Community Consolidated School District #59, a last-minute reprieve was granted by the state legislature, giving Marilyn's charter proposal an opportunity to be reviewed by the Illinois State Board of Education. There it was accepted. The Thomas Jefferson Charter School is scheduled to open in 1999.

No one can promise you a rose garden if you become a school activist. You may experience disappointment, rejection, vilification, and frustration. But you will make a difference.

I hope that the fifty plus suggestions and accompanying stories in this chapter have been motivating and inspirational to you. I hope you'll become involved in your community, not just for your own children but for the children who will attend your public schools in the next century. Take one step at a time. Read, study, learn, question, and network. Once you've done your homework, you will know the next step to take, whether it be joining an organization, designing a website, running for office, writing a newsletter, or putting your own creative spin on making a difference in the public schools. As you uncover the disarray in education, you may become impatient that not everyone sees what now seems obvious to you. Just remember the advice of one education activist: "I've decided that if it takes a principal four or five years to turn around a poorly achieving school, I have to be content with the slow progress we are making in our community. To expect too much change in a short period of time is unrealistic. I simply must be more patient with the long view in mind."

> Charter schools are held accountable for achieving educational results.

Publisher Karen Iacovelli, writing in the premier issue of *Crisis in Education*, encourages education activists to stay the course, no matter how discouraged they may become. She quotes her dear friend, the late Jack Pollard, who said, "Our mission is to be faithful, not successful." Karen goes on to say that "education reform activism has created a revolutionary spirit not witnessed since a solo horseback ride 200 years ago."[37] We need more revolutionaries to join the ride!

To a tireless education activist who had recently experienced a devastating setback in her efforts to establish a charter school, a friend and encourager wrote, "I have a book called *A Hero in Every Heart*,[38] and I cherish it for two quotes. They both apply to you." The first was from Teddy Roosevelt on courage:

> The credit belongs to those who are actually in the arena, who strive valiantly; who know the great enthusiasm, the great devotions, and spend themselves in a worthy cause; who at the best, know the triumph of high achievement; and who, at the worst, if they

fail, fail while daring greatly, so that their place shall never be with those cold and timid souls who know neither victory nor defeat.

The second quote came from Calvin Coolidge:

Nothing in the world can take the place of persistence. Talent will not; nothing is more common than unsuccessful men with talent. Genius will not; unrewarded genius is almost a proverb. Education will not; the world is full of educated derelicts. Persistence and determination alone are omnipotent.

The friend continued, "Three cheers for your tireless and worthwhile endeavors. And three more for anything you do in the future. I would always want a friend like you on my side."

Notes

1. The Annenberg Institute for School Reform at Brown University, *Reasons for Hope, Voice for Change* (Providence, RI: Annenberg Institute for School Reform, 1998).

2. Kathleen Kennedy Manzo, "New National Reading Panel Faulted before It's Formed," *Education Week* 18 Feb. 1998: 7.

3. National Right to Read Foundation, "News from the States," *Right to Read Report* Feb. 1998: 6.

4. National Right to Read Foundation, "Bulletin Board," *Right to Read Report* Feb. 1998: 7.

5. Ann Bradley, "Groups Outline Steps to Boost Reading, Math," *Education Week* 4 Feb. 1998: 1. Copies of "Every Child Reading—An Action Plan" can be obtained by calling the Learning First Alliance at (202) 822-8405 x40 or online at http://www.learningfirst.org

6. Ann Bradley, "Ed. Schools Getting Heat on Reading," *Education Week* 18 Feb. 1998: 1.

7. Dan Connell, "Some Teaching Methods Are Nonsense," *Kingsport Times-News* (TN) 22 Oct. 1997: 9A.

8. James Davison Hunter, *Culture Wars: The Struggle to Define America* (New York: BasicBooks, 1991) 203.

9. Barbara J. Hansen and Philip English Mackey, *Your Public Schools: What You Can Do to Help Them* (North Haven, CT: Catbird Press, 1993) 49.

10. Mortimer Smith, *A Citizen's Manual for Public Schools* (Boston: Little, Brown, Atlantic Monthly Press, 1965) 6.

11. Larry Cuban, "A Tale of Two Schools: How Progressives and Traditionalists Undermine our Understanding of What Is 'Good' in Schools," *Education Week* 28 Jan. 1998: 33. For a more complete description of the two schools described by Cuban, see David Ruenzel, "Two Schools of Thought," *Teacher Magazine* online, April 1995. Available: http://www.teacher.org

12. Mary Damer and Lynn Stuter, "Parent Meetings," *TAPIS Newsletter* 1.3 (May 1997): 2-3. Reprinted by permission.

13. Ann Bradley, "Educated Consumers," *Education Week* 26 Mar. 1997: 33.

14. Lynne Cheney, *Telling the Truth: A Report on the State of the Humanities in Higher Education* (Washington, DC: National Endowment for the Humanities, 1992).

15. Alan Bloom, *The Closing of the American Mind* (New York: Simon and Schuster, 1987).

16. Jean Jacques Rousseau, *The Emile of Jean Jacques Rousseau,* ed. William Boyd (New York: Teachers College Columbia University, 1956).

17. Walter D. St. John, "Dealing with Angry Adults," *Today's Education* 64.4 (Nov.-Dec. 1975): 82.

18. Anne Newman, communication with the author, 8 Jan. 1998.

19. Jeanne Donovan's website can be found at http://www.fastlane.net/~eca

20. Arizona Parents for Traditional Education can be found at http://www.theriver.com/Public/tucson_parents_edu_forum/

21. Find the Tennisons at http://www.rstenison.com

22. Anne Barbera, "Here's How to Lobby Your Elected Representatives," *Not with My Child You Don't: A Citizens' Guide to OBE and Restoring Education,* ed. Robert Holland (Richmond, VA: Chesapeake Capital Services, 1996) 10.12-10.14.

23. The Saxon Math Company website can be found at http://www.saxonpub.com

24. Scott Learn, "Reynolds Gives Maverick Teacher Two Years for Reading Experiment," *The Oregonian* 23 October 1997: 1, 8.

25. Information about the Texas Alternative Document and how to obtain a copy can be found at http://www.htcomp.net/tad
The story of Donna Garner and her efforts to change the course of English, Language Arts, and Reading Instruction in Texas can be found in Drew Lindsay, "Double Standards," online, 12 Nov. 1997. Available: http://www.edweek.org/

26. Available from Margaret Brown, 4200 Stone River Circle, Birmingham, AL 35213.

27. For more information on the Ball Charter School

initiative, contact Dr. Percy Clark, The Ball Foundation, 800 Roosevelt Rd., Glen Ellyn, IL 60137.

28. Richard G. Innes, "Did Kentucky Ever Score 'at the Bottom' of the National Assessment of Educational Progress?" unpublished, 9 Dec. 1997.

29. Bonnie Grossen, "Making Research Serve the Profession," *American Educator* 20.3 (Fall 1996): 7-8, 22-27.

30. Ernesto Cortes, Jr., "Making the Public the Leaders in Education Reform," *Education Week* online, 22 Nov. 1995. Available: http://www.edweek.org/

31. National Right to Read Foundation, "Phonics Legislation and State Regulation Approved in 1996" online. Available: http://www.jwor.com/nrrf.htm

32. Arizona Parents for Traditional Education can be found at http://www.theriver.com/Public/tucson_parents_edu_forum/

33. The Right to Read Foundation can be contacted at P.O. Box 490, The Plains, VA 20198, (540) 349-1614. To order materials, call (800) 468-8911. Their website can be found at http://www.jwor.com/nrrf.htm

34. Clifford B. Janey, "Seeking Customer Satisfaction," *Education Week* 1 Oct. 1997: 39.

35. Joe Nathan, *Charter Schools: Creating Hope and Opportunity for American Education* (San Francisco: Jossey-Bass Publishers, 1996) 1.

36. Ibid.

37. Karen Iacovelli, "Splendor in the Grassroots," *Crisis in Education* Feb. 1998: 60.

38. H. Jackson Brown, Jr., and Robyn Spizman, *A Hero in Every Heart* (Nashville, TN: Thomas Nelson Publishers, 1996) 29, 51.

APPENDIX A

Phonics/Whole-Language Survey

Here are the original quotations from which the survey statements were developed. The authors cited have written widely about whole-language and are considered to be the "experts" in the field.

1. Children must develop reading strategies by and for themselves.[1]

2. It is easier for a reader to remember the unique appearance and pronunciation of a whole word like "photograph" than to remember the unique pronunciations of meaningless syllables and spelling units.[2]

3. One word in five can be completely eliminated from most English texts with scarcely any effect on its overall comprehensibility.[3]

4. English is spelled so unpredictably that there is no way of predicting when a particular spelling correspondence applies.[4]

5. Children can develop and use an intuitive knowledge of letter-sound correspondences [without] any phonics instruction [or] without deliberate instruction from adults.[5]

6. Sounding out a word is a cumbersome, time-consuming, and unnecessary activity.[6]

7. Matching letters with sounds is a flat-earth view of the world, one that rejects modern science about reading.[7]

8. There is nothing unique about reading, either visually or as far as language is concerned.[8]

Notes

1. Constance Weaver, *Reading Process and Practice* (Exeter, NH: Heinemann, 1988) 178.

2. Frank Smith, *Reading without Nonsense* (New York: Teachers College Press, 1985) 146.

3. Frank Smith, *Psychology and Reading* (New York: Holt, Rinehart, & Winston, 1973) 79.

4. Smith, *Psychology* 53.

5. Weaver, *Reading Process* 86.

6. Ibid.

7. Kenneth Goodman, *What's Whole in Whole Language* (Exeter, NH: Heinemann, 1986) 37.

8. Frank Smith, *Understanding Reading* (Hillsdale, NJ: Lawrence Earlbaum, 1986) 188.

Phonics Instructional Materials

Action Reading
(800) 378-1046

Alphabetic Phonics (Texas
   Scottish Rite Hospital for
   Children, Dyslexia Therapy)
2222 Welborn St.
Dallas, TX 75219-3993
(214) 559-7425

Chall/Popp Reading
(800) 233-0759

Discover Intensive Phonics for
   Yourself
(800) 333-0054

The Herman Method Institute
4700 Tyrone Ave.
Sherman Oaks, CA 91423
(818) 784-9566
Renee Herman

Home Quest Learning Labs
(800) 767-7409
Jolly Phonics
(800) 488-2665

Language Tune-Up Kit
(800) 334-7344

Lindamood-Bell Learning
   Processes
416 Higuera St.
San Luis Obispo, CA 93401
(805) 541-3836
(800) 233-1819
Pat Lindamood

Nanci Bell

Merrill Linguistics (K-3)
(800) 772-4543
Modern Curriculum Press
(800) 321-3106

Open Court (Breaking the Code)
(800) 722-4543

Orton-Gillingham Academy
1322 7th St. S.W.
Rochester, MN 55902
(507) 288-5271

Phonics Pathways & Pyramids
Dorbooks Publishing
(510) 449-6983
(800) 852-4890 Credit card
   orders

Phono-Graphix/Read America
   Inc.
P. O. Box 1246
Mount Dora, FL 32757
(407) 332-9144
(800) 732-3868
Carmen McGuinness
Geoffrey McGuinness

Primary Phonics/Explode the
   Code
(800) 225-5750

Project Read/Language Circle
P. O. Box 20631
Bloomington, MN 55420
(612) 884-4880

Reading Mastery/Rainbow
  Edition
(800) 772-4543

Saxon Phonics
(800) 284-7019

Sing, Spell, Read, and Write
(800) 321-8322

Slingerland Institute
One Bellevue Center
411 108th Ave. NE 230
Bellevue, WA 98004
(206) 453-1190
Clara McCulloch

The Spalding Education
  Foundation
2814 W. Bell Rd.
Suite 1405
Phoenix, AZ 85023
(602) 866-7801

Total Reading
(800) 358-7323

Wilson Language Training
162 West Main St.
Milbury, MA 01527
(508) 865-5699
Barbara A. Wilson
(800) 899-8454

Zoo Phonics
(800) 622-8104

Suggested Book List on Reading Instruction

Adams, Marilyn Jager. *Beginning to Read: Thinking and Learning about Print.* Cambridge, MA: MIT Press, 1990. This well-written and eminently readable book summarizes many of the critical issues that have swirled about the "great debate," as well as updating Jeanne Chall's *Learning to Read: The Great Debate.* Adams comes down on the side of a balanced approach to reading instruction that manages to offend just about everybody who wants "their way" to be first, best, and only.

Balmuth, Miriam. *The Roots of Phonics.* New York: McGraw-Hill Book Company, 1982. This is a straightforward volume of history and scholarship. If you want to understand at what point in history we lost confidence in the alphabetic code, and the roles that Horace Mann and John Dewey played in its demise, check out this book.

Chall, Jeanne. *Learning to Read: The Great Debate.* New York: McGraw-Hill Book Company, 1967, 1983. Don't even bother with the first edition. The second edition is basically the same except for an updated summary. You will need to read this book as background (cultural literacy for educators if you will) to understand all of the subsequent discussion and argument that has ensued.

Flesch, Rudolph. *Why Johnny Can't Read.* New York: Harper, 1955, and *Why Johnny Still Can't Read: A New Look at the Scandal of Our Schools.* New York: Harper and Row, 1981. Both of these books are somewhat inflammatory and may raise your blood pressure, but they are instructive in understanding some of the political issues involved. They will definitely cause you to think.

Goodman, Ken. *What's Whole about Whole Language?* New York: Scholastic Press, 1986, and *Phonics Phacts.* New York: Scholastic Press, 1993. Goodman, a whole-language proponent, has written widely and his breezy, conversational style makes for interesting reading. Don't take someone else's word for what "whole-language" is; don't even think you already understand what it is; read what one of the founding fathers has to say.

Honig, Bill. *Teaching Our Children to Read: The Role of Skills in a Comprehensive Reading Program.* Thousand Oaks, CA: Corwin Press,

1996. Honig is on a mission to help educators remain research based while combining the best of both worlds—"a comprehensive, organized skill development and a literature driven and language rich language arts program" (vii). This is a readable book and an excellent desk resource.

Juel, Connie. *Learning to Read and Write in One Elementary School.* New York: Springer Verlag, 1994. This well-written book is an outstanding ethnographic study describing what it takes to bring the children of the poor to reading competency. The author believes that first-grade reading comprehension is almost always a matter of word recognition.

Routman, Regie. *Literacy at the Crossroads: Crucial Talk about Reading, Writing, and Other Teaching Dilemmas.* Portsmouth, NH: Heinemann, 1996. Routman is first a teacher and, because of her grounding in the realities and practicalities of making something work on a daily basis, brings a measure of common sense to the debate. Although Routman is a strong advocate for whole-language instruction, she also has a clear understanding of where it went wrong and what can be done to fix it. She is honest and plain speaking.

Smith, Frank. *Reading without Nonsense: Making Sense of Reading.* New York: Teachers College Press, 1985. Smith is a psycholinguist and, along with Kenneth Goodman, one of the guiding lights of the whole-language movement. If you hate research studies and citations, you'll love reading this book by Smith. He offers scarcely more than a page of suggestions for further reading and not a single footnote. If you want his technical discussions and supporting arguments, check out *Understanding Reading.* New York: Holt, Rinehart, & Winston, 1982.

Spalding, Romalda Bishop, and Walter T. Bishop. *The Writing Road to Reading.* New York: William Morrow & Company, 1990. If you don't really understand phonemic awareness and haven't a clue about what phonics really is, find this updated and revised classic from 1957 and read it. You'll be intrigued by what you find.

Education Websites

The following websites offer information, discussion, documents, and thought-provoking ideas about all of the education issues raised in this book. While each of the sites was operable and provided the indicated information at time of publication, let me make my apologies for any changes that may have occurred since then. Websites, unlike printed documents, are constantly under construction. They are moved to new locations or even shut down. Visiting a website is like going on a treasure hunt. Once you arrive at the location, you will often be pointed in a dozen different directions (links) that uncover further goodies. Plan to spend several hours exploring. When you find a particularly noteworthy site, don't forget to mark it with a "bookmark" so you can return to it quickly. I have identified sites that sell products and services by labeling it "commercial."

Included along with a brief description of what can be found on each website is the URL (Uniform Resource Locator). This is a standard address for anything on the Internet. A URL has three parts: 1) the name of the Internet protocol used (e.g., HTTP); 2) the name of the Internet host (e.g., www.edweek.org); and 3) the folders, if any, your browser has to go through to find the file you're looking for (e.g., /homepages/math man).

Nearly all of the URLs in this list are on the web and begin with HTTP, which stands for HyperText Transfer Protocol. This is the system by which information is transmitted on the web.

Please disregard any periods at the end of URLs in this list. URLs never have periods at the end. I have only included periods where necessary to make them part of a complete sentence.

ADVANCE Educational Spectrums
A commercial site offering products and services related to School-to-Work and SCANS (Secretary's Commission on Achieving Necessary Skills) for both education and business. Chosen in 1996 as a Technical Assistance Provider to the National School-to-Work Office of the United States Department of Education. Contains multiple links to workforce development sites, education sites, and government and grant resources sites. Visiting this site will make you aware of how School-to-Work is already creating its own set of consultants, workshops, and products.

http://www.advedspec.com/aesindex.htm

AMATH

Ward Woodruff's commercial remedial math program site. AMATH is a self-paced, computer driven, adult-level course designed as an intervention device to help those who have completed the course work in K-8 math but still cannot do the work. There's a 20-minute quiz to determine if you or your children could benefit from the course content of AMATH.

http://www.amath.com/index.html

America Reads Challenge

An initiative of the federal government under the Clinton administration that calls on all Americans to support teachers and help ensure that every American child can read well and independently by the end of third grade. This site describes the legislation, answers questions, and provides research and publication information.

http://www.ed.gov/inits/americareads/index.html

American Association of School Administrators

The professional organization for school superintendents. Particularly good source for tracking federal legislation relative to education.

http://www.aasa.org/

American Mathematical Society

Professional association for mathematicians. Contains two important reports prepared by AMS Committe to Comment on the NCTM Standards, referred to as NCTM2000.

http://www.ams.org/government/nctm2000.html

Arizona Parents for Traditional Education

Provides information on reading research and illustrates how activist parent Steve Goss is using the web to influence reading instruction. The group is based near where Kenneth Goodman teaches, which makes for an interesting perspective on the whole-language and phonics debate. The site contains articles from newspapers and magazines, and many interesting links.

http://www.theriver.com/Public/tucson_parents_edu_forum/

Block Scheduling Sources and Connections

This site was developed by parents in Flordia and is an outstanding source of research, information, and links related to block scheduling. If your community is considering block scheduling, this site is a must.

http://www.jbit.com/bs2.htm

The Case against Block Scheduling

This is another absolutely essential location to visit if you want a complete understanding of the implications of block scheduling in the high school. The site is maintained by Jeff Lindsay of Appleton, Wisconsin. It contains links to other sites as well as valuable student achievement research.

http://athnet.net/ ~jlindsay/Block.shtml#wronko

Center for Education Reform

National nonprofit education advocacy group and an active broker in school reform nationwide. Promotes school choice and charter schools and does a lot of grassroots work with schools and parents. Published "School Reform in the United States: State by State," an excellent guide to the educational reform movement. Contains many articles and news alerts.

http://www.edreform.com/

Center for the Future of Teaching and Learning

Contains an excellent synthesis of research on reading instruction from the National Institute of Child Health and Human Development.

http://www.cftl.org/

Center on Education and Work

Headquartered at the University of Wisconsin in Madison. Numerous articles and links to School-to-Work related topics.

http://www.cew.wisc.edu/

The Christian Conscience

Online publication dedicated to encouraging Christian believers to lead godly lives in the midst of a decadent culture. Features the writing of national authors and researchers such as Anita Hoge, Charlotte Iesrbyt, Dr. Dennis Cuddy, and Berit Kjos, and examines Outcome-Based Education, the New Age movement, and many other social/cultural issues. Provides articles and links to other sites.

http://www.netins.net/showcase/conscience

Core Knowledge Home Page

Contains a planned progression of specific knowledge covering history, geography, mathematics, science, and the arts for each grade level. Founded by E. D. Hirsch, author of *Cultural Literacy* and *The Schools We Need and Why We Don't Have Them,* the Core Knowledge Foundation is helping parents and teachers establish Core Knowledge schools around the country.

http://www.coreknowledge.org

Appendix D

Eagle Forum
An important site. Contains a wealth of information in easy-to-understand lanaguage. Includes articles on crucial issues like Outcome-Based Education and School-to-Work.

http://www.eagleforum.org/

Education Excellence Network
Sponsored by the Thomas B. Fordham Institute and the Hudson Institute. Visit this site regularly to check out postings of "This Week's Articles"—complete reprints of articles pertinent to educational reform. Chester Finn, Diane Ravitch, and Bruno Manno are regularly featured. Excellent articles, good links, and worthwhile information on standards and charter schools.

http://www.edexcellence.net

Education Reform Links
Contains links to topics in the areas of education reform that are currently of interest in Louisiana and across the United States. Great info on block scheduling, School-to-Work, and Certificate of Initial Mastery, along with a listing of websites of concerned parents from Maine to California. If you're thinking of creating your own website, check these out for ideas.

http://www.beaulib.dtx.net/ ~edu/

Education Week
Contains the entire archives of the *Education Week* newspaper since its inception. If you're looking for up-to-date education news, this is the place to find it.

http://www.edweek.org/

EdWeb Home Page
The place to find information on education reform as it relates to information technology. The *Harvard Educational Review* describes this site as "an intelligent, detailed, informed and practical guide to education related issues concerning the Internet and to educational resources on the World Wide Web." The K-12 Education Resource Guide and WWWEDU (pronounced "We Do"), an online discussion group that explores the role of the worldwide web in education, are especially noteworthy.

http://www.edweb.gsn.org

Electronic School
The quarterly technology magazine of the National School Boards Association. You can gain access to all of the articles from the current

print edition. Covers such issues as Internet safety and censorship.

    http://www.electronic-school.com

Empire State Task Force for Excellence in Educational Methods

Hours of reading with wonderful guest viewpoint articles and news reports. This site keeps the folk in New York state up-to-date. You shouldn't miss it either.

    http://www.netcom.com/~efny/esteem.html

Employment and Training Administration

Gain a sense of the spreading web of School-to-Work initiatives and job training programs.

    http://www.doleta.gov/

ERIC

Educational Resources and Information Clearinghouse websites are located on a variety of university campuses and each one covers a specific area of study. The ERIC Homepage (http://www.aspen sys.com/eric2/welcom/html) will give you access to all of the sites. The ERIC Elementary and Early Childhood site can be found at http://ericps.edu.uciuc.edu/ericeece.html. Resources and research about phonics and its use in the classroom can be located at the ERIC Clearinghouse on Reading, English, and Communication (http://www.indiana.edu/~eric_rec/ieo/bibs/phonics.html). The ERIC Clearinghouse on Assessment and Evaluation can be found here:

    http://www.cua.edu/www/eric_ae/

The Family Research Council

Research on pro-family issues. Articles, links, and copies of president Gary Bauer's latest monthly letter.

    http://www.frc.org/

HOLD

Stands for "Honest Open Logial Debate" on math reform. Founded in Palo Alto, California, in response to the introduction of fuzzy-math in that community. You can spend hours with the information and links on this site, and when you finish you'll be as concerned as the parents in Palo Alto.

    http://www.rahul.net/dehnbase/hold/

I Can Read

An example of what one concerned parent is doing in his area to respond to the lack of phonics instruction in the public schools. There are a variety of interesting links on this site as well as information about "direct instruction."

http://projectpro.com/icanread.htm

International Dyslexia Association

International, nonprofit, scientific, and educational organization dedicated to the study and treatment of dyslexia. The IDA was first established nearly 50 years ago to continue the pioneering work of Dr. Samuel T. Orton, who was one of the first to identify dyslexia and its remediation.

http://www.interdys.org/

The International Mathematics and Science Study (TIMSS)

Contains the results of the U.S. Department of Education's report "Pursuing Excellence: A Study of U.S. 12th Grade Mathematics & Science Achievement in International Context." 14 Feb. 1998.

http://nces.ed.gov/timss/

International Reading Association

Mission is to promote literacy. Supports a whole-language philosophy.

http://www.reading.org/

Japanese Math Challenge

Provides an opportunity to check out math problems translated from Japan's Junior High School math placement test given to twelve year olds. The 225 problems are logic-based and consist of about 20 different types of story problem. This commerical site is designed to provide American students with quality math content based on world standards. After you've worked the problems on the site, you can purchase more problems from Pacific Software Publishing.

http://www.japanese-online.com/math/index.htm

Kansas Education Watch Network

The network's primary objective is to secure the right and duty of parents to birth, nurture, teach, and provide for their own children in every way without unwarranted intervention of the state. You can sign up for the statewide Kansas conservative e-mail network, read articles about the Kansas Quality Performance Accreditation system, as well as be linked to sites on topics of interest to every parent.

http://www2.southwind.et/~kewnet

Kossor Education Newsletter

Published by Steve Kossor, the newsletter is featured on this web site along with dozens of articles and links to other sites.

http://www.voicenet.com/_sakossor

Lindamood-Bell Learning Processes
Offers information on the Phoneme Sequencing and the Visualizing-Verbalizing (reading comprehension) components of their program.
http://www.lblp.com

Mathematically Correct
A "must" visit for every parent and educator concerned about mathematics achievement in the United States. Prepare to spend an evening browsing this site. It is a gold mine.
http://www.mathematicallycorrect.com

National Center for Education Statistics
Collects and reports statistics and information showing the condition and progress of education in the United States and other nations in order to promote and accelerate the improvement of American education. You can access a variety of studies and reports; if you like statistics, this is the place for you.
http://nces.ed.gov/

National Center on Education and the Economy
The organization that brought us School-to-Work under the leadership of Marc Tucker. He started it all with his report: "A Human Resource Development Plan for the United States." Check out this report as well as "The Certificate of Initial Mastery: A Primer," "States Begin Developing the Certificate of Initial Mastery," and "Designing the New American High School."
http://www.ncee.org

National Council of Teachers of English
This is for teachers of English at all levels. The organization works to increase the effectiveness of instruction of English, language, and literature and to provide information and aids to teachers involved in formulating curriculum objectives. This organization strongly supports whole-language.
http://www.ncte.org/

National PTA
The National Parent Teacher Association is ostensibly a parent advocacy group. Check out this site to find out what agendas it is promoting before you send off your membership dues.
http://www.pta.org/

National Right to Read Foundation

Its mission is to return phonics and good literature to every school in the nation. There are a variety of interesting links on this site as well as materials for purchase.

http://www.jwor.com/nrrf.htm

National School Boards Association

Lots of information about schools from the insiders' perspective. Check out "Connecting with the Community" materials about school boards developed specifically for parents.

http://www.nsba.org/

Parents for Improved Education in Fairfax County

This is another example of how concerned parents are questioning the state of reading instruction. There is an especially interesting analysis of the three reading programs used in the Fairfax County (VA) Public Schools.

http://www.geocities.com/capitolhill/9155/

Parents Raising Education Standards in Schools

Nonprofit, statewide organization that addresses with a national perspective educational concerns in Wisconsin. Good articles and information coordinated by PRESS president and activist Leah Vukmir.

http://www.execpc.com/~presswis/

Riggs Institute

Nonprofit organization that promotes the teaching of phonics. Lots of information and links to other phonics sites.

http://www.riggsinst.org

Saxon Publishers, Inc.

Commercial website featuring the Saxon math materials that are widely used by homeschoolers and public schools tired of fuzzy-math. The site includes a diagnostic math test designed for students in fourth to eighth grades.

http://www.saxonpub.com

School-to-Career

The programs, plans, and documents of the California version of School-to-Work.

http://www.stc.cahwnet.gov/

Spalding Education Foundation

Founded by Romalda Spalding to ensure that her teaching methodologies and philosophies might be used by the widest number of educators. The Spalding Method is a multisensory, integrated total language arts approach validated by current research on the way children learn to read. The site provides a description of the Spalding Method of reading instruction and supporting research. Visitors to the website are also able to view a catalog and order materials.

http://www.spalding.org

Special Education Resources on the Internet
A collection of Internet-accessible information resources of interest to those involved in fields related to special education.

http://www.hood.edu/seri/

Surfing the Education Waves
Sponsored by the Thomas B. Fordham Foundation. If you have a limited amount of time to browse, go here first. It's organized into four categories: Organizations, Think Tanks, Federal & State Government Sites, and Publications.

http://www.edexcellence.net/surfing/surfing.htm

TAGFAM (Talented and Gifted Families)
Contains information for parents of gifted students on how to deal with schools.

http://www.access.digex.net/~king/tagfam.html

Tangled Web
An amazing chronology of School-to-Work put together by Joe Esposito who got his education while sitting on the Oklahoma School-to-Work Executive Council.

http://www.ionet.net/~study/tang.htm

Tennisons' Home Page
Describes the experiences of Bob and Barbara Tennison of Cottage Grove, Oregon. They have been on the forefront of educational activism in their state fighting Outcome-Based Education and School-to-Work. Excellent articles and great links. This site provides an interesting peek into the future for those who live in states where the reforms the Tennisons have been fighting in Oregon are only now arriving.

http://www.rstenison.com

Texas Alternative Document
A marvelous set of language arts curriculum standards written by a group of educators who objected to the "official" version, the Texas Essential Knowledge and Skills (TEKS), which can be viewed at

http://www.tea.state.tx.us/teks. Both documents are comprehensive and worth examining as you consider what you want your students to know when they leave your school. A Harvard professor who helped write the Massachusetts standards described the Texas Alternative Document as "the finest standards document in the country."

http://www.htcomp.net/tad

Texas Education Consumers Association
The story of tireless education activist Jeanne Donovan and her involvement in reform in Texas. Includes a variety of interesting links.

http://www.fastlane.net/ ~eca

United States Department of Education
Contains the agenda of the President and Secretary of Education along with research and statistics, publications and products, and links to other sites.

http://www.ed.gov/

Where's the Math?
Created by the parents of Petaluma, California, in response to their district's adoption of the Mathland program.

http://www.intres.com/math/

More Tales from the Trenches

Whole-Language at the Fork in the Road

Cathy Froggatt
Parent
The National Right to Read State Director

The purpose of this satire is to paint a clear picture of the anguish experienced by hundreds of thousands of young Americans as they advance through and leave school ill equipped to handle the very real demands and requirements of school and life beyond:

One day Dr. Goodguess died. The Gatekeeper to the afterlife told him that before entering the afterlife, he, like everyone, would be granted one wish to change one thing about his previous life on earth.

"What a wonderful surprise!" Dr. Goodguess exclaimed "My greatest regret in life was that I didn't learn to read with whole-language. As you undoubtedly know," he said. "I 'mainstreamed' that philosophy into nearly every classroom in the English-speaking world."

"Your wish is granted," responded the Gatekeeper. "From this moment on, you will find that your brain has been altered. Now you will read the whole-language way. You must now travel down the path you see before you for a short distance. There you will find a fork in the road. One path leads to Perdition, the other to Paradise. Signs are posted that clearly mark the paths. Choose carefully, because once you have chosen a path to travel, you can never turn back."

Dr. Goodguess marched off confidently until he reached the fork in the road. The left fork was marked with a sign that said "Perdition." The road to the right said "Paradise."

As he stood there, a look of puzzlement and then worry spread over his face. He scratched his head and thought, *They both start with 'P,' now what do I do? I've always been a risk-taker but this is a frightfully important decision. I cannot make a mistake.*

Just then, another founder of whole-language, Dr. Sample, died and stood before the Gatekeeper. "The hallmark of my life," he told the Gatekeeper with pride, "was the widespread influence my theories have had on reading instruction. I only wish that I had actually learned to read in a manner consistent with my theories: you know . . . naturally . . . without having to be forced to learn those low-level phonics sub-skills."

His wish was immediately granted, and in a moment he joined Dr. Goodguess at the fork in the road. "Thank goodness you're here, Dr. Sampler," exclaimed Dr. Goodguess. "I am in dire need of some cooperative learning."

"Why, Dr. Goodguess, what is the matter? You look very distraught! What has happened to your self-esteem?"

"Well, Dr. Sampler, it's these darn words-in-isolation. You'd think there would be at least one picture clue somewhere!"

"Hmm, I see what you mean, Dr. Goodguess. Oh, no! Both signs have words that start with the same letter, and the words are about the same length." As they stood pondering their dilemma, the earthly life of a College Professor of Education came to an end. As Professor Indoctrinate stood before the Gatekeeper, she stated with a rather high degree of confidence: "I have been completely happy with my earthly life. The life of a tenured professor, with the academic freedom it brings, was near perfect bliss. I wouldn't have changed a thing."

"So be it," said the Gatekeeper, "but I'm afraid the fork in the road ahead is becoming choked with people. Perhaps you can assist them by bringing this 'context clue' to help them decide which path to take." With that, the Gatekeeper gave her a sign that said: "Pandemonium.*" "Take this sign with you and place it at the left fork in the path. Do you understand?"

"Certainly," said Dr. Indoctrinate, and she did as she was asked.

Needless to say, Drs. Goodguess and Sampler were delighted to see help coming, but they were immediately confounded when they found themselves with yet another *P* word.

Professor Indoctrinate, unwilling to provide any phonics information due to her thorough disdain for such "lower order subskills," encouraged Drs. Goodguess and Sampler to use the Whole-Language cueing system they knew so well. In an attempt to reassure them, she said, "Don't be upset if you can't read the signs just yet. After all, reading is developmental. In time it will all begin to click, maybe next year or the year after."

Now they knew they were in need of a "real" reading expert, particularly one who had been intensely trained, preferably at

*Pandemonium is the capital of Hell in Milton's *Paradise Lost.*

Ohio State. So without hesitation, even though their self-esteem was becoming badly damaged, Drs. Goodguess and Sampler fell to their knees and began praying loudly. As if on cue, a Reading Recovery teacher appeared on the pathway.

At first she was a bit intimidated to be in the presence of the founders of whole-language. After all, she knew quite well that Reading Recovery owed its very existence to the theories and strategies taught by these experts.

Fortunately, her extensive training allowed her to quickly regain her composure and to focus on the reading problems the gentlemen were experiencing. "I am sure I need not remind you, gentlemen," she began, "that comprehension and meaning-making are of primary importance when reading a word you have not seen before. You must just answer the question: 'What would make sense here?'"

With the path behind them filling up with people impatiently awaiting their turn to pass through the fork, Drs. Goodguess and Sampler cried out in despair, "What we desperately need is more context!"

Just then they heard the soft voice of a child. A little six-year-old boy walked up to them, looked at the sign on the right and said with great pride, "I was taught to read with explicit, systematic phonics. I can sound out any word. The sign on the right says 'Paradise' and that's the way I'm going." And off he went.

Drs. Goodguess and Sampler looked at each other with knowing smirks. Their need for context had surely been met. Dr. Goodguess whispered excitedly, "Did you hear him say 'explicit, systematic phonics'? The path he took must be the road to Perdition! Quickly now, let's take the other path!"

Where Are the Disciplines in Interdisciplinary Instruction?

Stephen Kern
Parent
Professor of History

Dr. Kern wrote this letter to the editor of the local newspaper upon reading an article in the newspaper that a neighboring school district was planning to become a part of the Basic School Network. The network is a project of the Carnegie Foundation. It began with sixteen schools from various parts of the country and is now up to nearly thirty. The network's vision of a school community is one in which all subjects are interrelated through eight "universal topics" that are common to all people. Although the name implies a focus on traditional skill-based education with traditional values, such is not the case. Dr. Kern's letter will explain.

Dear Editor,

I am deeply troubled by a recent letter suggesting that the ABC School District join the Basic School Network in which "all subjects are interrelated, community service is emphasized, and the curriculum includes integrity and honesty." For lack of space I concentrate on the first goal.

It is impossible to interrelate all subjects; that's why we have disciplines, which make it possible to focus on logical divisions of human experience. They go back to antiquity, and they are the foundation for learning. The current fad of interdisciplinary instruction, also the rage in my city, may create an inspired combination of subjects with one or two energetic teachers, but such a unique pedagogical concoction cannot be reproduced from teacher to teacher or from generation to generation, and so it cannot be the basis of a coherent, sequential education. The conventional disciplines are the basis of all classification and codification of knowledge.

Libraries, university departments, scholarly journals, research institutes, textbooks, most high school courses (and transcripts), college courses, professions, and the entire history of thought are organized according to these classifications. Tampering with them will create educational and professional chaos.

I was particularly disturbed by the arrogance and lack of foundation for the listing of "eight universal topics that are common to all people: life cycle, sense of time and space, use of symbols, membership in groups, producing and consuming, connection to nature, appreciation of aesthetic, and living with a purpose." I believe there are universals, and I've spent thirty years writing histories of them, but during my research I selected my universals with extreme care, and I would never have the audacity to suggest that I found the basic eight. By what authority does anyone pose these eight as universals and then propose to organize children's education around them? I find these topics to be capricious and of dubious universality. "Life cycle" is vague. "Time and space" ground the others. "Living with a purpose" is moralizing. "Membership in groups" overlaps with "producing and consuming," and recent scholarship has emphasized how consumption is emphatically historical, not universal. Why these eight? Are there rigorous philosophical criteria for this selection or did some overpaid "change agent" pick them out of a hat?

Don't be fooled. The Basic School Movement is not about developing basic skills or grounding education on truly basic concepts, but about presenting a distinctly nonuniversal moral and political agenda under the guise of universal concepts.

Against the specific suggestion that time and space are good topics around which to organize education, I offer myself as an expert. I spent ten years writing *The Culture of Time and Space: 1880-1918,* which is documented with sources from many disciplines. Over the past ten years it has been assigned in over a hundred colleges in many departments—history, literature, art, architecture, science, sociology, geography, photography, and communications as well as many interdisciplinary courses. In private moments I have fantasized about history departments reorganizing the study of history around changing conceptions of time and space and related "basic topics," but wisdom prevailed, and I realized that to do so would create chaos for students, who have to relate their understanding of history to the conventional dividers of human experience according to which history has been organized for centuries. There are no "time and space" history textbook chapters, journals, college departments, or sections in libraries. Nor are there job openings for "time and space experts." A single college course might be organized creatively around time and space, but these topics cannot work as one out of eight on which to base the education of children from the earliest years.

The interdisciplinary thinking that grounds the Basic School Network is flawed for two reasons. First, as the basis for its intellectually liberating function it assumes that the conventional disciplines are air-tight boxes that artificially divide experience, but in fact every discipline is itself richly interdisciplinary. For example, a narrowly focused event in military history such as the bombing of Hiroshima involves understanding political, social, economic, military, and diplomatic history as well as atomic physics, trauma psychology, the Cold War, and radiation sickness. Since the disciplines are already interdisciplinary, why take a crow bar to the well-tested, logical divisions that enable us to find the sources that are necessary for understanding that interdisciplinary experience? If I need a history of aerial bombing or war medicine, I must be able to find it, and that investigation will be impossible if scholars do not stay at home in conventional disciplines and write about experience in a way that is thematically familiar. I would not be able to find information as efficiently if early education and the higher learning that presumably will derive from it are based on the Basic School Network "big eight."

Secondly, there is no need to strain to inculcate interdisciplinary thinking at the curriculum level, because that function is already built into the human mind. Human beings are interdisciplinary entities who are constantly unifying disparate information. But that information must be located in conventional categories so that people can find and absorb that information. The Basic School Network is a bad idea because it will make that access and absorption unnecessarily difficult, and so I urge ABC District not to adopt it.

The runaway interdisciplinary movement can only create confusion out of the elegant division of thought and experience that has been crafted throughout history. No matter how hard curriculum experts try, the clarity and intelligence of that division will prevail, even if a generation of children is sacrificed along the way. Our children's miraculous minds will continue struggling to interrelate whatever interdisciplinary piffle is presented in their classrooms. To the interdisciplinary zealots who are imperiling their education, I say try living in a house with the toilet in the kitchen.

Sincerely,
Dr. Stephen Kern

The Educrats' Alphabet

Continued from Chapter 2

L is for License to change the rules—as soon as anyone spots loopholes we missed.

M is for Money-Money-Money, the trinity we worship.

N is for Never, Never deviate from our intended path unless we set the parameters of the deviation.

O is for Outcome-Based Education in all its varied costumes; and also for Obfuscation when asked to explain what OBE is and why outcomes are so vague . . .

P is for Pilot Programs and the Public Relations we generate to ensure their immediate, Pre-Planned success.

Q is for quick; have the vote before "they" get to the meeting.

R is for the 4 R's we must never allow back in schools: Real Readin', Real Writin', Real 'rithmetic; and any Religion which objects to social agendas or promiscuous behaviors.

S is for the new 21st century paradigm: The Three S's: Sex Ed, Surveys, and Snow Jobs.

T is for Tell politicians what they want to hear; Tell parents and taxpayers to get lost; also for requiring students to Tell all personal details they can dredge up about parents, families, and home life.

U is for Unless you cooperate, we'll label your kids "At Risk."

V is for Visions of sugar candy perfection, dangled before every budget and bond vote, only to evaporate shortly thereafter.

W is for Write reports and books intended for Royal We; not the peasant parents and taxpayers.

X is for marking the spot where we used to stand, before anyone deciphered any of our buzzwords.

Y is for You'll never find out where our frivolous expenses are buried or how large the real total is.

Z is for Zilch in curriculum content, to ensure the need for lifelong learning, directed by educrats, of course.

An Insider's View of Cooperative Learning

Marie Becker
Student

One of the hottest buzzwords in education nowadays is "cooperative learning." The theory behind these group projects is that this teaches us how to work together, especially with people we wouldn't necessarily choose ourselves, and helps us learn cooperation and leadership. As these projects very often involve a class presentation, we will also improve our verbal skills and encourage creativity. Research is often needed, so we get to review those very necessary skills, too, right?

Sorry. It just doesn't work that way, at least not in my experience. In my entire life I have not had a pleasant, useful experience with a group project in the everyday classroom. In fact, I have had many miserable experiences with them.

As a student who is considered academically gifted, I pressure myself to get excellent grades. One of my main objections to group projects stems from that. I've simply spent too much time and energy trying to salvage projects and make peace among group members for the sake of an A or at least a passing grade. Also, because I am considered to be gifted and get good grades, I have had the very unpleasant and discouraging experience of realizing group members are perfectly content to leave me all the work—I'll probably do a great job, right? My experience has been that a lot of kids just don't care about learning, grades, or cooperation. I am deeply disturbed by the feeling that to save my own grade, I have to cover for them.

Some kids care a little more, but many of them don't pay attention in class, don't listen, are easily distracted, and simply haven't developed adequate work habits. This past weekend I worked on a science project with two girls who had this problem (a third girl simply didn't show up). Even though I was absent the day the project was assigned, I had to infer what was wanted since no one could explain it to me. I spent hours trying to explain the concepts we have studied since the first week of school, which, I discovered today when we began our presentation, they still don't get. I phrased ideas, spelled words, designed the visual aids, tried to explain tactfully why certain ideas were just wrong, and did almost everything else. However, in my attempts not to be bossy, I realized that I didn't give the girls enough structure. The presentation was messy and disorganized, with enormous errors and poorly planned and designed games.

This brings me to a problem I've had a lot of trouble with. Like many middle-school students, I find the lines between being a leader and being bossy to be blurry and, as a result, I'm scared to take charge. In fourth grade I had a terrible experience with this while working on a project with four other people. Absences had made it impossible for us to complete the project in school, so I spent a weekend desperately trying to pull things together. Only one girl made time to work, so I did my best to organize our presentation, again without seeming bossy. In class, our presentation started to crumble and I took over, since no one else in the group seemed willing to do so. I corrected errors, made suggestions, and tried to pull stuff together in an organized, interesting way. For my efforts, I got yelled at by my teacher for trying to take over and exclude other people; during a class wrap-up of the activity, she didn't discuss poor organization or how important it is that people follow through. She talked about being too bossy, and someone said that it was the GRC (Gifted Resource Center) kids who took over.

Now I know it was silly to let that affect me as much as it has over the past three years. After all, I reasoned, if a teacher, an educated, fair, authoritative person, thought that and encouraged other people to think that, did everyone see me that way? Was it wrong to try to correct errors, help people come up with creative ideas, try to keep people on task? Apparently so. By now I know that many people think of me as a fair, intelligent, and organized person, so I feel a little better about taking charge, but that teacher's words still affect me.

Many gifted kids I know also question the value of group projects, as do some parents. The only truly positive experience most of us have had with group projects has been through GRC. I realize that in my life I may often have to work with disorganized people who really aren't focused or particularly interested in the outcome of a project. But why should it be necessary for me to spend valuable time trying to teach someone how to use the card catalog, take notes, or go over what we did in class? And be nice and tactful about it, too? It's not fun.

I firmly believe that every complaint carries more weight when some kind of alternative to it is proposed. These are my suggestions for alternatives. First, the most important is to teach us how to work in groups. Most of us have been doing group projects since first or second grade, but a lot of people just haven't picked up cooperative learning skills yet. If someone hasn't learned by doing after all this time, they're not likely to learn it all of a sudden. Give us some basic techniques and procedures to use for every group project which we can use for the rest of our lives. For example, choose a leader. The way I see it, a leader should be fair, organized, a good listener but able to make decisions. If the group can't decide on one in ten minutes, pick a name out of a hat or have the teacher choose. Once work has started, we shouldn't argue about anything for more than ten minutes. If two people have different ideas, each gets five minutes to make a case, then the group should vote. In the event of a tie, the leader decides. Tell us what we can do if people don't follow through. The present system of doing group projects doesn't help anyone, neither the more academically talented nor the less academically talented.

Second, work should be divided among all group members. It isn't fair for some students to spend hours agonizing over whether they seem too bossy or whether the teacher will lower grades if group members argue. Students should know they won't be blamed for others' incompetence, lack of interest, or lack of responsibility to make the group project a success.

Whatever is necessary must be done in our school settings to ensure that the terms "cooperative learning" and "working together" mean just that.

Bibliography

Adams, Marilyn. *Beginning to Read: Thinking and Learning about Print.* Cambridge, MA: MIT Press, 1990.

Addison-Wesley. *Secondary Math: An Integrated Approach: Focus on Algebra.* Reading, MA: Addison-Wesley, 1997.

Adler, Jerry. "The Tutor Age." *Newsweek* 30 Mar. 1998: 48.

American Federation of Teachers. "True Standards That Parents Can Use" 6 Oct. 1996, online. Available: http://www.mathematicallycorrect.com

Archer, Jeff. "Students' Fortunes Rest with Assigned Teacher." *Education Week* 18 Feb. 1998: 3.

Barbera, Anne. "Here's How to Lobby Your Elected Representative." *Not with My Child You Don't: A Citizens' Guide to OBE and Restoring Education.* Ed. Robert Holland. Richmond, VA: Chesapeake Capital Services, 1996. 10.12-10.14.

Beard, Charles. *The Unique Function of Education in American Democracy.* Washington, DC: National Educational Association, 1937.

Beck, Joan. "Let Bright Pupils Move Ahead, Even If It Seems Unfair." *Chicago Tribune* 8 Feb. 1998: A13.

Benne, Kenneth. "Democratic Ethics in Social Engineering." *Progressive Education* 26.7 (May 1949): 201-7.

Bennet, Christine. *Comprehensive Multicultural Education.* Boston: Allyn and Bacon, 1990.

Berliner, David, and Bruce J. Biddle. *The Manufactured Crisis: Myths, Fraud, and the Attack on America's Public Schools.* Reading, MA: Addison-Wesley, 1995.

Bernstein, Richard. *The Dictatorship of Virtue: Multiculturalism and the Battle for America's Future.* New York: Knopf, 1994.

Bestor, Arthur. *Educational Wastelands: The Retreat from Learning in Our Public Schools.* Urbana, IL: Univ. of Illinois Press, 1953.

Bloom, Alan. *The Closing of the American Mind.* New York: Simon and Schuster, 1987.

Bloom, Benjamin. *All Our Children Learning: A Primer for Parents, Teachers, and Other Educators.* New York: McGraw-Hill, 1981.

Blumenfeld, Samuel. *The Whole Language/OBE Fraud: The Shocking Story of How America Is Being Dumbed Down by Its Own Educational System.* Boise, ID: Paradigm Company, 1996.

Bode, Boyd H. *Progressive Education at the Crossroads.* New York: Newson & Co., 1938.

Boschee, Floyd and Mark A. Baron. *Outcome-Based Education: Developing Programs through Strategic Planning.* Lancaster, PA: Technomic Publishing Co., 1993.

Bradley, Ann. "Educated Consumers." *Education Week* 26 Mar. 1997: 33.

_____. "Groups Outline Steps to Boost Reading, Math." *Education Week* 4 Feb. 1998: 1.

Brandt, Ron. "On Outcome-Based Education: A Conversation with Bill Spady." *Educational Leadership* Dec. 1992/Jan. 1993: 66-70.

Brederkamp, Sue, ed. *Developmentally Appropriate Practice in Early Childhood Programs Serving Children from Birth through Age 8.* Washington, DC: National Association for the Education of Young Children, 1988.

Brennan, Jacqueline, and Martin G. Brooks. *In Search of Understanding: The Case for Constructivist Classrooms.* Alexandria, VA: Association for Supervision and Curriculum Development, 1993.

Bruner, Jerome. *The Process of Education.* Cambridge, MA: Harvard Univ. Press, 1963.

Brunner, Michael. *Retarding America: The Imprisonment of Potential.* Portland, OR: Halcyon House, 1993.

Burns, Douglas. "Ames Parents Angry Over Drop in Basic Math Skills." *The Daily Tribune* [Ames, IA] 21 Feb. 1995: A1.

Byrne, Dennis. "No Winners—and No Losers." *Chicago Sun Times* 8 Feb. 1998: 35.

California State Board of Education. *Math Frameworks.* Sacramento, CA: California State Board of Education, 1992.

Carpenter, B., ed. *Reading Recovery Task Force Report.* San Diego, CA: San Diego County Office of Education, 1996.

Chall, Jeanne. *Learning to Read: The Great Debate.* New York: McGraw-Hill, 1967, 1983.

Chamberlain, Jenny. "Our Illiteracy: Reading the Writing on the Wall." *North and South Magazine* [Auckland, New Zealand] June 1993: 67-76.

Chamberlin, Leslie, and Ricardo Girona. "Our Children Are Changing." *Educational Leadership* 33.5 (Jan. 1976): 301-5.

Cheney, Lynne V. "The Latest Education Disaster: Whole Math." *The Weekly Standard* 4 Aug. 1997: 25-29.

_____. *Telling the Truth: A Report on the State of the Humanities in Higher Education*. Washington, D.C.: National Endowment for the Humanities, 1992. Government Document 92-0609-P.

Cizek, Gregory J. "S.A.T. 'Recentering': Baby Boomers Get a Break." *Education Week* 21 Sept. 1994, online. Available: http://www.edweek.org/

Clay, Marie. *Becoming Literate: The Construction of Inner Control*. Portsmouth, NH: Heinemann, 1991.

Colburn, Evangeline. *A Library for Intermediate Grades*. Chicago, IL: Laboratory Schools of the University of Chicago, 1930.

Collins, James. "How Johnny Should Read." *Time* 27 Oct. 1997: 78-81.

Concerned Women for America. *Outcome-Based Education: Remaking Your Children through Radical Educational Reform*. Washington, DC: Concerned Women for America, n.d.

Cornell, Dan. "Some Teaching Methods Are Nonsense." *Kingsport Times-News* [TN] 22 Oct. 1997: 9A.

Cortes, Ernesto, Jr. "Making the Public the Leaders in Education Reform." *Education Week* online, 22 Nov. 1995. Available: http://www.edweek.org/

Counts, George S. *Dare the School Build a New Social Order*. 1932; New York: Arno Press, 1969.

Craig, Susan, and Ann Haggart. *Inclusion: A Teacher's Guide*. Hampton, NH: AGH Associates, 1993.

Cuban, Larry. "A Tale of Two Schools: How Progressives and Traditionalists Undermine our Understanding of What Is 'Good' in Schools." *Education Week* 28 Jan. 1998: 33.

Cuddy, Dennis. "We Should Not Respect All Views." *American Commentary*. Oklahoma City, OK: Hearthstone Publishing, 1993.

Cunningham, Ann E., and Keith E. Stanovich. "Early Reading Acquisition and Its Relation to Reading Experience and Ability 10 Years Later." *Developmental Psychology* 33.6 (Nov. 1997): 934-45.

Custred, Glynn. "Onward to Adequacy." *Academic Questions*. Summer 1990.

Dewey, John. *Democracy and Education.* New York: Macmillan, 1916.

Diegmueller, Karen. "California Plotting New Tack on Language Arts." *Education Week* 14 June 1995, online. Available: http://www.edweek.org/

_____. "The Best of Both Worlds." *Education Week.* March 20, 1996, 33.

_____. "S.A.T. to Realign Scores for the First Time in Half a Century." *Education Week* 22 June 1994, online. Available: http://www.edweek.org/

Dietz, Diane. "Students Get Real Work Lessons." *Eugene Register Guard* [OR] 29 Dec. 1997: 1C.

Donohue, John W. "'Goals 2000: Educate America Act': Notes for a Chronicle." *America* 170.21 (18 June 1994): 61-63.

Doyle, Denis. "Issue." *Update* 36.8 (Oct. 1994). Alexandria, VA: Association for Supervision and Curriculum Development.

D'Souza, Dinesh. *Illiberal Education: The Politics of Race and Sex on Campus.* New York: The Free Press, 1991.

Durden, William G. "Where Is the Middle Ground? When Educational Either/Ors Hold Sway, Judgment Can Yield to Advocacy." *Education Week* 4 Oct. 1995: 48.

Editor. "National Testing Is No Magic Bullet." *Investors Business Daily.* 3 Sept. 1997: A32.

Editorial Projects in Education. "Public Agenda: Reality Check." *Quality Counts: '98 The Urban Challenge: Public Education in the 50 States* (Washington, DC: Editorial Projects in Education, 1998): 72-75.

Farney, Dennis. "For Peggy McIntosh, 'Excellence Can Be a Dangerous Concept.'" *Wall Street Journal* 14 June 1997: A1, A5.

Finn, Chester. "Testimony to the National Assessment Governing Board," online. Available: http://www.mathematicallycorrect.com

_____. *We Must Take Charge: Our Schools and Our Future.* New York: The Free Press, 1991.

Flesch, Rudolph. *Why Johnny Can't Read.* New York: Harper and Row, 1955.

Foorman, Barbara, et al. "The Role of Instruction in Learning to Read: Preventing Failure in At-Risk Children." *Journal of Educational Psychology* 90:37-55.

Bibliography

Gardner, Howard. *Frames of Mind: The Theory of Multiple Intelligences.* New York: BasicBooks, 1983.

_____. "Low Scores Are No Disgrace." *New York Times* 2 Mar. 1998: A19.

_____. *Multiple Intelligences: The Theory into Practice.* New York: BasicBooks, 1991.

_____. *The Unschooled Mind: How Children Think and How Schools Should Teach.* New York: BasicBooks, 1991.

Glasser, William. *Schools without Failure.* New York: Harper and Row, 1969.

Goodman, Ken. *What's Whole in Whole Language?* Exeter, NH: Heinemann, 1986.

Gray, William S. *On Their Own in Reading.* 2nd ed. Chicago: Scott, Foresman, 1948.

Groff, Patrick. Letter to the Editor. *Education Week* 3 Aug. 1994, online. Available: http://www.edweek.org/

_____. "Teachers' Opinions of the Whole Language Approach to Reading Instruction." *Annals of Dyslexia* 41 (1991): 83-95.

Grossen, Bonnie. "Making Research Serve the Profession." *American Educator* 20.3 (Fall 1996): 7-8, 22-27.

_____. "30 Years of Research: What We Now Know about How Children Learn to Read," online. Santa Cruz, CA: Center for the Future of Teaching and Learning. Available: http://www.cftl.org/reading.html

Grossen, Bonnie, et al. "Reading Recovery: An Evaluation of Benefits and Costs." *Effective School Practices* 15.3: 6-24.

Gurren, Louise, and Ann Hughes. "Intensive Phonics vs. Gradual Phonics in Beginning Reading." *A Review Journal of Educational Research* 58: 339-46.

Hambleton, Ronald K., et al. *Review of the Measurement Quality of the Kentucky Instructional Results Information System.* Frankfort, KY: Office of Education Accountability, 1995.

Hansen, Barbara J., and Philip English Mackey. *Your Public Schools: What You Can Do to Help Them.* North Haven, CT: Catbird Press, 1993.

Hayes, Donald P., and Loreen T. Wolfer. "Was the Decline in SAT Verbal Scores Caused by Simplified Textbooks?" Manuscript prepared for the *Journal of Educational Research* 31 Aug. 1993.

Hedges, William, and Marian Martinello. "What Schools Might Do: Some Alternatives for the Here and Now." Ed. Louise Berman and Jessie Roderick. *Feeling, Valuing and the Art of Growing: Insights into the Affective.* Washington, DC: Association for Supervision and Curriculum Development, 1977: 229-247.

Hirsch, E. D. *The Schools We Need and Why We Don't Have Them.* New York: Doubleday, 1996.

_____. *What Your Kindergartner Needs to Know: Fundamentals of a Good Kindergarten Education.* New York: Doubleday, 1996.

_____. *What Your 1st Grader Needs to Know: Fundamentals of a Good First Grade Education.* New York: Doubleday, 1991.

_____. *What Your 2nd Grader Needs to Know: Fundamentals of a Good Second Grade Education.* New York: Doubleday, 1991.

_____. *What Your 3rd Grader Needs to Know: Fundamentals of a Good Third Grade Education.* New York: Doubleday, 1992.

_____. *What Your 4th Grader Needs to Know: Fundamentals of a Good Fourth Grade Education.* New York: Doubleday, 1992.

_____. *What Your 5th Grader Needs to Know: Fundamentals of a Good Fifth Grade Education.* New York: Doubleday, 1993.

_____. *What Your 6th Grader Needs to Know: Fundamentals of a Good Sixth Grade Education.* New York: Doubleday, 1993.

Holden, Greg. *Publishing on the World Wide Web.* Indianapolis, IN: Hayden Books, 1995.

Holland, Robert. *Not with My Child You Don't: A Citizens' Guide to Eradicating OBE and Restoring Education.* Richmond, VA: Chesapeake Capital Services, 1996.

_____. "Stealth Takeover of Education?" *Washington Times* 8 Feb. 1994.

Holt, John. *Escape from Childhood.* New York: E. P. Dutton, 1974.

_____. *The Underachieving School.* New York: Pitman Publishing Corporation, 1969.

Howse, Brannon. *Reclaiming a Nation at Risk: The Battle for Your Faith, Family, and Freedoms.* Chandler, AZ: Bridgestone Multimedia Group, 1995.

Huey, Edmund Burke. *The Psychology and Pedagogy of Reading.* New York: Macmillan, 1908.

Huizinga, David. *Program of Research on the Causes and Correlates of Delinquency, Urban Delinquency and Substance Abuse.* Washington, D.C.: U.S. Department of Justice, 1991.

Hunter, James Davison. *Culture Wars: The Struggle to Define America.* New York: BasicBooks, 1991.

Iacovelli, Karen. "Splendor in the Grassroots." *Crisis in Education* Feb. 1998: 60.

Innerst, Carol. "Students Fall Behind All Along the Way." *Washington Times* 20 Oct. 1997: A1.

Innes, Richard. "Did Kentucky Ever Score 'At the Bottom' of the National Assessment of Educational Progress?" Unpublished manuscript, 9 Dec. 1997.

Interactive Mathematics: Activities and Investigations. New York: Glencoe/McGraw-Hill, 1995.

Janey, Clifford B. "Seeking Customer Satisfaction." *Education Week* 1 Oct. 1997: 39.

Jennings, Marianne Moody. "MTV Math Doesn't Add Up." *Wall Street Journal* 17 Dec. 1996.

Jennings, Marianne Moody. "A Test Is Not Necessarily a Test." *Arizona Republic* 12 Jan. 1997. Portions of the text that did not appear in the newspaper are reprinted with permission of the author, online, Arizona Parents for Traditional Education. Available: http://www.theriver.com/ Public/tucson_parents_edu_forum/

Johnson, David, Roger Johnson, and Edythe Holubec. *Cooperation in the Classroom.* Edina, MN: Interaction Book Company, 1988.

Kagan, Robert. "A Relic of the New Age: The National Education Association." *American Spectator* Feb. 1982: 14-18.

Kaufman, Jonathan. "Suburban Parents Shun Many Public Schools, Even the Good Ones." *Wall Street Journal* 1 Mar. 1996: A1, A6.

Kilpatrick, William Heard. *Foundations of Method.* New York: The Macmillan Company, 1925.

Kliebard, Herbert H. *Success and Failure in Educational Reform: Are There Historical Lessons?* East Lansing, MI: The Holmes Group, 1989.

Kohn, Alfie. *No Contest: The Case Against Competition.* Boston: Houghton Mifflin Company, 1986.

_____. "Only for My Kid: How Privileged Parents Undermine School Reform." *Phi Delta Kappan* Apr. 1998: 570.

_____. *Punished by Rewards: The Trouble with Gold Stars, Incentive Plans, A's, Praise and Other Bribes*. New York: Houghton Mifflin, 1993.

Kulik, James, and Chen-Lin Kulik. *Research on Ability Grouping: Historical and Contemporary Perspective*. Ann Arbor: Univ. of Michigan Press, 1991.

Lally, Kathy, and Debbie M. Price. "The Brain Reads Sound by Sound." *Baltimore Sun* online, 3 Nov. 1997. Available: http://www.read-ingb9.com/

Lauchner, A. H. "How Can the Junior High Curriculum Be Improved?" *Bulletin of the National Association of Secondary School Principals* 35.177 (Mar. 1951): 299-300.

Lawton, Millicent. "Calif. Education Officials Approve Back to Basics Standards in Math." *Education Week* online, 14 Jan. 1998. Available: http://www.edweek.org/

Learn, Scott. "Reynolds Gives Maverick Teacher Two Years for Reading Experiment." *The Oregonian* 23 Oct. 1997: 1, 8.

Ledell, Marjorie, and Arleen Arnsparger. *How to Deal with Community Criticism of School Change*. Alexandria, VA: Association for Supervision and Curriculum Development, 1993.

Lefkowitz, Mary. *Not Out of Africa: How Afrocentrism Became an Excuse to Teach Myth as History*. New York: BasicBooks, 1996.

Levine, Art. "The Great Debate Revisited." *Atlantic Monthly* Dec. 1994: 38-44.

Lindamood, Phyllis, and Nanci Bell. "Sensory-cognitive Factors in the Controversy over Reading Instruction." *Journal of Developmental and Learning Disorders* 1 (1997): 143-82.

Lindsay, Drew. "Double Standards." *Teacher Magazine* online, Nov. 1997. Available: http://www.teachermagazine.org

Lipsey, Mark W., et al. "The Efficacy of Psychological, Educational, and Behavioral Treatment: Confirmation from Meta-analysis." *American Psychologist* 48.12 (1993): 1181-1209.

Lynd, Albert. *Quackery in the Public Schools*. Boston: Little, Brown and Company, 1953.

McGuinness, Diane. *Why Our Children Can't Read and What We Can Do about It: A Scientific Revolution in Reading*. New York: Free Press, 1997.

McKeown, Mike. "Letter to President Clinton," online. Available: http://www.mathematicallycorrect.com

Bibliography

McPike, Elizabeth. "Learning to Read: Schooling's First Mission." *American Educator* Summer 1995: 3-6.

Maeroff, Gene. "Assessing Alternative Assessments." *Phi Delta Kappan* 73.4 (1991): 273-81.

Manzo, Kathleen Kennedy. "Calif. Text Adoption Puts Emphasis on Phonics." *Education Week* online, 15 Jan. 1997. Available: http://www.edweek.org/

————. "New National Reading Panel Faulted before It's Formed." *Education Week* 18 Feb. 1998: 7.

Martinez, Pila. "Universities' Reading Ethos Shuns Extremes." *Arizona Daily Star* 16 Feb. 1997: A11.

Marzano, Robert J., Debra Pickering, and Jay McTighe. *Assessing Student Outcomes: Performance Assessment Using the Dimensions of Learning Model.* Alexandria, VA: Association for Supervision and Curriculum Development, 1993.

Mathematically Correct. "The Northridge Chronicles: A Virtual Play," online. Available: http://www.mathematicallycorrect.com

Mathews, Mitford McLeod. *Teaching to Read: Historically Considered.* Chicago: Univ. of Chicago Press, 1966.

Miller, George A. "Varieties of Intelligence." *New York Times Review of Books* 25 Dec. 1983: Sect. 7, 5:1.

Mitchell, James, ed. "Phoenicia." *Random House Encyclopedia.* New York: Random House, 1977.

Mlawer, Mark A. "My Kid Beat Up Your Honor Student." *Education Week* online, 13 July 1994. Available: http://www.edweek.org/

Montgomery, Zach. *Poison Drops in the Federal Senate. The School Question from a Parental and Non-Sectarian Stand-Point.* Washington, DC: Gibson Bros. Printers and Bookbinders, 1889; New York: Arno Press, 1972.

Moore, Randy. "Grades and Self-Esteem." *American Biology Teacher* Oct. 1993: 388-89.

Morissey, Biobhan. "A Cartoonist Can't Worry about the Good of the Country." *Washington Post* 14 July 1985: B3.

Nathan, Joe. *Charter Schools: Creating Hope and Opportunity for American Education.* San Francisco: Jossey-Bass Publishers, 1996.

National Academy of Education Commission on Reading. *Becoming a Nation of Readers: The Report of the Commission on Reading.* Washington,

DC: National Academy of Education, National Institute of Education, Center for the Study of Reading, 1995.

National Commission on Excellence in Education. *A Nation at Risk: The Imperative for Educational Reform*. Washington, DC: GPO, 1983.

National Council of Teachers of Mathematics. *Curriculum and Evaluation Standards*. Reston, VA: National Council of Teachers of Mathematics, 1989.

National Education Association. *Report of the Committee on Secondary School Studies Appointed at the Meeting of the National Education Association*. Washington, DC: National Education Association, 9 July 1892.

The National Right to Read Foundation. "Bulletin Board." *Right to Read Report* Feb. 1998: 7.

_____. "News from the States." *Right to Read Report* Feb. 1998: 6.

_____. "Phonics Legislation and State Regulation Approved in 1996" online. Available: http://www.jwor.com/ nrrf.htm

Neill, A. S. *Summerhill: A Radical Approach to Child Rearing*. New York: Hart Publishing, 1960.

Oakes, Jeannie. *Keeping Track: How Schools Structure Inequality*. New Haven, CT: Yale Univ. Press, 1985.

Office of Educational Research and Improvement. "NAEP 1994." *Reading Report Card for the Nation and States*. Washington, DC: U.S. Department of Education.

Office of Educational Research and Improvement. "NAEP 1996." *Math and Science Report Card for the Nation and States*. Washington, DC: U.S. Department of Education.

Olson, Lynn. *The School-to-Work Revolution: How Employers and Educators Are Joining Forces to Prepare Tomorrow's Skilled Workforce*. Reading, MA: Addison-Wesley, 1997.

Palmaffy, Tyce. "No Excuses." *Policy Review* online. Available: http://www.heritage.org/heritage/p_review/jan98/noexcuses.html

Patrick, James, ed. *America 2000/Goals 2000: Moving the Nation Educationally to a "New World Order."* Moline, IL: Citizens for Academic Excellence, 1994.

Patterson, Chris. "School-to-Work: The Coming Collision." San Antonio: Texas Public Policy Foundation, 1998.

Popp, Helen M. "Current Practices in the Teaching of Beginning Reading." ed. John B. Carroll and Jeanne S. Chall. *Toward a Literate*

Society: The Report of the Committee on Reading of the National Academy of Education. New York: McGraw-Hill, 1975.

Project R.E.A.D. *To Make a Difference.* Silver Spring, MD: READ, Inc., 1978.

Public Agenda. *The Basics: Parents Talk about Reading, Writing, Arithmetic and the Schools.* New York: Public Agenda, 1996.

_____. *First Things First: What Americans Expect from Their Public Schools.* New York: Public Agenda, 1994.

_____. *How Teachers of Teachers View Public Education.* New York: Public Agenda, 1997.

Rafferty, Max. *What Are They Doing to Your Children?* New York: New American Library, 1963.

Raspberry, William. "'Reform' or Good Traditional Education." *Washington Post* 23 Mar. 1990: A23.

Ravitch, Diane. *Learning from the Past: What History Teaches Us about School Reform.* Baltimore: Johns Hopkins Univ. Press, 1995.

Rogers, Laura. "In Loco Parentis." Ed. James Patrick. *America 2000/Goals 2000: Moving the Nation Educationally to a "New World Order."* Moline, IL: Citizens for Academic Excellence, 1994. 540-46.

Rose, Lowell C., Alec M. Gallup, and Stanley M. Elam. "The 29th Annual Phi Delta Kappa/Gallup Poll of the Public's Attitudes Toward the Public Schools." *Phi Delta Kappan* Sept. 1997: 41-58.

Rousseau, Jean Jacques. *The Emile of Jean Jacques Rousseau.* Ed. William Boyd. New York: Teacher College Columbia Univ., 1956.

Rushdoony, Rousas J. *The Messianic Character of American Education.* Nutley, NJ: Craig Press, 1972.

St. John, Walter D. "Dealing with Angry Adults." *Today's Education.* 64.4 (Nov.-Dec. 1975): 82.

Sanders, William L., and Sandra Horn. *An Overview of the Tennessee Value-Added Assessment System.* Knoxville, TN: Univ. of Tennessee, n.d.

Schafly, Phyllis. "What's Wrong with Outcome-Based Education?" *The Phyllis Schafly Report.* 26.10 (May 1993).

Shavelson, Richard, et al. "Performance Assessments: Political Rhetoric and Measurement and Reality." *Educational Researcher* 21.4 (1992): 22-27.

Simon, Barry. "Modern Mathematicians Have Lost Value of Proofs." *Binghamton Sunday Press and Sun Bulletin* 17 Feb. 1998: E4.

Singal, Daniel J. "The Other Crisis in American Education." *Atlantic Monthly* Nov. 1991: 59-69.

Smith, Donna. "Schoolteacher Wants 'Just the Facts.'" Oklahoma Council of Public Affairs, online, 1997. Available: http://www.ocpathink.org

Smith, Frank. *Reading without Nonsense.* New York: Teachers College Press, 1985.

_____. *Understanding Reading: A Psycholinguistic Analysis of Reading and Learning to Read.* 5th ed. Hillsdale, NJ: Lawrence Erlbaum, 1994.

Smith, Mortimer. *A Citizen's Manual for Public Schools.* Boston: Little, Brown, Atlantic Monthly Press, 1965.

_____. *And Madly Teach: A Layman Looks at Public School Education.* Chicago: Henry Regnery, 1949.

Sommerfeld, Meg. "Calif. Parents Target Math Frameworks." *Education Week* online, 24 Apr. 1996. Available: http://www.edweek.org/

Sommers, Christina Hoff. *Who Stole Feminism? How Women Have Betrayed Women.* New York: Simon and Schuster, 1994.

Sowell, Thomas. *Inside American Education: The Decline, the Deception, the Dogmas.* New York: The Free Press, 1993.

Spalding, Romalda Bishop, and Walter T. Spalding. *The Writing Road to Reading: The Spalding Method of Phonics for Teaching Speech, Writing, and Reading.* 4th ed. New York: William Morrow, 1990.

Spitz, Jill Jorden. "Sixth-grade Jury Deadlocked on President's Guilt." *Arizona Daily Star* 29 Jan. 1998: 1A, 5A.

Stahl, Steven. "Does Whole Language or Instruction Matched to Learning Styles Help Children Learn to Read?" *School Psychology Review* 24: 393-405.

Stanovich, Keith. "Matthew Effects in Reading: Some Consequences of Individual Differences in the Acquistion of Literacy." *Reading Research Quarterly* 21 (1986): 360-407.

_____. "Does Reading Make You Smarter? Literacy and the Development of Verbal Intelligence." *Advances in Child Development and Behavior* Ed. Hayne W. Reese San Diego, CA: Academic Press, 1993. 133-80.

Steinke, Peter. *Healthy Congregations: A Systems Approach.* Washington, DC: Alban Institute, 1996.

Bibliography

Stevenson, Harold W. "Children Deserve Better Than Phony Self-Esteem." *Education Digest* Dec. 1992: 12-13.

Stevenson, Harold W., and James W. Stigler. *The Learning Gap: Why Our Schools Are Failing and What We Can Learn from Japanese and Chinese Education.* New York: Summit Books, 1992.

Sunseri, Ron. *Outcome Based Education: Understanding the Truth about Educational Reform.* Sisters, OR: Questar Publishing, 1994.

Tennebaum, Samuel. *William Heard Kilpatrick: Trail Blazer in Education.* New York: Harper & Bros., 1951.

Texas Alternative Document, online. Available: http://www.htcomp.net/tad

Thomson-Myers, Charlene. "Paper Airplanes Let Fifth-graders' Imaginations Soar." *Binghamton* [NY] *Press & Sun Bulletin* 19 Feb. 1998: B1.

Thomson, Scott, and Nancy DeLeonibus. *Guidelines for Improving SAT Scores.* Reston, VA: National Association of Secondary School Principals, 1978.

Thorndike, Edward, and Arthur Gates. *Elementary Principles of Education.* New York: Macmillan, 1929.

Toch, Thomas. "The Perfect School." *U.S. News and World Report* 11 Jan. 1993: 46-59.

Tucker, Marc S. "Letter to Hillary Clinton, The Governor's Mansion, Little Rock, AR." National Center on Education and the Economy, online, 11 Nov. 1992. Available: http://www.sover.net/~nbrook/Hillary.html

Tyack, David, and Larry Cuban. *Tinkering toward Utopia: A Century of Public School Reform.* Cambridge, MA: Harvard Univ. Press, 1995.

Tyack, David, Michael W. Kirst, and Elisabeth Hansot. "Educational Reform: Retrospect and Prospect." *Teachers College Record* 81 (Spring 1980): 253-269.

U.S. Department of Education. *America 2000: An Education Strategy.* Washington, DC: U.S. Department of Education, 1991.

_____. "Mathematics Equals Opportunity," White Paper, online, 10 Oct. 1997. Available: http://www.ed.gov/pubs/ math/

_____. "Pursuing Excellence: A Study of U.S. 12th Grade Mathematics & Science Achievement in International Context" online, 14 Feb. 1998. Available: http://nces.ed.gove/timss/

_____. *Life Adjustment for Every Youth*. Washington, DC: United States Office of Education, 1945.

West, Peter. "Palo Alto Parents Square Off over Math Curriculum." *Education Week* 7 June 1995: 7.

Wood, Regna Lee. "20th Century America Illiteracy." Briefing 01. The Plains, VA: National Right to Read Foundation, 1997.

Zandt, Dorothy. "Reports on Famous People Bring Learning into Homes." *Binghamton [NY] Press & Sun Bulletin* 6 Mar. 1998: 1B.

Index

Index

Index

Index

Phillips, Sarah, 205-9
Phoenicians, 87
Phoneme, 85
Phonemic awareness
    definition, 79, 85, 96
    materials, 252-53
Phonics
    definition, 79, 85
    materials, 252-53
Phono-Graphix, 97
Pickerig, Debra, 179
PIE. *See* Parents Involved in
    Education
Pilot programs, 230-31
Pinnell, Gay Su, 182
Placebo math, 114
Political correctness, 125
Politicians, role in education
    crisis, 67-68
Portfolios, 180-81
"Power to the Consumer," 240-
    41
Print awareness, 96
Professional organizations, role
    in education crisis, 70-71
Professors, role in education
    crisis, 68-70
Profits, role in education crisis,
    70
Progressive education,
    critique of, 59, 66, 177,
    description, 48-49
    history, 55-60
    relationship to traditional
        education, 52-53
Project READ, 80
Prosser Resolution, 58

Quality Schools. *See* Mastery
    Learning

Rafferty, Max, 62
Rainforest Algebra, 114
Raspberry, William, 65

Reading
    achievement related to
        delinquency, 80
    amount of, 100
    components of ideal
        program, 95-103
    omprehension in, 98
    definition of, 85
    how children learn, 93, 99
    interpretation in, 100-101
    strategies, 101
    wars, 81, 86-92
Reading Competency Test, 102
Reading Excellence Act, 198
Reading Recovery, 181-82
Research
    dissemination of, 198
    evaluation of, 233-34
Restructured education. *See*
    Mastery Learning and
    Outcome-Based Education
Results-Based Curriculum. *See*
    Mastery Learning and
    Outcome-Based Education
Results Oriented. *See* Mastery
    Learning and
    Outcome-Based Education
Riggs Institute, 263
Rittmeyer, Marilyn Keller,
    240-41, 244
Roosevelt, Teddy, 245
Rosen, Jerry, 14
Rousseau, Jean Jacques, 220
Rudman, Herbert, 20

SAT. *See* Scholastic Aptitude Test
Saxon, John, 230
Saxon Publishing, Inc., 263
Scheffers, Lauren, 117
Scholastic Aptitude Test, 17-18
School boards
    campaigns, 227-29
    election to, 227-28
    meetings, 201-4